discover
PARIS

CAROLINE SIEG
STEVE FALLON, CATHERINE LE NEVEZ,
CHRIS PITTS, NICOLA WILLIAMS

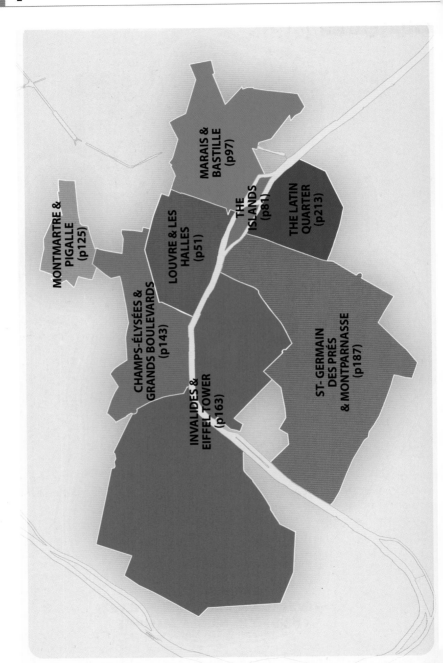

MONTMARTRE & PIGALLE (p125)

MARAIS & BASTILLE (p97)

THE ISLANDS (p81)

THE LATIN QUARTER (p213)

LOUVRE & LES HALLES (p51)

CHAMPS-ÉLYSÉES & GRANDS BOULEVARDS (p143)

INVALIDES & EIFFEL TOWER (p163)

ST-GERMAIN DES PRÉS & MONTPARNASSE (p187)

DISCOVER PARIS

Louvre & Les Halles (p51) The heart of Paris, with the lion's share of major sights and museums.

The Islands (p81) One boasts the landmark Notre Dame, while the other sits elegantly in the background.

Marais & Bastille (p97) Lively shopping and dining with one landmark resident: the acoustically superior Opéra Bastille.

Montmartre & Pigalle (p125) The Paris of myth and films, adjacent to the tame red-light district.

Champs-Élysées & Grands Boulevards (p143) Paris' most glamorous department store and opera, and the Champs-Élysées.

Invalides & Eiffel Tower (p163) Home to the iconic, spiky tower and brilliant rectangles of green.

St-Germain des Prés & Montparnasse (p187) Former literary haunts, now chi-chi venues, in the shadow of a skyscraper.

The Latin Quarter (p213) The hub of Paris' academia, crisscrossed by eclectic, multicultural foodie haunts.

↘ CONTENTS

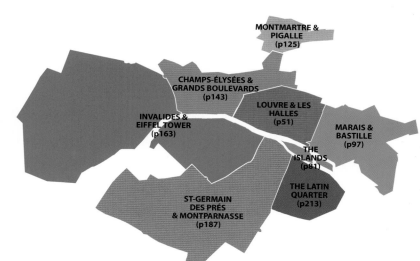

MONTMARTRE &
PIGALLE
(p125)

CHAMPS-ÉLYSÉES &
GRANDS BOULEVARDS
(p143)

LOUVRE & LES
HALLES
(p51)

INVALIDES &
EIFFEL TOWER
(p163)

MARAIS &
BASTILLE
(p97)

THE
ISLANDS
(p81)

THE LATIN
QUARTER
(p213)

ST-GERMAIN
DES PRÉS
& MONTPARNASSE
(p187)

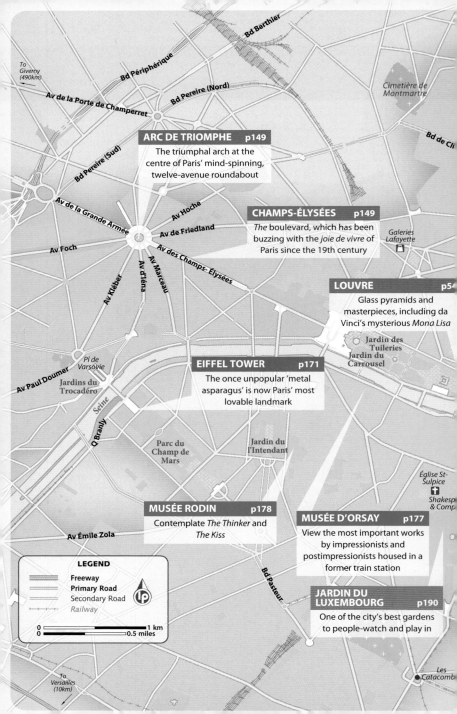

ARC DE TRIOMPHE p149

The triumphal arch at the centre of Paris' mind-spinning, twelve-avenue roundabout

CHAMPS-ÉLYSÉES p149

The boulevard, which has been buzzing with the *joie de vivre* of Paris since the 19th century

LOUVRE p5[4]

Glass pyramids and masterpieces, including da Vinci's mysterious *Mona Lisa*

EIFFEL TOWER p171

The once unpopular 'metal asparagus' is now Paris' most lovable landmark

MUSÉE RODIN p178

Contemplate *The Thinker* and *The Kiss*

MUSÉE D'ORSAY p177

View the most important works by impressionists and postimpressionists housed in a former train station

JARDIN DU LUXEMBOURG p190

One of the city's best gardens to people-watch and play in

LEGEND

Freeway
Primary Road
Secondary Road
Railway

0 ——— 1 km
0 ——— 0.5 miles

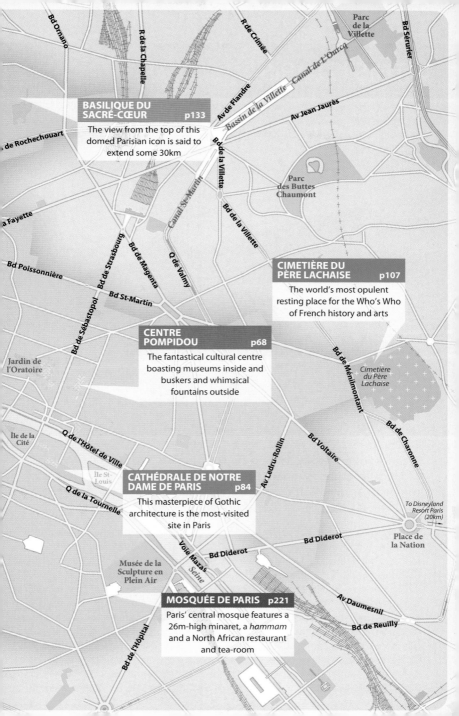

BASILIQUE DU SACRÉ-CŒUR p133

The view from the top of this domed Parisian icon is said to extend some 30km

CIMETIÈRE DU PÈRE LACHAISE p107

The world's most opulent resting place for the Who's Who of French history and arts

CENTRE POMPIDOU p68

The fantastical cultural centre boasting museums inside and buskers and whimsical fountains outside

CATHÉDRALE DE NOTRE DAME DE PARIS p84

This masterpiece of Gothic architecture is the most-visited site in Paris

MOSQUÉE DE PARIS p221

Paris' central mosque features a 26m-high minaret, a *hammam* and a North African restaurant and tea-room

⬊THIS IS PARIS

Well informed, eloquent and oh-so-romantic, the Ville-Lumière (City of Light) is a philosopher, a poet, a crooner...a million different things to a million different people. It has all but exhausted the superlatives that can reasonably be applied to any city.

Notre Dame and the Eiffel Tower – at sunrise, at sunset, at night – have been described countless times, and at length, as have the Seine and the subtle (and not-so-subtle) differences between its Left and Right Banks. But what writers really cannot capture is the grandness and the magic of this incomparable city. You must experience it for yourself.

The French capital probably has more familiar landmarks than any other city in the world. As a result, first-time visitors often arrive with all sorts of expectations: of grand vistas, of intellectuals discussing weighty matters in cafés, of romance along the Seine, of naughty nightclub revues, of rude people who won't speak English... If you look hard enough, you can probably find all of those things. But a better approach is to set aside the preconceptions of Paris and explore the city's avenues and backstreets without constantly looking for the tip of the Eiffel Tower or the spire of Notre Dame to pop into view at any moment. Then you'll be set to uncover the magic of simple, au-

thentic Parisian pastimes such as poking into quirky boutiques and sipping aperitifs at Lilliputian wine bars, or thumbing through old paperbacks in dusty, ancient bookshops and strolling through leafy hidden squares.

> **'Paris is enchanting almost everywhere, at any time'**

You'll soon discover (as so many have before you) that Paris is enchanting almost everywhere, at any time, even 'in the winter, when it drizzles' and 'in the summer, when it sizzles' as Cole Porter put it. And, like a good meal, it excites, it satisfies and the memory lingers.

↘ PARIS' TOP 25 EXPERIENCES

`1`

⬎ LA TOUR EIFFEL

Ascend to the tip of the iconic **Eiffel Tower** (p171) for a spectacular 360-degree panorama of Paris' boulevards and monuments. By night the tower's twin searchlights beam an 80km radius around the illuminated city, and every hour on the hour for 10 minutes the spire glitters like a diamond, with 20,000 gold-toned lights.

⬊ JOIN PARISIANS AT PLAY

The merest ray of sunshine draws apartment-dwelling Parisians outdoors to **Jardin du Luxembourg** (p198). Join them prodding little wooden sail boats on the octagonal pond, watching marionettes perform Punch & Judy or riding the *carrousel* (merry-go-round), or corral one of the iconic 1923-designed sage-green metal chairs and find your own favourite part of the park.

⬊ HIT THE FOOD MARKETS

Feast your senses during a wander through Paris' **food markets** (p257). Trestle tables groan under the weight of perfectly stacked delicacies, such as spit-roasted fowl, sun-ripened produce, pâtés and wedges and wheels of aromatic cheese. Pick up picnic supplies and edible gifts while enjoying the convivial, social atmosphere.

1 WILL SALTER; 2 BRUCE BI; 3 WILL SALTER

1 Eiffel Tower (p171); 2 Grand Bassin in Jardin du Luxembourg (p198), with Palais du Luxembourg (p190) in the background; 3 Food markets on rue Montorgueil (p76)

⬎ EXPLORE MOSQUÉE DE PARIS

4

Revitalise your mind, body and soul at Paris' art-deco Moorish **mosque** (p221). Wander through the colonnaded court-yards, pamper yourself with a massage or Turkish steam bath in its mosaic-and-marble *hammam* (a series of Turkish steam baths, each successively hotter) and check out the authentic *souq* (Moroccan-style market) overflow-ing with colourful fabrics, crockery and trinkets.

5

⬎ ISLANDS & ICE CREAM

Pick up a scoop of fruit sorbet or rich, organic ice cream from esteemed, family-owned *glacier* (ice-cream maker) **Berthillon** (p94) and enjoy it stroll-ing the narrow, tranquil streets of **Île St-Louis** (p92), which are dotted with old travel-book and antique shops, or watching the riverboats glide by from its busker-filled banks and bridges.

↘ SHAKESPEARE & CO'S MAGIC

This charming, cluttered **bookshop's** (p233) enchanting nooks and crannies overflow with new and secondhand English-language books. In their midst you'll also find a wishing well and a miniature staircase leading to an attic-like reading library. At night, its couches turn into beds where writers stay for free in exchange for working in the shop.

6

4 BRUCE BI; 5 DENNIS JONES; 6 BRUCE BI

4 Minaret of Mosquée de Paris (p221); 5 Berthillon ice-cream shop (p94), Île St-Louis; 6 Shakespeare & Company bookshop (p233)

PARIS' TOP 25 EXPERIENCES

↘ NAVIGATE THE LABYRINTHINE LOUVRE

Marvel at the futuristic glass pyramids sitting atop the world's largest **museum** (p61) – which covers a whopping 700m stretch of Seine riverbank – and at its works of art from Europe, the Middle East and ancient civilisations. The astounding collection of paintings and artefacts on display span multiple lifetimes, from the Middle Ages to the late 19th century.

7

◥ VISIT A CELEBRITY TOMBSTONE

8

Pay homage to the famous departed at Cimetière du Père Lachaise (p107), a 48-hectare cemetery of cobbled lanes and elaborate tombs the size of small houses. It's the city's most-fashionable final address; celebrity 'residents' range from writers Molière and Proust to singer Édith Piaf and rock god Jim Morrison.

◥ ASCEND PARIS' LANDMARK BASILICA

9

Climb the steps or ascend the 90-second funicular to Montmartre Hill's Basilique du Sacré Cœur (Sacred Heart Basilica; p133). Dizzying vistas of the city's rooftops unfurl from the front steps, and the views are even better if you climb the 234 steps inside the basilica's Roman-Byzantine dome. You can see for 30km on a clear day.

7 SGI/IMAGEBROKER; 8 DENNIS JOHNSON; 9 NEIL SETCHFIELD

7 Inside the Musée du Louvre (p61); 8 Doors' singer Jim Morrison's headstone, Cimetière du Père Lachaise (p107); 9 Basilique du Sacré Cœur (p133)

10

↘ SKIRT THE SEINE

There are at least 101 different ways to woo France's timeless river. Walk, bike or sail along it (p166); revel in its riverbanks' richest museum, the **Musée du Quai Branly** (p172); brunch on the quays at **Le Baba Bourgeois** (p230); or flop on the sand of **Paris Plages** (p166).

↘ NOTRE DAME CATHEDRAL

11

Discover **Cathédrale de Notre Dame de Paris'** (p89) sublime balance: meander to Square Jean XXIII, the lovely little park behind the cathedral, and let your soul fly with the extraordinary flying buttresses encircling the cathedral's chancel, walls and roof. This masterpiece of French Gothic architecture has been the focus of Catholic Paris for seven centuries.

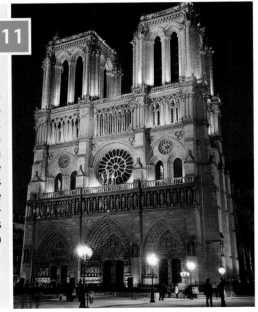

↘ PONDER THE KISS

12

Musée Rodin (p178), with its stellar pieces dotted about tranquil gardens, is one of the most relaxing museums in the city. Contemplate the incomparable *The Thinker* and *The Kiss,* alongside Rodin's other masterpiece bronze and marble sculptures.

↘ ROAM THE MUSÉE D'ORSAY

13

Venture through this erstwhile train station turned **museum** (p177) to explore some of the most important impressionist and postimpressionist works – its collection is the country's premier showcase for art from 1848 to 1914 and includes works by Monet, Renoir, Van Gogh and Matisse.

10 Bateaux-Mouches tour boat (p273) on the Seine; 11 Notre Dame Cathedral (p89) illuminated at dusk; 12 Musée Rodin (p178) sculpture garden; 13 Inside the Musée d'Orsay (p177)

PARIS' TOP 25 EXPERIENCES

14

↘ FIND THE RUBY-RED LIPS

You'll find fabulous modern art and spectacular rooftop views at the **Centre Pompidou** (p68), the talk of the town for years after it opened. The surrounding streets and squares buzz with cafés, buskers, musicians, jugglers and mime artists. Don't forget to check out the fanciful mechanical fountains featuring skeletons, hearts and a big pair of ruby-red lips.

↘ CHÂTEAU DE VERSAILLES

There are magnificent frescoes, opulent halls and gilded everything at the extravagant **Palace of Versailles** (p238) – from a 75m long Hall of Mirrors to its overdone King and Queen State Apartments and surrounding formal French-style gardens, it's a study of pure decadence.

15

14 JONATHAN SMITH; 15 JOHN ELK III

14 Centre Pompidou (p68); 15 Grand Apartments at the Château de Versailles (p238)

↘ STROLL MONET'S GARDEN

Visiting impressionist painter Claude Monet's home (where he painted some of his most famous pieces, including *Water Lilies*) and symmetrically laid out gardens in **Giverny** (p241) is a treat in any season. Look out for especially magnificent rows of daffodils in the spring; wisteria, roses and sweet peas in June; and sunflowers and hollyhocks in September.

16

↘ UNDERGROUND BONES

17

Wander through **Les Catacombes** (p195), down below the streets of Paris. These skull- and bone-lined tunnels are former quarries that served as the headquarters of the Resistance during WWII. The remnants of exhumed bodies (relocated here due to overflowing cemeteries) are horrid yet intriguing.

↘ ARC DE TRIOMPHE

18

Admire the four high-relief panels at the base – don't miss François Rude's *Departure of the Volunteers of 1792*, otherwise known as *La Marseillaise,* and the frieze depicting hundreds of 2m-high figures – before heading up to the top of this **triumphal arch** (p149), which anchors Paris' busiest intersection.

16 JOHN HAY; 17 DENNIS JONES; 18 KARL BLACKWELL

16 Garden at Maison de Claude Monet (p241), Giverny; 17 Les Catacombes (p195); 18 Arc de Triomphe (p149)

↘ AVENUE DES CHAMPS-ÉLYSÉES

Amble down Paris' bustling, tree-lined **boulevard** (p149). Crazy wide and overwhelming with its mammoth shops, it's oh so impressive. It especially comes to life on New Year's Eve, and one Sunday late in July when the last stage of the prestigious Tour de France cycling event takes place here.

19

20

⭙ JARDIN DES TUILERIES

There is no lovelier spot in Paris to stroll, mooch or jog between sculptures and flowerbeds than this, a riverside **garden** (p66) safeguarded as the 'Banks of the Seine' Unesco World Heritage Site.

19 MICHELLE LEWIS; 20 BRUCE BI

19 Av des Champs-Élysées (p149); 20 Sculpture by Aristide Maillol in Jardin des Tuileries (p66)

PARIS' TOP 25 EXPERIENCES

21

⬎ CRACK THE CODE

Relive the famous murderous scene, pivoting around the Rose Line, from Dan Brown's book-turned-film *The Da Vinci Code* at Église St-Sulpice (p198). Paris' second-largest church, Italianate outside, neoclassical in, this 18th-century stunner also boasts spectacular frescoes by Eugène Delacroix.

⬎ TAKE A COOKING COURSE

22

Come on, admit it. The Eiffel Tower might have views and the Louvre may have the Mona Lisa, but you really came for the food. Learn how to whip up the sublime flavours of a hearty, classic *boeuf bourguignon* or the secret to a crowd-pleasing *béarnaise* sauce at a cooking course (p271).

↘ SHOP 'TIL YOU DROP

Do it all – shop the **Champs-Élysées** (p161), boutique-hop the speciality shops and small fashion labels in the **Marais** (p122), putter through secondhand finds at **Marché aux Puces de la Porte de Vanves** (p212) and tool around Paris' grandest department store, **Galeries Lafayette** (p161).

↘ STE-CHAPELLE

Tucked away within the walls of the Palais de Justice (Law Courts) on Île de la Cité, **Ste-Chapelle** (p92) is Paris' most exceptional Gothic building. Its intricate stained glass is at its most magnificent on a sunny day, when it glows with rich, glorious colour.

21 KRZYSZTOF DYDYNSKI; 22 KRZYSZTOF DYDYNSKI; 23 KRZYSZTOF DYDYNSKI; 24 GLENN BEANLAND

21 Église St-Sulpice (p198); 22 Cooking course (p271); 23 Louis Vuitton (p162), Av des Champs-Élysées; 24 Ste-Chapelle (p92)

⬎ CHILL AT A CAFÉ

It's the quintessential Parisian experience: grab a magazine or newspaper, settle inside a cosy café and press pause. Or perch at an outdoor café table and watch the parade of Parisians go about their daily lives. Whatever you do, you can stay as long as you want for the price of a *café au lait*.

25

25 JONATHAN SMITH

25 Reading at a café near Place des Vosges (p105)

↘ PARIS' TOP ITINERARIES

A SHORT BREAK

TWO TO THREE DAYS
THE ISLANDS TO MONTMARTRE

With two to three days, you can hit all the major sights on this whistle-stop tour, which boasts two awe-inspiring views of the City of Light. And you'll still have time for some cultural pursuits or bar action.

❶ THE ISLANDS

Twins separated at birth, the Islands consist of chi-chi Île St-Louis and tourist-packed Île de la Cité, with its plethora of sights. Snap pictures of the Seine and its arched bridges from the magnificent **Pont Neuf** (p91), which connects Île de la Cité with the left and right banks. On Île de la Cité, take in the Gothic splendour of **Notre Dame** (p89), the most-visited site in Paris, with its delicate architecture and eerie gargoyles. Next, head over to admire ethereal **Ste-Chapelle's** (p92) intricate stained glass, before crossing over to Île St-Louis. Unwind with a stroll along tranquil Rue St Louis en Île, an arrow-straight thoroughfare peppered with fine food shops and gourmet restaurants to nourish natives and locals alike.

❷ EIFFEL TOWER

Hop on the metro over to the **Eiffel Tower** (p171), the one landmark that symbolises Paris like no other. Check out the arches of the 'Metal Asparagus' at ground level before climbing up (or riding in the lift) for sweeping views of the capital. Relax with a warm cup of goodness at **Café de Flore** (p209), a former bohemian haunt in St Germain, before

GLENN BEANLAND

Upper chapel of Ste-Chapelle (p92)

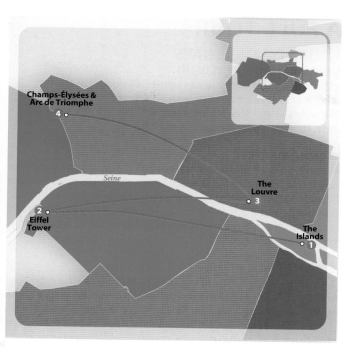

taking in a concert, ballet or opera at **Palais Garnier** (p150). The hopping **Bastille** (p97) is another option for a night out.

❸ THE LOUVRE

Visit the mammoth **Musée du Louvre** (p61), but don't even try to cover it all in one sitting. Enter through IM Pei's glass **Grand Pyramide** and make your first stop da Vinci's sly *Mona Lisa*. After seeing the lady, choose your passions (the antiquity wing's *Venus de Milo* or Renaissance-master Michelangelo's *The Dying Slave*?) and focus on one or two sections to avoid burnout. If you have another day free, consider returning to see more of this massive museum.

❹ CHAMPS-ÉLYSÉES & ARC DE TRIOMPHE

Brush out those museum cobwebs with an amble down the buzzing **Champs-Élysées** (p149), Paris' most-famous boulevard, to the dizzy traffic circle surrounding the **Arc de Triomphe** (p149). Climb to the top of the triumphal arch for a stellar view of 12 avenues and three arrondissements. Round out the day with dinner at an ethnic restaurant in the **Latin Quarter** (p213).

A FULL TOUR

FOUR TO SEVEN DAYS
MONTMARTRE TO VERSAILLES

In four to seven days, you can immerse yourself in the full gamut of France's capital. Spend your first few days exploring the sights in our Short Break itinerary, then hit the second-most famous sights in and around Paris.

❶ MONTMARTRE

Montmartre is the quintessential Parisian neighbourhood. Wind your way through the cobbled streets of this artists' enclave up to **Sacré Cœur** (p133), the domed basilica gracing the neighbourhood's hill. Afterwards, wander through convivial **Place du Tertre** (p133) and grab a bite at a cosy restaurant nearby. Finish off with a cabaret show in adjacent **Pigalle** (p141).

❷ CENTRE POMPIDOU

Head to the **Centre Pompidou** (p68), with its colourful tubes and massive exhaust pipes, and revel in its forward-thinking art at the **Musée National d'Art Moderne** (National Museum of Modern Art). Watch buskers earning their keep at the **Place Georges Pompidou** and relax in front of the whimsical **mechanical fountains** propelling water this way and that.

❸ PÈRE LACHAISE

This cemetery's residents may be deceased, but they still fill our hearts. **Père Lachaise** (p107) is the final resting place of celebrities of all walks

BÉTHUNE CARMICHAE

Château de Versailles (p238)

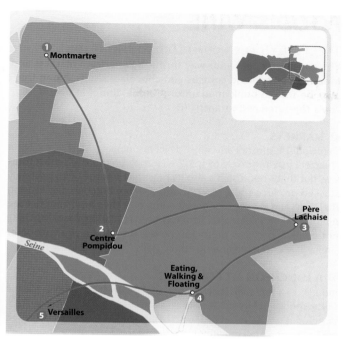

of life. Among its 69,000 tombs lie the graves of writers, actors, paint-ers and singers, including Balzac, Delacroix, Wilde, Édith Piaf and Jim Morrison.

❹ EATING, WALKING & FLOATING

Food goes hand-in-hand with Paris, and a ride along the Seine is a must-do. Nosh your way through cheese, breads and ethnic fare at Paris' eye-popping, open-air **Marché Bastille** (p257), the food mar-kets where the locals go. Walk off your feast with a stroll along the Seine and take a ride on a Batobus, a glassed-in boat with over half a dozen hop-on, hop-off stops peppered along the river. Grab dinner in the lively **St-Germain and Montparnasse** (p187) area or a drink in trendy **Marais** (p119).

❺ VERSAILLES

The palace to rival all others – spend your last day on a day trip to the resplendent **Château de Versailles** (p238), with Greek and Roman de-tails exuding from every cornice and door in its Grands Appartements du Roi et de la Reine, and 99 fountains filling Neptune's pool in its ornate gardens.

FOOD & WINE

TWO DAYS RUE MOUFFETARD TO BERTHILLON

You could easily eat your way through Paris, from markets and food halls to cooking courses and chocolate shops. Along the way, be sure to book in an unforgettable dinner at one of the city's top-rated restaurants.

❶ MARKETS

Take your pick from Paris' most delicious markets. Start at the Latin Quarter's **rue Mouffetard** (p228) – it may be the city's most touristy, but that's because it's also its most picturesque, with pristinely stacked produce stalls, straight-out-of-a-film butchers showcasing their fowl and cheese mongers tending over their aromatic cheeses. Alternatively, on Tuesday or Saturday head to **Marché Bastille** (p257), not quite as postcard-pretty but no less fun, where you encounter similar fare peppered among ethnic stalls.

❷ A LUNCHEON FIT FOR KINGS

Indulge in a top-shelf lunch at one of Paris' best bistros, such as **Le Comptoir du Relais** (p204), where you can sample its seasonal, creative menus, or **Le Cristal de Sel** (p205), where you can see for yourself why everyone's talking about its rising-star chef.

❸ WINE & THE FOOD HALL

Head to the **Musée du Vin** (p176) to learn everything you ever wanted to know about viniculture, before hitting **La Grande Épicerie** (p184), Paris' most outrageous food hall.

KRZYSZTOF DYDYNSK

Wine for sale, rue Mouffetard (p228)

La Grande Épicerie (p184)

JEAN-BERNARD CARILLET

❹ SWEET GIFTS

Pick up an edible gift to take home to your sweet-tooth friends. Explore renowned *chocolatier* **Cacao et Chocolat** (p96), which churns out eccentric flavoured bars such as citrus, spice and chilli. Alternatively, choose among delicate green-tea chocolates or from over 72 flavours of sculpture-like macaroons at **Pâtisserie Sadaharu Aoki** (p212).

❺ A WINE-FILLED EVENING OUT

Spend an evening wine-bar hopping in the Marais and Bastille area. For sipping in tranquil belle époque surrounds head to **Le Bistrot Du Peintre** (p121). Those wanting oodles of wine options shouldn't miss **Le Café du Passage** (p121), which boasts a menu of hundreds, many served by the glass. **La Tartine** (p120) feels like a wine bar from the past, with old gas lighting and a small but quality choice of wines served by the *pot* (46cL).

❻ COOKING COURSE

Can you think of a better place to indulge in a **cooking course** (p271)? Most run from a few hours to roughly half a day. The question is price and time, really. One thing is certain: you'll learn why food is such an important part of French culture, and walk away armed with a new recipe. **Cours de Cuisine Olivier Berté** (p271) offers excellent courses in English, well-suited to visitors keen for a short class to learn the basics.

❼ ICE CREAM & ISLANDS

Head to Île St-Louis (p92), the smaller of the two islands between the left and right banks, and unwind with a stroll along tranquil Rue St Louis en Île, a foodie-heaven street filled with fine food shops. Then, tuck into a scoop at **Berthillon** (p94), Paris' most famous *glacier* (ice-cream maker) – it's tough to choose between *marron glacés* (candied chestnuts), *chocolat* or fruit flavours, such as lemon or cassis, but it sure is fun.

❽ DECADENT DINING

Treat yourself to a lavish dinner feast at one of Paris' best restaurants. The Ducasse-and-Starck-inspired **Spoon** (p156) is renowned for its outstanding fusion fare – you can mix and match main meals with your favourite sauce to create a masterpiece. Alternatively, wine connoisseurs should spend an evening at **Bistrot Du Sommelier** (p155), where one of the world's most-talented sommeliers matches velvety wines with hearty bistro fare.

JEAN-BERNARD CARILLET

Interior of Spoon fusion restaurant (p156)

PARIS' BEST...

⬎ CAPITAL VIEWS

- **Top of the Eiffel Tower** (p171) Has to be done at least once – by lift or on foot.
- **Basilique du Sacré Cœur** (p133) Climb 234 steps up into the dome of this iconic basilica in Montmartre.
- **Cathédrale de Notre Dame de Paris** (p89) Scale 422 steps inside the cathedral's north tower for a view you'll never forget.
- **Arc de Triomphe** (p149) Little known fact: you can climb to the top of the arch.
- **Tour Montparnasse** (p196) Spectacular views of the capital from the top of an eyesore 1970s skyscraper.

⬎ PARISIAN CAFÉ LIFE

- **Les Deux Magots** (p209) Too famous, but a must-visit-once address in literary St-German des Prés.

- **Le Bistrot du Peintre** (p121) A favourite since the belle époque.
- **Le Café qui Parle** (p139) Best for breakfast and brunch.
- **Café De Flore** (p209) Sartre and de Beauvoir's former haunt.
- **Café La Fusée** (p77) A relaxed escape from the bustle of Centre Pompidou.

⬎ TRADITIONAL BISTROS

- **Le Trumilou** (p116) A century old, with same-era dishes to match.
- **Bofinger** (p115) Paris' oldest, established 1864.
- **Bouillon Racine** (p206) An art nouveau 'soup kitchen' from 1906; end with an old-fashioned sherbet.
- **Le Roi du Pot au Feu** (p158) The address for authentic *pot au feu* (beef stew).
- **Crèmerie Restaurant Polidor** (p205) The most famous *tarte tatin* in Paris.

WILL ROBB

View of Paris from the Eiffel Tower (p171)

PARISIAN QUIRKS

- **Clos du Montmartre** (p130) A *petite* vineyard in the middle of Montmartre.
- **Les Catacombes** (p195) Skulls are everywhere.
- **Musée des Égouts de Paris** (p178) Immerse yourself in Paris' sewage system.
- **Paris Walks** (p274) Explore from a different perspective: fashion, chocolate, French Revolution…
- **Place Georges Pompidou's mechanical fountains** (p68) Whimsical and utterly entertaining.

SHOP 'TIL YOU DROP

- **Galeries Lafayette** (p161) Paris' most famous department store; stop and gape at its magnificent art nouveau cupola.
- **Tati** (p142) Hunt down a bargain with savvy Parisians– you're new favourite top might be lurking at the bottom of that bin.
- **Shakespeare & Company** (p233) Pick up a tattered copy of a classic at this dusty old library.
- **Marché aux Puces de la Porte de Vanves** (p212) One of Paris' tiniest flea markets.

- **La Grande Épicerie de Paris** (p184) Go gaga over gourmet goodies.

HOLY MONUMENTS

- **Basilique du Sacré Cœur** (p133) Paris' landmark basilica.
- **Église St-Sulpice** (p198) Looks familiar, right? You saw it in the film adaptation of Dan Brown's *The Da Vinci Code*.
- **Cathédrale de Notre Dame de Paris** (p89) The capital's most iconic cathedral.
- **Ste-Chapelle** (p92) A hidden Gothic gem.
- **Mosquée de Paris** (p221) The Moorish Paris mosque.

ART & MUSEUMS

- **Musée d'Orsay** (p177) Housed in a former railway station.
- **Louvre** (p61) The mother-lode of all Parisian museums.
- **Musée du Quai Branly** (p172) One of the newest arts and culture museums to join the gang.
- **Montmartre** (p125) Art takes to the streets.
- **Versailles** (p238) France's most-famous, grandest, busiest palace.

THINGS YOU NEED TO KNOW

AT A GLANCE

- **ATMs** Omnipresent
- **Credit Cards** Visa and MasterCard widely accepted at restaurants and hotels, Amex at more upmarket places. Cafés, bars and smaller shops may not accept cards.
- **Currency** The euro
- **Electricity** 220V at 50Hz AC; two-round-pin plugs
- **Language** French
- **Tipping** Not necessary, but many Parisians leave a few coins at the end of a meal.
- **Population** 2.177 million
- **Smoking** No-go in public places; OK on alfresco café terraces.
- **Visas** Not required for most nationalities.

ADVANCE PLANNING

- **As early as possible** Book accommodation.
- **One month before** Book a cooking or wine-tasting course (p271), organise tickets for the opera or ballet and make reservations for a gastronomic feast.
- **One week before** Cut queues in situ by buying admission tickets online for Château de Versailles (p238) and the Louvre (p61); book a city tour (p273).
- **One day before** Pack your comfiest pair of shoes for all that walking you'll be doing.

BE FOREWARNED

- **Museums** Closed Monday or Tuesday (days to avoid Versailles); all museums and monuments shut their doors 30 minutes to one hour before listed closing times.
- **Bars & cafés** A drink costs more sitting at a table than standing, on a fancy square than a back street.
- **Shopaholics** Sales start mid-January and second week of June.
- **Metro stations** Worth skipping late at night: Châtelet-Les Halles

TGV trains, Gare de Lyon railway station

JEAN-BERNARD CARILLET

PLANNING YOUR TRIP

THINGS YOU NEED TO KNOW

and its seemingly endless corridors, Château Rouge (Montmartre), Gare du Nord, Strasbourg St-Denis, Réaumur Sébastopol and Montparnasse Bienvenüe.

COSTS

- **Baguette** from €1.20
- **Coffee** from €1.30
- **Small beer** from €5
- **Glass of wine** from €4
- **Métro ticket good for 1½ hours** €1.60
- **Taxi to/from Charles de Gaulle airport** €45-60
- **Taxi to/from Orly airport** €35-50
- **Substantial sit-down lunch** under €15
- **Satisfying 3-course dinner** around €35

EMERGENCY NUMBERS

- **Ambulance** ☎ 15
- **Fire** ☎ 18
- **Police** ☎ 17
- **SOS Helpline** (☎ 01 47 23 80 80; ☽ 3-11pm daily)
- **Urgences Médicales de Paris** (Medical Emergencies; ☎ 01 53 94 94 94; www.ump.fr)

GETTING AROUND

- **Metro & RER** Get around underground between 5.30am and midnight (p278).
- **Bicycle** Paris' self-service bike rental scheme, Vélib' (p277), makes freewheeling a breeze (and a joy).
- **Boats** Cruise along the Seine (p273).

GETTING THERE & AWAY

- **Eurostar** The swiftest way from London (p279).
- **Thalys** Will get you to Brussels, Amsterdam and Cologne (p279).
- **SNCF** France's national train service (p279).

TECH STUFF

- **Wi-fi** Free in more and more hotels, train stations and airports.
- **Wireless hotspots** Track them down at www.wifinder.com.
- **Internet cafés** See p272; pay €2 to €6 per hour to surf.
- **Hotels** In this guide a computer icon (🖳) means hotel has a computer guests can use; wi-fi icon (📶) means guests can access wi-fi with their own computer.

WHEN TO GO

- **Spring** One of the most glorious seasons, although April can be rainy.
- **Summer** Long days, warm weather and Paris Plages; downside is that prices are high, the city is packed with fellow visitors and many smaller shops, cafés and restaurants shut in August.
- **Autumn** Quiet but pleasant weather, although many larger hotels are booked solid for business conferences.
- **Winter** Oodles of cultural events (p46); the frigid weather means more time indoors – more time to eat, drink and visit museums.

GET INSPIRED

PLANNING YOUR TRIP

GET INSPIRED

BOOKS

- **Is Paris Burning?** (Larry Collins & Dominique Lapierre, 1965) The last days of the Nazi occupation of Paris.
- **The Flâneur: A Stroll Through the Paradoxes of Paris** (Edmund White, 2001) Loving portrait of White's adopted city.
- **The Death of French Culture** (Donald Morrison, 2010) Suggests that France and its culture no longer speak to the world.
- **The French** (Theodore Zeldin, 1983) Acclaimed survey of French passions, peculiarities and perspectives by a British scholar.

FILMS

- **Last Tango in Paris** (USA, 1972) Bernardo Bertolucci's classic with Marlon Brando.
- **Les Quatre Cents Coups** (The 400 Blows; France, 1959) The semi-autobiographical story of a down-trodden and neglected Parisian teenage boy who turns to outward rebellion.
- **Le Fabuleux Destin d'Amélie Poulain** (Amélie; France, 2001) Jean-Pierre Jeunet's feel-good story of a winsome young Parisian do-gooder named Amélie takes viewers on a colourful tour.
- **La Môme** (La Vie en Rose; 2007) Édith Piaf's bio played by the highly honoured (and deservedly so) Marion Cotillard.

MUSIC

- **Édith Piaf** *Live at the Paris Olympia* The belle of Belleville's classics, including 'Milord', 'Hymne à l'Amour' and, of course, 'Non, Je Ne Regrette Rien'.
- **Georges Brassens** *Le Disque d'Or* Everything you need to know about one of France's greatest

LOU JONES

Rental bikes (p277)

performers (and the inspiration for Jacques Brel) is in this 21-track double helping.

- **Serge Gainsbourg** *Anthologie* Three-CD anthology includes the metro man's most famous tracks, including 'Le Poinçonneur des Lilas' and 'Je t'aime…Moi Non Plus' in duet with Brigitte Bardot.
- *La Nouvelle Chanson Française* Five-pack by various artists representing the way vocals are heading in French music, with everything from traditional and cabaret to folk-electronic and Paris club sound.

⤵ WEBSITES

- **Paris Convention & Visitors Bureau** (www.parisinfo.com) City tourist office.
- **Espace du Tourisme d'Île de France** (www.new-paris-ile-de-france.co.uk) Tourist office for surrounding Île de France area.
- **Paris.fr** (www.paris.fr) Paris city information.
- **Go Go** (www.gogoparis.com) Fashion, food, arts, gigs and gossip.

PLANNING YOUR TRIP

↘ CALENDAR

CALENDAR

Runners on the Champs-Élysées during the Paris International Marathon

↘ JANUARY–FEBRUARY

GRANDE PARADE DE PARIS
1 JANUARY

The Great Paris Parade (www.parispa rade.com), relatively subdued after the previous night's shenanigans, features marching and carnival bands, dance acts and so on, on the afternoon of New Year's Day.

FASHION WEEK

Fashion houses showcase their new collections twice a year (in late January and again in September) – a must for fashion buffs. For info on ready-to-wear shows, see Prêt-à-Porter (www.pretparis.com); for haute couture, see Mode à Paris (www.modeaparis.com).

↘ MARCH–APRIL

PRINTEMPS DU CINÉMA

Over three days (usually Sunday, Monday and Tuesday) sometime around 21 March (www.printempsducinema.com, in French) selected cinemas across Paris offer filmgoers a special discounted entry fee of €3.50.

MARATHON INTERNATIONAL DE PARIS

The Paris International Marathon (www.parismarathon.com, in French), usually held on the first or second Sunday of April, starts on the av des Champs-Élysées, 8e and finishes on av Foch, in the 16e, and attracts some 40,000 runners from around the world.

MAY	JUN	JUL	AUG	SEP	OCT	NOV	DEC

⇘ MAY

LA NUIT EUROPÉENNE DES MUSÉES
Key museums across Paris throw open their doors at 6pm (and don't close till late) for European Museums Night (www.nuitdesmusees.culture.fr) one Saturday night in mid-May.

ART DT-GERMAIN DES PRÉS
Some 70 St-Germain des Prés galleries (www.artsaintgermaindespres.com) come together in mid-May to showcase their top artists.

FRENCH TENNIS OPEN
The glitzy Internationaux de France de Tennis (www.rolandgarros.com) – the Grand Slam – takes place over two weeks from late May to early June at Stade Roland Garros at the southern edge of the Bois de Boulogne in the 16e.

⇘ JUNE–AUGUST

FÊTE DE LA MUSIQUE   21 JUNE
This national music festival (www.fetedelamusique.fr, in French), now in its third decade, welcomes in summer on the summer solstice and caters to a great diversity of tastes (jazz, reggae and even classical). Staged and impromptu live performances take place all over the city.

GAY PRIDE MARCH
Marche des Fiertés is a colourful Saturday-afternoon parade through the Marais to Bastille held in late June to celebrate Gay Pride Day (www.gaypride.fr, in French), with various bars and clubs sponsoring floats, and participants in some pretty outrageous costumes.

French Tennis Open (Internationaux de France de Tennis)

CALENDAR

PLANNING YOUR TRIP

CALENDAR

FOIRE ST-GERMAIN
This six-week-long **festival** (www.foire saintgermain.org, in French) of concerts and theatre from early June to mid-July takes place on the place St-Sulpice, 6e and various other venues in the quartier St-Germain.

PARIS CINÉMA
This 12-day **festival** (www.pariscinema. org) in the first half of July sees rare and restored films screened in selected cinemas across Paris.

BASTILLE DAY   14 JULY
France's national day boasts a 10am military and fire-brigade parade along av des Champs-Élysées, accompanied by a fly-past of fighter aircraft and helicopters and a huge display of *feux d'artifice* (fireworks) on the Champ de Mars at 11pm.

PARIS PLAGES (PARIS BEACH)
From mid-July to mid-August, 2.5km of the banks of the Seine transform into sand and pebble 'beaches' with beach umbrellas and palm trees. One section (1er to the 4e) boasts a tropical feel, while a second strip (19e) is devoted to water sports.

◥ SEPTEMBER

JOURNÉES EUROPÉENNES DU PATRIMOINE
The third weekend in September, Paris opens the doors to buildings normally off-limits to outsiders (eg embassies, government ministries, corporate offices – even the Palais de l'Élysée) on **European Heritage Days** (www.journ eesdupatrimoine.culture.fr, in French).

JOHN ELK III

Paris Plages along the Seine

| MAY | JUN | JUL | AUG | SEP | OCT | NOV | DEC |

White-cap soldiers of the Foreign Legion marching in Bastille Day parade

PLANNING YOUR TRIP

CALENDAR

⬊ OCTOBER

NUIT BLANCHE
White Night (or more accurately in French 'All Nighter'; www.paris.fr) is a cultural festival that takes place on the first Saturday and Sunday of October. Museums and recreational facilities join bars and clubs and stay open until sunrise.

FÊTE DES VENDANGES DE MONTMARTRE
This festival (www.fetedesvendanges demontmartre.com, in French) is held over five days (Wednesday to Sunday) over the second weekend in October, following the harvesting of grapes from the Clos du Montmartre (p130), with costumes, speeches and a parade.

FOIRE INTERNATIONALE D'ART CONTEMPORAIN
Better known as FIAC (www.fiac.com), this huge contemporary art fair is held over four days in late October, with some 160 galleries represented at the Louvre (p61) and the Grand Palais (p151).

⬊ DECEMBER

CHRISTMAS EVE MASS
24 DECEMBER
Christmas Eve midnight Mass is celebrated at many Paris churches, including Notre Dame. Get there by 11pm.

NEW YEAR'S EVE   31 DECEMBER
Blvd St-Michel (5e), place de la Bastille (11e), the Eiffel Tower (7e) or av des Champs-Élysées (8e) are the places to be to welcome in the New Year.

LOUVRE & LES HALLES

LOUVRE & LES HALLES

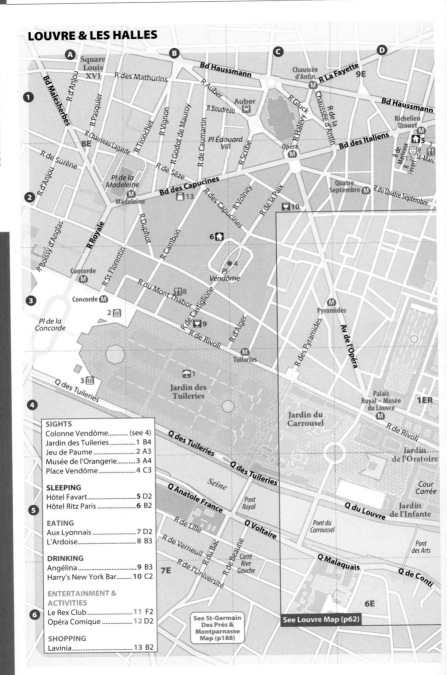

See St-Germain
Des Prés &
Montparnasse
Map (p188)

See Louvre Map (p62)

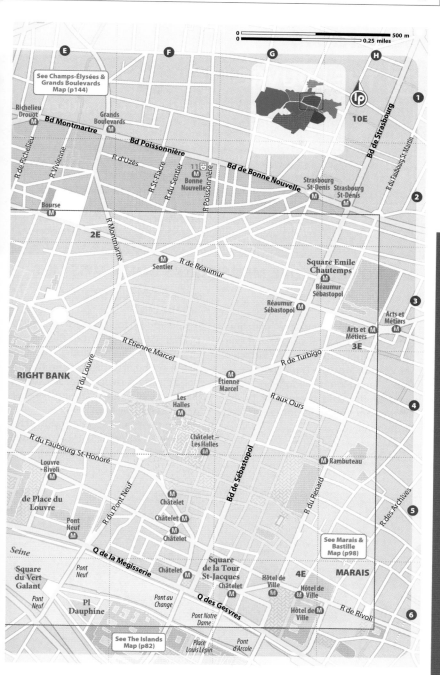

See Champs-Élysées &
Grands Boulevards
Map (p144)

10E

Richelieu
Drouot
Bd Montmartre
Grands
Boulevards
Bd Poissonnière
R d'Uzès
Bd de Bonne Nouvelle
Bonne
Nouvelle
Strasbourg
St-Denis
Strasbourg
St-Denis
Bd de Strasbourg
R du Faubourg St-Martin
R de Richelieu
R Vivienne
R St-Fiacre
R du Sentier
R Poissonnière
Bourse
2E
R Montmartre
Sentier
R de Réaumur
Square Emile
Chautemps
Réaumur
Sébastopol
Réaumur
Sébastopol
Arts et
Métiers
Arts et
Métiers
3E
RIGHT BANK
R du Louvre
R Étienne Marcel
R de Turbigo
Étienne
Marcel
Les
Halles
R aux Ours
Châtelet –
Les Halles
Rambuteau
R du Renard
Louvre
-Rivoli
de Place du
Louvre
R du Pont Neuf
Châtelet
Bd de Sébastopol
R des Archives
Pont
Neuf
Châtelet
Châtelet
See Marais &
Bastille
Map (p98)
Seine
Q de la Megisserie
Châtelet
Square
de la Tour
St-Jacques
Châtelet
Hôtel de
Ville
4E
MARAIS
Square
du Vert
Galant
Pont
Neuf
Pont au
Change
Q des Gesvres
Hôtel de
Ville
Hôtel de
Ville
R de Rivoli
Pont
Neuf
Pl
Dauphine
Pont Notre
Dame
See The Islands
Map (p82)
Place
Louis Lépin
Pont
d'Arcole

HIGHLIGHTS

1 THE LOUVRE

BY NIKO SALVATORE MELISSANO, MUSÉE DU LOUVRE

I've worked at the Louvre for 10 years and each day I still experience many emotions: we're in the heart of Paris; it is a magical place, charged with history and very intimate... The Louvre was a 12th-century fortress, then a royal palace, today one of the most famous art museums in the world, an unforgettable place with magnificent gardens.

↘ NIKO SALVATORE MELISSANO'S DON'T MISS LIST

❶ WINGED VICTORY OF SAMOTHRACE

It's impossible to reduce the collections of the Louvre to a hit parade... A definite highlight is the *Winged Victory of Samothrace* atop the Daru Staircase (1st Floor, Denon Wing). I adore her wings. I just cannot stop contemplating her from all angles. She is, moreover, very photogenic.

❷ THE SEATED SCRIBE & MONA LISA

I could admire this statuette (Room 22, 1st Floor, Sully Wing) from the ancient Egyptian empire for hours. The face of the scribe, like his posture (a little 'yoga') and his deep stare, say several things to me: serenity, strength of character, eternal wisdom.

Then there is *La Joconde* (Mona Lisa; Room 6, 1st Floor, Salle de la Joconde, Denon Wing) and that amazing fasci-

Clockwise from top: Exterior of the Louvre and IM Pei's Grande Pyramide (p62); Daru Staircase and *Winged Victory of Samothrace*; Interior gallery; Leonardo da Vinci's *La Joconde* (Mona Lisa)

nation of why and how she intrigues spirits with her mysteries.

❸ COUR KHORSABAD

With its enormous human-headed winged bulls, this courtyard on the Ground Floor of the Richelieu Wing is a jump in time into the cradle of one of the oldest cultures in the world: Mesopotamia. During the reign of King Sargon II in the 8th century, these bulls carved from alabaster guarded the Assyrian city and palace of Khorsabad (northern Iraq). A mix of force and serenity, perfectly balanced despite their colossal size, these protective monsters with four or five paws were a measure of the power of the Assyrian Empire in its heyday.

❹ GRANDE GALERIE

It's a real highlight, this gallery (1st Floor, Denon Wing), with masterpieces from the great masters of the Italian Renaissance: Leonardo da Vinci, Raphael, Arcimboldo, Andrea Mantegna... For more on all these works of art, borrow the Louvre's **multimedia guide** (http://monguide.louvre.fr; adult/under 18yr €6/2), available at the three main entrances (Richelieu, Sully and Denon), which makes for a fun visit at your own pace.

↘ THINGS YOU NEED TO KNOW

Hard facts 40 sq hectares, 60,000 sq m of gallery space, 35,000 art works **The brutal truth** One visit can in no way cover all the collections and the Louvre's extraordinary cultural richness **Forward plan** Take time to prepare your visit; study www.louvre.fr to optimise your time. **See our author's review, p61.**

HIGHLIGHTS

2

↘ MUSÉE DE L'ORANGERIE

The exquisite **Musée de l'Orangerie** (p67) is brimming with impressionist works. It's the best place in the world to enjoy the eight panels of Monet's sublime *Decorations des Nymphéas* (Water Lilies), as they are housed in two purpose-built, oval rooms here. It also boasts equally impressive Picassos, Matisses and more.

3

↘ CENTRE POMPIDOU

The **Centre Pompidou** (p68), a kind of Louvre for the 21st century, offers a day of culture and amusement for the whole family. From its National Museum of Modern Art to the whimsical mechanical fountains spewing water and silliness every which way and the buskers performing in the adjacent square, this is where art and fun fuse together seamlessly.

LOUVRE & LES HALLES

HIGHLIGHTS

↘ JARDIN DES TUILERIES

The Jardin des Tuileries' (p66) verdant oasis is a great place to recharge your batteries and enjoy Paris at its symmetrical best. Whilst wandering, you can admire its exquisite sculptures, such as Rodin's *The Kiss* and Louise Bourgeois' delicate, intertwined *Welcoming Hands*, and ponder its octagonal pond.

↘ ÉGLISE ST-EUSTACHE

Église St-Eustache (p70) is one of the least-known (and most-beautiful) churches in Paris. It's one of the best examples of early renaissance style on the right bank, with its magnificent mix of Flamboyant Gothic and neo-classical architectural work. Don't miss the colossal organ inside.

↘ PALAIS ROYAL

With pristine gardens, designer fashion shops, galleries, sculptures and history (the French Revolution effectively started at a café here), this former Royal Palace (p68) is a perfect hangout for a warm day. Don't miss the sculpture at the southern end of the garden: legend says if you can toss a coin onto one of the columns, your wish will come true.

2 WILL SALTER; 3 BRUCE BI; 4 WILL SALTER; 5 JONATHAN SMITH; 6 IZZET KERIBAR

2 Interior of Musée de l'Orangerie (p67); 3 Centre Pompidou (p68) at night; 4 Jardin des Tuileries (p66); 5 Église St-Eustache (p70); 6 Courtyard, Palais Royal (p68)

TREAD THE TIME PASSAGES

Step into the Right Bank's *passages couverts* (covered shopping arcades) for a feel of early-19th-century Paris. Tailor-made for rainy days (but best avoided on Sunday when galleries are shut), this walk – roughly 2km and one to 1½ hours – starts east of Métro Pyramides at Palais Royal and ends at Grands Boulevards.

❶ GALERIE DE MONTPENSIER

Galerie de Montpensier has several traditional shops, including A Bacqueville at Nos 6 to 8, with Légion d'Honneur–style medals and ribbons; Didier Ludot at both Nos 19 & 20 and 23 & 24, with exquisite antique clothes; and – in between at Nos 21 & 22 – Dugrenot, with curios and antiques.

❷ GALERIES DU PALAIS ROYAL

No 5 rue de Valois is one of the entrances to the Galeries du Palais Royal. Strictly speaking, these galleries are not *passages* as they are arcaded rather than covered, but since they date from 1786 they are considered the prototypes of what was to come.

❸ GALERIE DE VALOIS

This *passage* on the eastern side of the Galeries du Palais Royal – where Charlotte Corday, Jean-Paul Marat's assassin, once worked in a shop – is more upmarket, with posh galleries and designer shops, such as Stella McCartney at Nos 114 to 121 and Pierre Hardy, with bags and shoes, at Nos 155 to 161.

❹ PASSAGE DU PERRON

The tiny arcade that doglegs from the north of the Galeries du Palais Royal into rue de Beaujolais is Passage du Perron. The writer Colette (1873–1954) lived out her last dozen years in a flat above here (9 rue de Beaujolais), from which she wrote *Paris de Ma Fenêtre* (Paris from My Window), her description of the German occupation of Paris.

❺ GALERIE VIVIENNE

Diagonally opposite from where you exit Passage du Perron at 4 rue des Petits Champs is Galerie Vivienne. Built in 1826 and decorated on the upper walls with bas-reliefs of snakes (signifying prudence), anchors (hope) and beehives (industry) it has always been one of the poshest of the *passages*.

❻ GALERIE COLBERT

The major draw of the Galerie Colbert is its glass dome and rotunda. Check out the bizarre fresco above the exit to the rue des Petits

Champs; it's completely disproportionate. Enter and exit from rue des Petits Champs.

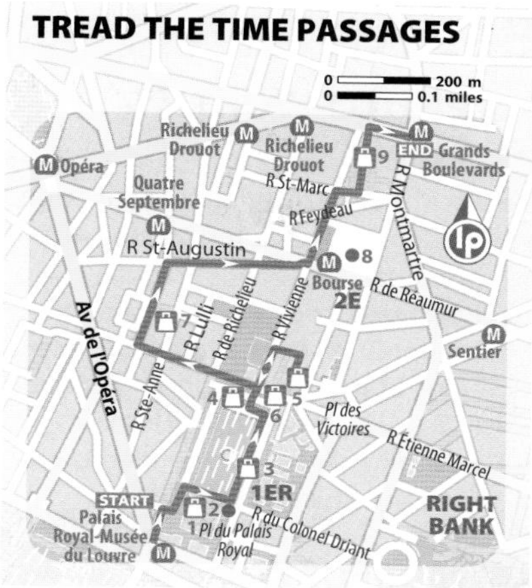

❼ PASSAGE CHOISEUL

No 40 rue des Petits Champs is the entrance to Passage Choiseul (1824), which contains scores of shops. The *passage* has a long literary pedigree: Paul Verlaine (1844–96) drank absinthe here, and Céline (1894–1961) grew up in his mother's lace shop at No 62, which now sells beads and costume jewellery.

❽ BOURSE DE COMMERCE

Leave passage Choiseul at 23 rue St-Augustin and walk eastwards to where the street meets rue du Quatre Septembre. The building across the square is the **Bourse de Commerce** (p71), built in 1826. Turn left and head north up rue Vivienne, and then east (right) along rue St-Marc.

❾ PASSAGE DES PANORAMAS

The entrance to the mazelike Passage des Panoramas is at 10 rue St-Marc. Built in 1800, Passage des Panoramas is the oldest covered arcade in Paris and the first to be lit by gas (1817). It was expanded in 1834 with the addition of four other interconnecting *passages:* Feydeau, Montmartre, St-Marc and Variétés.

TREAD THE TIME PASSAGES

LOUVRE & LES HALLES

BEST...

BEST...

⭨ PHOTO-WORTHY SPOTS

- **Jardin des Tuileries** (p66) Pristine gardens in measured swaths of greenery.
- **Pyramids above Musée du Louvre** (p62) IM Pei's dynamic protrusions of glass and stunning angles.
- **Place Vendôme** (p67) Home to the posh Ritz Hotel, colonnaded buildings and stunning bas-reliefs.

⭨ MUSEUMS

- **Musée du Louvre** (opposite) Magnificent art across five centuries.
- **Les Arts Décoratifs** (p64) Devoted to applied arts, design and advertising.
- **Louvre des Antiquaires** (p66) Museum with a difference – these antiquities and jewellery are all for sale.

⭨ THINGS FOR FREE

- **Jardin des Tuileries** (p66) An urban oasis and perfect post-museum break.
- **Centre Pompidou's mechanical fountains** (p68) Flamboyant, colourful expressions of art.
- **Place Vendôme** (p67) One of Paris' most-exquisite squares.

⭨ FRENCH FARE IN SUBLIME SURROUNDS

- **Café Marly** (p74) Sit and stare at the Louvre pyramids while nibbling on the classics.
- **Café Beaubourg** (p76) Café fare and a front-row seat to the Place Georges Pompidou action.
- **Aux Lyonnais** (p75) Lyonnais fare in art deco surrounds.

WILL SALTER

Jardin des Tuileries (p66)

DISCOVER LOUVRE & LES HALLES

The 1er arrondissement contains some of the most important sights for visitors to Paris. Though it can boast a wild and exciting side, it remains essentially a place where history and culture meet head on along the banks of the Seine. Sculptures merge with lawns, pools and fountains.

To the north, under the arcades of the rue de Rivoli, the pace quickens with bustling shops and chaotic traffic. The Forum des Halles and rue St-Denis seem kilometres away but are already visible, soliciting unwary passers-by with bright lights, jostling crowds and painted ladies. The mostly pedestrianised zone between the Centre Pompidou and the Forum des Halles is filled with people day and night, just as it was for the 850-odd years when part of it served as Paris' main *halles* (marketplace) for foodstuffs.

The Bourse (Stock Exchange) is the financial heart of the 2e arrondissement to the north, the Sentier district, the centre of the city's garment trade and the Opéra, its ode to music and dance.

SIGHTS

MUSÉE DU LOUVRE Map p62

☎ 01 40 20 53 17; www.louvre.fr; permanent collections/permanent collections & temporary exhibits adult €9.50/14, after 6pm Wed & Fri adult €6/12, permanent collections free for EU resident under 26yr, everyone under 18yr & after 6pm Fri for 18-25yr, 1st Sun of the month free for all; ⏰ 9am-6pm Mon, Thu, Sat & Sun, to 10pm Wed & Fri; Ⓜ Palais Royal-Musée du Louvre

The vast Palais du Louvre was constructed as a fortress by Philippe-Auguste in the early 13th century and rebuilt in the mid-16th century for use as a royal residence. The Revolutionary Convention turned it into a national museum in 1793.

The paintings, sculptures and artefacts on display in the Louvre Museum have been amassed by subsequent French governments. Among them are works of art and artisanship from all over Europe and collections of Assyrian, Etruscan, Greek, Coptic and Islamic art and antiquities. The Louvre's *raison d'être* is essentially to present Western art from the Middle Ages to about 1848 (at which point the Musée d'Orsay across the river in the 7e takes over), as well as the works of ancient civilisations that formed the starting point for Western art.

When the museum opened in the late 18th century it contained 2500 paintings and *objets d'art;* today some 35,000 are on display. The 'Grand Louvre' project inaugurated by the late President Mitterrand in 1989 doubled the museum's exhibition space, and both new and renovated galleries have opened in recent years devoted to *objets d'art* such as the crown jewels of Louis XV (Room 66, 1st floor, Apollo Gallery, Denon Wing).

Daunted by the richness and sheer size of the place (the south side facing the Seine is 700m long and it is said that it would take nine months to look at every piece of art in the museum), locals and visitors alike often find the prospect of an afternoon at a smaller museum far more inviting, meaning the Louvre may be the most actively avoided museum

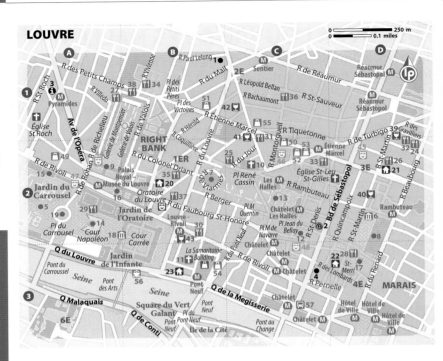

in the world. Eventually, most people do their duty and visit, but many leave overwhelmed, unfulfilled, exhausted and frustrated at having got lost on their way to da Vinci's *La Joconde,* better known as *Mona Lisa* (Room 7, 1st floor, Salle de la Joconde, Denon Wing; see the boxed text, p64). Since it takes several serious visits to get anything more than a brief glimpse of the works on offer, your best bet – after checking out a few that you really want to see – is to choose a particular period or section of the Louvre and pretend that the rest is in another museum somewhere across town.

The most famous works from antiquity include the *Squatted Scribe* (Room 22, 1st floor, Sully Wing), the *Code of Hammurabi* (Room 3, ground floor, Richelieu Wing) and that armless duo, the *Venus de Milo* (Room 7, ground floor, Denon Wing)

and the *Winged Victory of Samothrace* (opposite Room 1, 1st floor, Denon Wing). From the Renaissance, don't miss Michelangelo's *The Dying Slave* (Room 4, ground floor, Michelangelo Gallery, Denon Wing) and works by Raphael, Botticelli and Titian (1st floor, Denon Wing). French masterpieces of the 19th century include Ingres' *The Turkish Bath* (off Room 60, 2nd floor, Sully Wing), Géricault's *The Raft of the Medusa* (Room 77, 1st floor, Denon Wing) and works by Corot, Delacroix and Fragonard (2nd floor, Sully Wing).

The main entrance and ticket windows in the Cour Napoléon are covered by the 21m-high **Grande Pyramide**, a glass pyramid designed by the Chinese-born American architect IM Pei. You can avoid the queues outside the pyramid or at the Porte des Lions entrance by entering the

LOUVRE

Louvre complex via the **Carrousel du Louvre entrance** (Map p62), at 99 rue de Rivoli, or by following the 'Musée du Louvre' exit from the Palais Royal-Musée du Louvre metro station. Buy your tickets in advance online, from the ticket machines in the Carrousel du Louvre or by phoning ☎ 0 892 684 694 or ☎ 01 41 57 32 28, or from the *billeteries* (ticket offices) of Fnac or Virgin Megastores for an extra €1 to €1.60, and walk straight in without queuing. Tickets are valid for the whole day, so you can come and go as you please. They are also valid for the **Musée National Eugène Delacroix** (p200) on the same day.

The Louvre is divided into four sections: the Sully, Denon and Richelieu Wings and Hall Napoléon. **Sully** creates the four sides of the Cour Carrée (literally 'square courtyard') at the eastern end of the complex. **Denon** stretches along the Seine to the south; **Richelieu** is the northern wing running along rue de Rivoli.

The split-level public area under the Grande Pyramide is known as the **Hall Napoléon** (🕐 9am-10pm Wed-Mon, temporary exhibition galleries 9am-6pm Mon, Thu & Sun, 9am-10pm Wed, 9am-8pm Sat). The hall has a temporary exhibition hall, a bookshop and souvenir store, a café and auditoriums for lectures and films. The centrepiece of the **Carrousel du Louvre**, the shopping centre that runs underground from the pyramid to the **Arc de Triomphe du Carrousel** (p149), is the **pyramide inversée** (inverted glass pyramid), also by Pei.

Free English-language maps of the complex (entitled *Plan/Information Louvre*) can be obtained from the circular information desk in the centre of the Hall Napoléon. Excellent publications to guide you if you are doing the Louvre on

MONA LISA: THE TRUTH BEHIND THE SMILE

So much has been written about the painting the French call *La Joconde* and the Italians *La Gioconda,* yet so little is known of the lady behind that enigmatic smile. For centuries admirers speculated on everything from the possibility that the subject was mourning the death of a loved one to that she might have been in love – or in bed – with her portraitist, Leonardo da Vinci.

Mona (actually *monna* in Italian) is a contraction of *madonna,* while Gioconda is the feminine form of the surname Giocondo. With the emergence of several clues in recent years, it is has been established almost certainly that the subject was Lisa Gherardini (1479–1542?), the wife of Florentine merchant Franceso del Giocondo, and that the painting was done between 1503 and 1506 when she was around 25 years old. At the same time, tests done in 2005 with 'emotion recognition' computer software suggest that the smile on 'Madam Lisa' is at least 83% happy. And one other point remains unequivocally certain despite occasional suggestions to the contrary: she was not the lover of Leonardo, who preferred his *Vitruvian Man* to his *Mona.*

your own are the *Louvre Visitors' Guide* (€8), *Louvre Masterpieces* (€10), *Louvre: The 300 Masterpieces* (€12) and the hefty, 485-page *A Guide to the Louvre* (€17). An attractive and useful memento is the DVD entitled *Louvre: The Visit* (€26). All are available from the museum bookshop.

English-language **guided tours** (☎ 01 40 20 52 63) lasting 1½ hours depart from the area under the Grande Pyramide, marked *Acceuil des Groupes* (Groups Reception), at 11am, 2pm and (sometimes) 3.45pm Monday to Saturday, excluding of course Tuesday. Tickets cost €5 in addition to the cost of admission. Groups are limited to 30 people, so it's a good idea to sign up at least 30 minutes before departure time.

Self-paced audioguide tours in six languages, with 1½ hours of commentary, can be rented for €6 under the pyramid at the entrance to each wing.

LES ARTS DÉCORATIFS Map p62

☎ 01 44 55 57 50; www.lesartsdecoratifs.fr; 107 rue de Rivoli, 1er; permanent collections/per-

manent collections & temporary exhibits adult €9/13, 18-25yr €7.50/10.50, permanent collections free for EU resident under 26yr, everyone under 18yr; ⏲ 11am-6pm Tue, Wed & Fri-Sun, to 9pm Thu; Ⓜ Palais Royal-Musée du Louvre The Palais du Louvre contains three other privately administered museums collectively known as the Decorative Arts in its Rohan Wing. Admission includes entry to all three here as well as the Musée Nissim de Camondo in the 8e.

The **Musée des Arts Décoratifs** (Applied Arts Museum), which begins on the 3rd floor and continues over six more floors, displays furniture, jewellery and such *objets d'art* as ceramics and glassware from the Middle Ages and the Renaissance through the art nouveau and art deco periods to modern times.

The much smaller **Musée de la Publicité** (Advertising Museum), which shares the 3rd floor, has some 100,000 posters in its collection dating as far back as the 13th century, and innumerable promotional materials touting everything from 19th-century elixirs and early radio advertisements to Air France as well as electronic publicity. Only certain items are exhibited at any one time; most of the rest of the space is given over to special exhibitions.

The **Musée de la Mode et du Textile** (Museum of Fashion & Textiles) on ground through 2nd floors has some 16,000 costumes dating from the 16th century to today, including *haute couture* creations by the likes of Chanel and Jean-Paul Gaultier. Most of the outfits are warehoused, however, and displayed during regularly scheduled themed exhibitions.

ÉGLISE ST-GERMAIN L'AUXERROIS
Map p62

☎ 01 42 60 13 96; www.saintgermainauxerrois. cef.fr; 2 place du Louvre, 1er; ☯ 9am-7pm Mon-Sat, to 8pm Sun; Ⓜ Louvre-Rivoli or Pont Neuf

Built between the 13th and 16th centuries in a mixture of Gothic and Renaissance styles and with similar dimensions and ground plans to those of Notre Dame, this once royal parish church stands on a site at the eastern end of the Louvre that has been used for Christian worship since about AD 500. After being mutilated in the 18th century by clergy intent

LOUVRE & LES HALLES

SIGHTS

Viaduc des Arts

JEAN-BERNARD CARILLET

↘ IF YOU LIKE...

If you like what you see at **Les Arts Décoratifs** (opposite), ponder similar objects outside a museum setting at **Viaduc des Arts** (Map p98; Ⓜ Gare de Lyon or Daumesnil). The arches beneath this disused railway viaduct running along av Daumesnil southeast of place de la Bastille are a showcase for both designers and artisans – if you are in the market for your own decorative object, this is the place to come. Savvy locals also flock here for repairs to their cherished treasures – here they can get experts to restore Gobelins tapestries, repaint porcelain or re-copper the bottoms of antique saucepans. The top of the viaduct forms a leafy, 4.5km-long promenade called the **Promenade Plantée** (☯ 8am-sunset Mon-Fri, 9am-sunset Sat & Sun), which offers excellent views of the surrounding area. Don't miss the spectacular **art deco police station** (78 av Daumesnil, 12e) at the start of rue de Rambouillet, which is topped with a dozen huge, identical marble caryatids.

LOUVRE & LES HALLES

SIGHTS

on 'modernisation', and damaged during the Revolution, the church was restored by the Gothic Revivalist architect Eugène Viollet-le-Duc in the mid-19th century.

LOUVRE DES ANTIQUAIRES Map p62
☎ 01 42 97 27 27; www.louvre-antiquaires.com; 2 place du Palais Royal; ☺ 11am-7pm Tue-Sun Sep-Jun, to 7pm Tue-Sat Jul & Aug; Ⓜ Palais Royal-Musée du Louvre

A tourist attraction in itself, this elegant 'mall' houses some 70 antique shops spread over three floors, filled with *objets d'art,* furniture, clocks, classical antiquities and jewellery. Visit it as you would the Louvre across the road, bearing in mind that all the stuff here is up for grabs.

JARDIN DES TUILERIES Map p52
☎ 01 40 20 90 43; 113 rue de Rivoli, 1er; ☺ 7am-9pm Apr, May & Sep, 7am-11pm Jun-Aug, 7.30am-7.30pm Oct-Mar; Ⓜ Tuileries or Concorde

The formal, 28-hectare Tuileries Garden, which begins just west of the Jardin du Carrousel, was laid out in its present form, more or less, in 1664 by André Le Nôtre, who also created the gardens at **Versailles** (p238). The Tuileries soon became the most fashionable spot in Paris for parading about in one's finery; today it is a favourite of joggers and forms part of the Banks of the Seine World Heritage Site listed by Unesco in 1991. There are some lovely sculptures within the gardens, including Louise Bourgeois' *The Welcoming Hands* (1996), which faces place de la Concorde.

JEU DE PAUME Map p52
☎ 01 47 03 12 50; www.jeudepaume.org; 1 place de la Concorde, 8e; adult/senior, student & 13-18yr €7/5, free for student & under 26yr 5-9pm last Tue of month; ☺ noon-9pm Tue, to 7pm Wed-Fri, 10am-7pm Sat & Sun; Ⓜ Concorde

The Galerie du Jeu de Paume – Site Concorde (Jeu de Paume National Gallery at Concorde), which stages innovative exhibitions of contemporary art, is housed in an erstwhile *jeu de paume* (real, or royal, tennis court), built in 1861 during the reign of Napoleon III, in the northwestern corner of the Jardin des Tuileries.

KRZYSZTOF DYDYNSKI

Église St-Germain l'Auxerrois (p65)

Arc de Triomphe du Carrousel

LOUVRE & LES HALLES

SIGHTS

↘ ARC DE TRIOMPHE DU CARROUSEL

Erected by Napoleon to celebrate his battlefield successes of 1805, this triumphal arch, which is set in the Jardin du Carrousel at the eastern end of the Jardin des Tuileries, was once crowned by the ancient Greek sculpture called *The Horses of St Mark's*, 'borrowed' from the portico of St Mark's Basilica in Venice by Napoleon but returned after his defeat at Waterloo in 1815. The quadriga (the two-wheeled chariot drawn by four horses) that replaced it was added in 1828 and celebrates the return of the Bourbons to the French throne after Napoleon's downfall. The sides of the arch are adorned with depictions of Napoleonic victories and eight pink-marble columns, atop each of which stands a soldier of the emperor's Grande Armée.

Things you need to know: Map p62; Place du Carrousel, 1er; Ⓜ Palais Royal-Musée du Louvre

MUSÉE DE L'ORANGERIE Map p52
☎ 01 44 77 80 07; www.musee-orangerie.fr, in French; Jardin des Tuileries, 1er; adult/student & 18-25yr €7.50/5.50, permanent collections free for EU resident under 26yr, everyone under 18yr & 1st Sun of the month; Ⓨ 9am-6pm Wed-Mon; Ⓜ Concorde
This museum exhibits important impressionist works, including an eight-panel series of Monet's *Decorations des Nymphéas* (Water Lilies) in two huge oval rooms purpose-built in 1927 to the artist's specifications, as well as paintings by Cézanne, Matisse, Renoir, Rousseau, Soutine and Utrillo.

PLACE VENDÔME Map p52
Ⓜ Tuileries or Opéra
This octagonal square, and the arcaded and colonnaded buildings around it, was built between 1687 and 1721. In March 1796, Napoleon married Josephine, Viscountess of Beauharnais, in the building that's at No 3 in the southwest corner. Today, the buildings around the square

house some of the city's most fashionable boutiques, especially jewellery stores.

In the centre of the square stands the 43.5m-tall **Colonne Vendôme** (Vendôme Column) which consists of a stone core wrapped in a 160m-long bronze spiral that's made from hundreds of Austrian and Russian cannons captured by Napoleon at the Battle of Austerlitz in 1805. The 425 bas-reliefs on the spiral celebrate Napoleon's victories between 1805 and 1807. The statue on top depicts Napoleon in classical Roman dress.

PALAIS ROYAL Map p62

☎ 01 42 96 13 32; www.monuments-nationaux.fr; 6 rue de Montpensier, 1er; Ⓜ Palais Royal-Musée du Louvre

Mechanical fountains, Place Georges Pompidou
WILL SALTER

The Royal Palace, which accommodated a young Louis XIV for a time in the 1640s, lies to the north of place du Palais Royal and the Louvre. Construction was begun in 1624 by Cardinal Richelieu, though most of the present neoclassical complex dates from the latter part of the 18th century. Today it contains the governmental **Conseil d'État** (State Council; Map p62) and is closed to the public.

CENTRE POMPIDOU Map p62

☎ 01 44 78 12 33; www.centrepompidou.fr; place Georges Pompidou, 4e; Ⓜ Rambuteau

The Centre National d'Art et de Culture Georges Pompidou (Georges Pompidou National Centre of Art & Culture), also known as the Centre Beaubourg, has amazed and delighted visitors since it was inaugurated in 1977, not just for its outstanding collection of modern art but for its radical architectural statement.

The **Forum du Centre Pompidou** (admission free; ⏲ 11am-10pm Wed-Mon), the open space of the centre at ground level, has temporary exhibits and information desks. The 4th and 5th floors of the centre exhibit a fraction of the almost 65,000 works by 5700 artists of the **Musée National d'Art Moderne** (MNAM; National Museum of Modern Art; adult €10-12, 18-25yr €8-9, EU resident under 26yr & everyone under 18yr free & 1st Sun of the month free for all; ⏲ 11am-9pm Wed-Mon), France's national collection of art dating from 1905 onward, and including the work of the surrealists and cubists as well as pop art and contemporary works.

The huge **Bibliothèque Publique d'Information** (BPI; ☎ 01 44 78 12 33; www.bpi.fr; ⏲ noon-10pm Mon & Wed-Fri, 11am-10pm Sat & Sun), entered from rue du Renard, takes up part of the 1st as well as the entire 2nd and 3rd floors of the centre. The 6th floor has two galleries for **temporary exhibitions** (included in the higher entrance fee)

Musée des Arts Décoratifs (p64)

KRZYSZTOF DYDYNSKI

and a trendy restaurant called **Georges**, with panoramic views of Paris. (If you want a view of the view without eating, a ticket costs €3 for adults and is free for those under 26.) There are **cinemas** (adult/senior & 18-25yr €6/4) and other entertainment venues on the 1st floor and in the basement.

Atelier Brancusi (Map p62; 55 rue Rambuteau, 4e; admission free; ☽ 2-6pm Wed-Mon), across place Georges Pompidou to the west of the main building, is a reconstruction of the studio of Romanian-born sculptor Constantin Brancusi (1876–1957) designed by Renzo Piano. It contains some 160 examples of his work, including hundreds of drawings, sketches, paintings and photographs.

West of the centre, **Place Georges Pompidou** and the nearby pedestrian streets attract buskers, musicians, jugglers and mime artists, and can be a lot of fun. South of the centre on place Igor Stravinsky, the fanciful **mechanical fountains** (Map p62) of skeletons, hearts, treble clefs and a big pair of ruby-red lips,

created by Jean Tinguely and Niki de St-Phalle, are a positive delight.

MUSÉE DES ARTS ET MÉTIERS
Map p62

☎ 01 53 01 82 00; www.arts-et-metiers.net; 60 rue de Réaumur, 3e; permanent collections/permanent collections & temporary exhibits adult €6.50/7.50, 18-25yr €4.50/5.50; ☽ 10am-6pm Tue, Wed & Fri-Sun, to 9.30pm Thu; Ⓜ Arts et Métiers

The Arts & Crafts Museum, the oldest museum of science and technology in Europe, is a must for anyone with an interest in how things work. Housed in the 18th-century priory of St-Martin des Champs, some 3000 instruments, machines and working models from the 18th to 20th centuries are displayed according to theme (from Construction and Energy to Transportation) across three floors. Taking pride of place in the attached church of St-Martin des Champs is Foucault's original pendulum, which he introduced to the world in 1855, and Louis Blériot's monoplane from 1909. There are lots of workshops and other activities here for children.

FORUM DES HALLES Map p62

☎ 01 44 76 96 56; www.forum-des-halles.com; 1 rue Pierre Lescaut, 1er; 🕑 shops 10am-8pm Mon-Sat; Ⓜ Les Halles or Châtelet les Halles

Les Halles, the city's main wholesale food market, occupied the area just south of the Église St-Eustache from the early 12th century until 1969, when it was moved lox, stock and cabbage head to the southern suburb of Rungis, near Orly. In its place, this unspeakably ugly, four-level, underground shopping centre with some 170 shops was constructed in the glass-and-chrome style of the late 1970s; it's slated to be gutted and rebuilt by 2012, topped with La Canopée, an architecturally stunning 'canopy' above shop as well as public spaces such as an auditorium and conservatory. Topping the complex on the street level is a popular **garden**, also slated for a major facelift, with a rather stunning sculpture by Henri de Miller (1953–99) called *Listen*. In the warmer months, street musicians, fire-eaters and other performers display their talents here, especially at **place Jean du Bellay**, which is adorned by a multitiered Renaissance fountain, the **Fontaine des Innocents** (1549).

ÉGLISE ST-EUSTACHE Map p62

☎ 01 42 36 31 05; www.saint-eustache.org, in French; place du Jour, 1er; 🕑 9.30am-7pm Mon-Fri, 10am-7pm Sat, 9am-7.15pm Sun; Ⓜ Les Halles

This majestic church, one of the most beautiful in Paris, is just north of the gardens next to the Forum des Halles. Constructed between 1532 and 1637, St-Eustache is primarily Gothic, though a neoclassical facade was added on the western side in the mid-18th century. Inside, there are some exceptional Flamboyant Gothic arches holding up the ceiling of the chancel, though most of the ornamentation is Renaissance and even classical. Above the western entrance, the gargantuan organ, with 101 stops and 8000 pipes dating from 1854, is used for concerts (long a tradition here) and at Sunday Mass at 11am and 6pm.

Musée des Arts et Métiers (p69)

BRUCE BI

BOURSE DE COMMERCE Map p62

☎ 01 55 65 55 65; 2 rue de Viarmes, 1er; admission free; ⊙ 9am-6pm Mon-Fri; Ⓜ Les Halles

At one time the city's grain market, the circular Trade Exchange was capped with a copper dome in 1811. The murals running along internal walls below the galleries were painted by five different artists in 1889 and restored in 1998. They represent French trade and industry through the ages.

SLEEPING

This area is very central but don't expect to find tranquillity or many bargains here. While it is more disposed to welcoming top-end travellers, there are some decent midrange places to choose from.

HÔTEL RITZ PARIS Map p52   Hotel €€€

☎ 01 43 16 30 30; www.ritzparis.com; 15 place Vendôme, 1er; s & d €770-870, ste from €1020; Ⓜ Opéra; ▨ ☎ ▣

So famous it's lent its name to the English lexicon, the incomparable, the unmistakable Ritz has 161 sparkling rooms and suites. Its **L'Espadon** restaurant has two Michelin stars and the **Hemingway Bar** (☎ 01 43 16 30 50; ⊙ 6.30pm-2am Tue-Sat) is where the American author imbibed once he'd made a name for himself and took charge of the place during the liberation of Paris. The Ritz is celebrated for its cooking school. Wi-fi costs €25 extra.

LE RELAIS DU LOUVRE
Map p62   Hotel €€

☎ 01 40 41 96 42; www.relaisdulouvre.com; 19 rue des Prêtres St-Germain l'Auxerrois, 1er; s €125, d & tw €170-215, tr €215, ste €244-435; Ⓜ Pont Neuf; ▨ ☎

If you are someone who likes style but in a traditional sense, choose this lovely 21-room hotel just west of the Louvre and

Sculpture in front of Église St-Eustache
JOHN ELK III

south of the Église St-Germain l'Auxerrois. The nine rooms facing the street and the church are on the petite side; if you are looking for something more spacious, ask for one of the five rooms ending in a '2' (eg 52). Room 2 itself has access to the garden. The apartment on the top floor sleeps five, boasts a fully equipped kitchen and has memorable views over the rooftops.

HÔTEL ST-MERRY Map p62   Hotel €€

☎ 01 42 78 14 15; www.hotelmarais.com; 78 rue de la Verrerie, 4e; s & d €135-230, tr €205-275, ste €250-407; Ⓜ Châtelet; ▨ ☎

The interior of this 12-room hostelry, with beamed ceilings, church pews and wrought-iron candelabra, is a neo-Goth's wet dream; you have to see the architectural elements of room 9 (flying buttress

↘ UNDERGROUND ART

Almost half of Paris' 300 **metro stations** were given a face-lift to mark the centenary of the world-famous Métropolitain at the turn of the millennium. The following list is just a sample of the most interesting stations from an artistic perspective.

Abbesses (Map p126; line 12) The noodle-like pale-green metalwork and glass canopy of the station entrance is one of the finest examples of the work of Hector Guimard (1867–1942), the celebrated French art nouveau architect.

Assemblée Nationale (Map p164; line 12 platform) Gigantic posters of silhouettes in red, white and blue by artist Jean-Charles Blais represent the MPs currently sitting in parliament on the surface.

Bastille (Map p98; line 5 platform) A 180 sq metre ceramic fresco features scenes taken from newspaper engravings published during the Revolution, with illustrations of the destruction of the infamous prison.

Cluny-La Sorbonne (Map p214; line 10 platform) A large ceramic mosaic replicates the signatures of intellectuals, artists and scientists from the Latin Quarter through history including Molière, Rabelais and Robespierre.

Concorde (Map p52; line 12 platform) What look like children's building blocks in white-and-blue ceramic on the walls of the station are 45,000 tiles that spell out the text of the *Déclaration des Droits de l'Homme et du Citoyen* (Declaration of the Rights of Man and of the Citizen), the document setting forth the principles of the French Revolution.

Louvre-Rivoli (Map p62; line 1 platform & corridor) Statues, bas-reliefs and photographs offer a small taste of what to expect at the Musée du Louvre above ground.

Palais Royal-Musée du Louvre (Map p62; line 1) The zany entrance on the place du Palais by Jean-Nichel Othoniel is composed of two crown-shaped cupolas (one representing the day, the other night) with 800 red, blue, amber and violet glass balls threaded on an aluminium structure.

over the bed) and the furnishings of 12 (choir-stall bed board) to believe them. On the downside there is no lift connecting the postage-stamp lobby with the four upper floors, and only some of the rooms have air-conditioning.

HÔTEL FAVART Map p52   Hotel €€
☎ 01 42 97 59 83; www.hotel-favart.com; 5 rue Marivaux, 2e; s €105-130, d €135-160, tr €145-180, q €155-200; Ⓜ Richelieu Drouot; ⌘ ⌘ ⌘

This stylish art nouveau hotel with 37 rooms facing the Opéra Comique feels like it never let go of the belle époque. It's an excellent choice if you're interested in shopping, being within easy walking distance of the *grands magasins* on blvd Haussmann. We like the prints of Parisian scenes on the walls in the lobby and the dramatic wrought-iron staircase leading up to the 1st floor, but not those fake books. Goya slept here in 1824.

HÔTEL DU SÉJOUR BEAUBOURG

Map p62   Hotel €€

☎ 01 48 87 40 36; www.hoteldusejour.com; 36 rue du Grenier St-Lazare, 3e; s €78-95, d €90-97; Ⓜ Rambuteau; 🛜

This bright and cheerful 20-room property offers a warm welcome and excellent value just minutes from the Centre Pompidou. Rooms, at the top of a wooden staircase (no lift), are simple but some have had a recent refit and cherry seems to be the colour of choice. Double-glazing keeps the din out on the street where it belongs.

HÔTEL DE LILLE Map p62   Hotel €

☎ /fax 01 42 33 33 42; 8 rue de Pélican, 1er; s €39-43, d €50-55, tr €85; Ⓜ Palais Royal-Musée du Louvre

This old-fashioned but spotlessly clean 13-room hotel is down a quiet side street from the Louvre in a 17th-century building. A third of the rooms have just a washbasin and bidet (communal showers cost €3), while the rest have en suite showers. Some of the rooms, like No 1 with its Moroccan theme, have been refitted.

The friendly and helpful manager speaks good English.

EATING

The area between Forum des Halles (1er) and the Centre Pompidou (4e) is filled with a number of trendy restaurants, but most of them cater to tourists and few of them are especially good. Streets lined with places to eat include rue des Lombards, the narrow streets to the north and east of Forum des Halles and pedestrian-only rue Montorgueil, a market street that's probably your best bet for something quick.

Those in search of Asian food should head for rue Ste-Anne and other streets of Paris' so-called Japantown.

CHEZ LA VIEILLE Map p62   French €€€

☎ 01 42 60 15 78; 1 rue Bailleul & 37 rue de l'Arbre Sec, 1er; starters €15-23, mains €24-30, menu €26 (lunch only); ⏰ lunch Mon-Fri, dinner to 9.45pm Mon, Tue, Thu & Fri; Ⓜ Louvre-Rivoli

'At the Old Lady's', a favourite little restaurant south of Bourse, is on two floors,

CHRISTINE OSBORNE

Bourse de Commerce (p71)

but don't expect a slot on the more rustic ground floor; that's reserved for regulars. The small menu reflects the size of the place but is universally sublime.

LE GRAND COLBERT

Map p62   French €€€

☎ 01 42 86 87 88; www.legrandcolbert.fr; 2 rue Vivienne, 2e; starters €9.20-23.50, mains €21.50-35, 2-/3-course menus €22.50 & €29.50 (lunch only); ⏰ noon-1am; Ⓜ Pyramides

This former workers' *cafétéria* transformed into a *fin de siècle* showcase is more relaxed than many similarly restored restaurants and a convenient spot for lunch if visiting Galerie Vivienne and Galerie Colbert or cruising the streets relatively late at night (last orders: midnight).

CAFÉ MARLY Map p62   French, Café €€€

☎ 01 46 26 06 60; cour Napoléon du Louvre, 93 rue de Rivoli, 1er; starters €10-26, mains €20-30; ⏰ 8am-2am; Ⓜ Palais Royal-Musée du Louvre

This classic venue facing the Louvre's inner courtyard serves contemporary French fare throughout the day under the palace col-

onnades. The views of the glass pyramid are priceless – if you don't know you're in Paris now, you never will – and depending on how *au courant* (familiar) you are with French starlets and people who appear in *Match,* you should get an eyeful.

DERRIÈRE Map p62   French €€€

☎ 01 44 61 91 95; 69 rue des Gravilliers, 3e; starters €12-15, mains €18-26; ⏰ lunch Tue-Fri, dinner to 11pm daily; Ⓜ Arts et Métiers

So secretive it's almost a speakeasy, 'Behind' is just that – set in a lovely courtyard between (and behind) the **404** (p76) restaurant and the **Andy Walhoo** (p77) bar and club. Chilled in a 'shoes-off' kind of way with distressed arm chairs and newspapers on the coffee tables, this place is a lot more serious behind the scenes, serving up both classic French bistro dishes and more inventive ones (eg suckling pig braised in ginger and lime with lentils, macaroni gratin with taramasalata). Vegetarians: more than half of the starters are meatless. Smokers: there's a *fumoir* behind the closet door upstairs.

WILL SALTER

Café Marly

AUBERGE NICOLAS FLAMEL

Map p62   French €€€

☎ 01 42 71 77 78; www.auberge-nicolas-flamel.
fr, in French; 51 rue de Montmorency, 3e; starters €10, mains €17; 2-/3-course menu €18.50/25
(lunch only); ☺ lunch & dinner to 11pm Mon-
Sat; Ⓜ Rambuteau or Arts et Métiers

A visit to this charming restaurant, with its
higgledy-piggledy rooms on two floors,
is not so much about the food but the location: once the residence of celebrated
alchemist and writer Flamel (1330–1417),
it's the oldest building still standing in
Paris. Expect correct but not earth-moving
dishes – duck foie gras, lamb cooked in a
tajine and so on. Ask about wine tastings
in the atmospheric (read: spooky) cellar.

AUX LYONNAIS

Map p52   French, Lyonnais €€

☎ 01 42 96 65 04; www.auxlyonnais.com; 32
rue St-Marc, 2e; starters €10.50-14, mains €19-
25, 2-/3-course menus €26/34; ☺ lunch Tue-Fri,
dinner to 11pm Tue-Sat; Ⓜ Richelieu Drouot

This is where Alain Ducasse (who's got
three Michelin stars at his restaurant over
at the Plaza Athénée) and his followers
'slum' it. The venue is an art nouveau masterpiece that feels more real than movie
set and the food is restructured Lyonnais
classics on the short, seasonal menu; any
item based on *cochon* (pig) comes with an
ironclad guarantee to satisfy and everything goes well with Beaujolais.

L'ARDOISE Map p52   French, Bistro €€

☎ 01 42 96 28 18; www.lardoise-paris.com; 28
rue du Mont Thabor, 1er; menu €34; ☺ lunch
Tue-Sat, dinner to 11pm Tue-Sun; Ⓜ Concorde
or Tuileries

This is a lovely little bistro with no menu as
such (*ardoise* means 'blackboard', which
is all there is), but who cares? The food –
fricassee of corn-fed chicken with morels,
pork cheeks in ginger, hare in black pep-

per, prepared dextrously by chef Pierre
Jay (ex-Tour d'Argent) – is superb, the
menu changes every three weeks and
the three-course *prix fixe* (set menu) offers good value.

WILLI'S WINE BAR

Map p62   French, Bistro €€

☎ 01 42 61 05 09; www.williswinebar.com; 13
rue des Petits Champs, 1er; starters €10, mains
€18.50, menus €20 & €26 (lunch only), €32 & €35;
☺ lunch & dinner to 11pm Mon-Sat; Ⓜ Bourse

This civilised and very convivial wine bar-
cum-bistro was opened in 1980 by British
expats who introduced the wine-bar concept to Paris. The food by chef François
Yon is still excellent, the wines (especially
Côtes du Rhône) well chosen and Willi's
legendary status lives on.

AU PIED DE COCHON

Map p62   French, Brasserie €€

☎ 01 40 13 77 00; www.pieddecochon.com; 6
rue Coquillère, 1er; starters €6.90-18.50, mains
€17.20-35.90, menus €16.30 (lunch only) &
€21.90; ☺ 24hr; Ⓜ Les Halles

This venerable establishment, which once
satisfied the appetites of both market por-
ters and theatre-goers with its onion soup
and *pieds de cochon* (pig's feet or trotters),
has become more uniformly upmarket
and touristy since Les Halles was moved
to the suburbs, but it still opens round the
clock seven days a week as it has since the
end of WWII.

L'ÉPI D'OR Map p62   French, Bistro €€

☎ 01 42 36 38 12; 25 rue Jean-Jacques Rousseau, 1er; starters €6-16, mains €17-24,
2-/3-course menus €17/23; ☺ lunch Mon-Fri,
dinner to 11.30pm Mon-Sat; Ⓜ Louvre-Rivoli

'The Golden Sword' has been an institution since the belle époque, when it
would open at 10pm to serve the *'forts des
halles'*, the brutes who stacked the *'devils'*,

huge bags of potatoes and cabbage, all night at the old Marché des Halles. Today it's an oh-so-Parisian bistro with 1940s decor and well-prepared, classic dishes.

COMPTOIR DE LA GASTRONOMIE

Map p62   French €€

☎ 01 42 33 31 32; www.comptoir-gastronomie. com, in French; 34 rue Montmartre, 1er; starters €6-16, mains €16-25; ☺ noon-11pm Mon-Thu, to midnight Fri & Sat; Ⓜ Les Halles

This striking art nouveau establishment, here since 1894, has an elegant dining room where dishes are constructed around delicacies such as foie gras, truffles and caviar. The adjoining **épicerie fine** (specialist grocer; ☺ 6am-8pm Mon, 9am-8pm Tue-Sat) stocks a scrumptious array of gourmet goods to take away.

404 Map p62   North African, Moroccan €€

☎ 01 42 74 57 81; 69 rue des Gravilliers, 3e; starters €7-9, couscous & tajines €15-24, menus €17 (lunch only); ☺ lunch Mon-Fri, dinner to midnight daily, brunch noon-4pm Sat & Sun; Ⓜ Arts et Métiers

As comfortable a Maghreb (North African) caravanserai as you'll find in Paris, the 404 not only has excellent couscous and *tajines* but superb grills (€13 to €24) and fish *pastilla* (€18). The *brunch berbère* (Berber brunch; €21) is available at the weekend. You'll just love the One Thousand and One Nights decor with antiques and curios.

CAFÉ BEAUBOURG

Map p62   French, International €€

☎ 01 48 87 63 96; 100 rue St-Martin, 4e; starters €9-14, mains €15-21; ☺ 8am-1am Sun-Wed, to 2am Thu-Sat; Ⓜ Châtelet–Les Halles

This upbeat minimalist café across from the Centre Pompidou has been drawing a well-heeled crowd for breakfast and

brunch (from €13 to €24) on its terrace for some two dozen years now.

JOE ALLEN Map p62   American €€

☎ 01 42 36 70 13; www.joeallenrestaurant.com; 30 rue Pierre Lescot, 1er; starters €7.90-11.10, mains €14-26.50, menus €14 (lunch only), €18.10 & €22.50; ☺ noon-2am; Ⓜ Étienne Marcel

An institution in Paris since 1972, Joe Allen is a little bit of New York in Paris, with a great atmosphere and a good selection of Californian wines. There's an excellent brunch (€19.50 to €23.50) from noon to 4pm at the weekend, where many can be seen slumped over a Bloody Mary and trying to make sense of the night – or was that the morning? – before.

BAAN BORAN Map p62   Thai €

☎ 01 40 15 90 45; www.baan-boran.com, in French; 43 rue de Montpensier, 1er; starters €8-20, mains €11.40-21; ☺ lunch Mon-Fri, dinner to 11pm Mon-Sat; Ⓜ Palais Royal–Musée du Louvre or Pyramides

The fare at this eatery behind the Palais Royal is provincial Thai and about as authentic as you'll find in this part of Paris. It makes a convenient stop before or after touring the Louvre.

SCOOP Map p62   International €

☎ 01 42 60 31 84; www.scoopcafe.com, in French; 154 rue St-Honoré, 1er; dishes €9.90-15.50; ☺ 11am-4pm Tue, 11am-4pm & 7-10pm Wed-Sat, 11am-5pm Sun; Ⓜ Louvre-Rivoli

This American-style ice-cream parlour has also been making quite a splash with its excellent wraps, burgers, tarts and soups and central, very fashionable location.

SELF-CATERING

Rue Montorgueil (Map p62; rue Montorgueil btwn rue de Turbigo & rue Réaumur, 2e; ☺ 8am-7.30pm Tue-Sat, to noon Sun; Ⓜ Les Halles or Sentier), one of the busiest and best-

Comptoir de la Gastronomie

GREG ELMS

stocked *rues commerçantes* (commercial streets, not unlike open-air markets) in Paris, is north of Les Halles.

DRINKING

Some great bars skirt the no-man's-land of Les Halles, but avoid crossing the garden above the Forum des Halles at night. Rue des Lombards is celebrated for its jazz venues, while sophisticated bars are grouped towards the Louvre and Palais Royal. Rue Tiquetonne and rue Montorgueil in the Étienne Marcel area have a fine selection of hip cafés.

LE CŒUR FOU Map p62   Bar
☎ 01 42 33 91 33; 55 rue Montmartre, 2e;
⏰ 5pm-2am; Ⓜ Étienne Marcel
'The Crazy Heart' is hip without attaining that too-cool-by-half pretentiousness that reigns in the Étienne Marcel environs. It's a tiny, gallery-like bar with little candles nestled in whitewashed walls, a dapper late-20s crowd that doesn't keep to itself, and rotating art exhibitions.

CAFÉ LA FUSÉE Map p62   Bar, Café
☎ 01 42 76 93 99; 168 rue St-Martin, 3e;
⏰ 10am-2am; Ⓜ Rambuteau or Étienne Marcel
Close to the Pompidou Centre but away from the crowds, this hip café, strung with coloured lights, is a lively and laid-back local hangout. The wine selection is particularly good and the music excellent.

LE COCHON À L'OREILLE
Map p62   Bar, Café
☎ 01 42 36 07 56; 15 rue Montmartre, 1er;
⏰ 10am-11pm Tue-Sat; Ⓜ Les Halles or Étienne Marcel
A Parisian *bijou* (jewel), this heritage-listed hole-in-the-wall retains its belle époque tiles with market scenes of Les Halles and just eight tiny tables.

ANDY WALHOO Map p62   Cocktail Bar
☎ 01 42 71 20 38; 69 rue des Gravilliers, 3e;
⏰ 5.30pm-2am Tue-Sat; Ⓜ Arts et Métiers
Casablanca meets pop-artist Andy Warhol in this cool, multicoloured cocktail lounge hidden away just north of the Centre Georges Pompidou. Its clever name

Angélina tearoom

WILL SALTER

LE FUMOIR Map p62 · Cocktail Bar
☎ 01 42 92 00 24; 6 rue de l'Amiral de Coligny, 1er; ☽ 11am-2am; Ⓜ Louvre-Rivoli
This colonial-style bar-restaurant opposite the eastern flank of the Louvre is a fine place to sip top-notch gin from quality glassware while nibbling on olives from the vintage mahogany bar. There's a buoyant, corporate crowd on weekday evenings. The restaurant is popular for late breakfast during the week and brunch on Sundays; try to get a seat in the 'library'.

ANGÉLINA Map p52 · Tearoom
☎ 01 42 60 82 00; 226 rue de Rivoli, 1er; ☽ 8am-7pm Mon-Fri, 9am-7pm Sat & Sun; Ⓜ Tuileries
Line up for a table at Angélina, along with lunching ladies, their posturing poodles and half the students from Tokyo University. This beautiful, high-ceilinged tearoom has exquisite furnishings, mirrored walls and fabulous fluffy cakes.

ENTERTAINMENT & ACTIVITIES

LE REX CLUB Map p52 · Clubbing
☎ 01 42 36 10 96; www.rexclub.com; 5 blvd Poissonnière, 2e; admission free-€12; ☽ 11.30pm-6am Wed-Sat; Ⓜ Bonne Nouvelle
The Rex reigns majestic in the house and techno scene, always has and probably always will. The sound system is impeccable but getting in is more a question of lining up than looking right. Friday nights are a techno institution in Paris.

LES BAINS DOUCHES Map p62 · Clubbing
☎ 01 48 87 01 80; www.lesbainsdouchesparis.com, in French; 7 rue du Bourg l'Abbé, 3e; admission €10-20; ☽ 11.30pm-5am Wed-Sun; Ⓜ Étienne Marcel

means 'I have nothing' in Arabic and is a major misnomer: the acid colours, sweet cocktails, pushy staff and loud house music may be a bit too much for some palates. Happy hour is 5pm to 8pm. The courtyard behind is paradise for smokers and pullers.

HARRY'S NEW YORK BAR
Map p52 · Cocktail Bar
☎ 01 42 61 71 14; 5 rue Daunou, 2e; ☽ 10.30am-4am; Ⓜ Opéra
One of the most popular American-style bars in the prewar years (when there were several dozen in Paris), Harry's once welcomed such habitués as writers F Scott Fitzgerald and Ernest Hemingway, who no doubt sampled the bar's unique cocktail creation: the Bloody Mary (€12.50).

Housed in a refitted old Turkish *hammam,* this darling of the 1990s, famous for its glamorous clientele and impassable door complete with blocking limo, has sought to shake off its inaccessible image with a new mix of theme nights, Sunday morning 'afters' and gay soirées. It's working, but just and memories do linger: Friday is still 'Famous Club' night.

SUNSET/SUNSIDE Map p62   Jazz & Blues
☎ 01 40 26 46 60; www.sunset-sunside.com; 60 rue des Lombards, 1er; admission free-€25; ⏱ 8pm-4am; Ⓜ Châtelet
It's two venues in one at this trendy, well-respected club. The Sunset downstairs has electric jazz and fusion. The Sunside picks things up upstairs with jazz acoustics.

OPÉRA COMIQUE Map p52   Opera
☎ 0 825 010 123; www.opera-comique.com; 1 place Boïeldieu, 2e; tickets €6-108; Ⓜ Richelieu Drouot
This century-old hall has premiered many important French operas and continues to host classic and less-known works. Buy tickets online or from the **box office** (⏱ 11am-7pm Mon-Sat, to 5pm Sun) on the other side of the square from the theatre. Subject to availability, students and those under 28 can buy tickets from €15 (but often not for weekend performances).

COMÉDIE FRANÇAISE
Map p62   Theatre
☎ 0 825 101 680; www.comedie-francaise.fr; place Colette, 1er; tickets €5-37; ⏱ box office 11am-6pm; Ⓜ Palais Royal–Musée du Louvre
Founded in 1680 under Louis XIV, the 'French Comedy' theatre bases its repertoire around the works of classic French playwrights such as Molière, Racine, Corneille, Beaumarchais, Marivaux and Musset, though in recent years contemporary and even – shock, horror! – non-

French works (in translation, of course) have been staged.

There are three venues: the main **Salle Richelieu** on place Colette just west of the Palais Royal; the **Studio Théâtre** (Map p62; ☎ 01 44 58 98 58; Galerie du Carrousel du Louvre, 99 rue de Rivoli, 1er; ⏱ box office 2-5pm Wed-Sun; Ⓜ Palais Royal-Musée du Louvre) and the **Théâtre du Vieux Colombier** (☎ 01 44 39 87 00; 21 rue du Vieux Colombier, 6e; ⏱ box office 11am-6pm; Ⓜ St-Sulpice).

SPA NUXE Map p62   Hammams & Spas
☎ 01 55 80 71 40; www.nuxe.com; 32 rue Montorgueil, 1e; massage from €80; ⏱ 9.30am-9pm Mon-Fri, 9.30am-7.30pm Sat; Ⓜ Les Halles
A regular in *Elle* and other French glossies, this recently overhauled spa lounging in a medieval wine cellar with old stone walls and wood-beamed ceilings is where stars and supermodels find peace. An orgy of 45-minute massages (Thai, ayurvedic, Californian, shiatsu), including rhythmic ones to music; skin treatments; French pedicures and manicures; and so on.

SHOPPING

The 1e and 2e arrondissements are mostly about fashion. Indeed, the Sentier garment district has become a centre for fashion, while rue Étienne Marcel, place des Victoires and rue du Jour offer prominent labels and shoe shops. Nearby rue Montmartre and rue Tiquetonne are known for their streetwear and avant-garde designs. Les Halles itself, once the city's food market, is now a vast underground shopping complex.

Most of the many museums in this neighbourhood have excellent in-house shops. For a preview of what to expect, check out the **Les Boutiques de Musées** (www.boutiquesdemusees.fr/en) website.

LOUVRE & LES HALLES

SHOPPING

BARBARA BUI
Map p62   Fashion & Accessories
☎ 01 40 26 43 65; www.barbarabui.com; 23 rue Étienne Marcel, 2e; ⏱ 11am-7.30pm Mon-Sat; Ⓜ Étienne Marcel

Franco-Vietnamese Barbara Bui's nearby Kabuki Femme was an instant success here in Paris and she went on to open her own shops, known for their elegant modernism and beautifully cut trousers. There's also a **Marais branch** (☎ 01 53 01 88 05; 43 rue des Francs Bourgeois, 4e; ⏱ 12.30-7pm Mon, 10.30am-7pm Tue-Sat, 1-7pm Sun; Ⓜ St-Paul).

BONPOINT Map p62   Fashion & Accessories
☎ 01 40 26 20 90; www.bonpoint.com; 50 rue Étienne Marcel; ⏱ 10am-7pm Mon-Sat; Ⓜ Étienne Marcel

This is an immaculate collection of classic children's clothes (newborn to 14 years). It's a longstanding tradition for the chic *bébés* of Paris to be besuited by their grannies in Bonpoint.

KABUKI FEMME
Map p62   Fashion & Accessories
☎ 01 42 33 55 65; www.barbarabui.com; 25 rue Étienne Marcel, 2e; ⏱ 11am-7.30pm Mon-Sat; Ⓜ Étienne Marcel

Opened some 20 years ago, this is the shop that brought Barbara Bui to world attention. Her own eponymous store is next door and you'll find **Kabuki Homme** (Map p62; ☎ 01 42 33 13 44; 21 rue Étienne Marcel, 2e), for men, two doors down. In addition to Bui's own designs there's a judicious selection from other brands, including Prada, Balenciaga, Stella McCartney, Yves Saint Laurent and Dior.

KENZO Map p62   Fashion & Accessories
☎ 01 40 28 11 80; www.kenzo.com; 1 rue du Pont Neuf, 1er; ⏱ noon-7.30pm Mon, 11am-7.30pm Tue-Sat; Ⓜ Pont Neuf

While Kenzo himself may have retired from designing some time ago, his successor Antonio Marras has brought a new *joie de vivre* to the label. The Pont Neuf flagship store is spread over five floors and is a tantalising temple to fashion and beauty for both men and women.

KILIWATCH
Map p62   Fashion & Accessories
☎ 01 42 21 17 37; www.kiliwatch.fr, in French; 64 rue Tiquetonne, 2e; ⏱ 2-7pm Mon, 11am-7.30pm Tue-Sat; Ⓜ Étienne Marcel

A Parisian institution, Kiliwatch is always packed to the rafters with hip guys and gals rummaging through rack after rack of new and used streetwear and designs. There's a startling vintage range including hats and boots, as well as art and photography books, eyewear and the latest sneakers.

LAVINIA Map p52   Food & Drink
☎ 01 42 97 54 50; www.lavinia.com, in French; 3 bd de la Madeleine, 1er; ⏱ 10am-8pm Mon-Sat; Ⓜ Madeleine

Among the largest (and certainly most exclusive) drinks shops is this bastion of booze near Madeleine. To be sure, come here for the fruit of the vine but we usually visit to top our collection of exclusive *eaux-de-vie* (fruit brandies).

ASTIER DE VILLATTE
Map p62   Home & Garden
☎ 01 42 60 74 13; www.astierdevillatte.com; 173 rue St-Honoré, 1er; ⏱ 11am-7.30pm Mon-Sat; Ⓜ Palais Royal-Musée du Louvre

The only Parisian outlet of the exclusive manufacturer of ceramic tableware displays its settings (and candles and beauty products) in a wonderfully old-fashioned shop just west of the Palais Royal.

THE ISLANDS

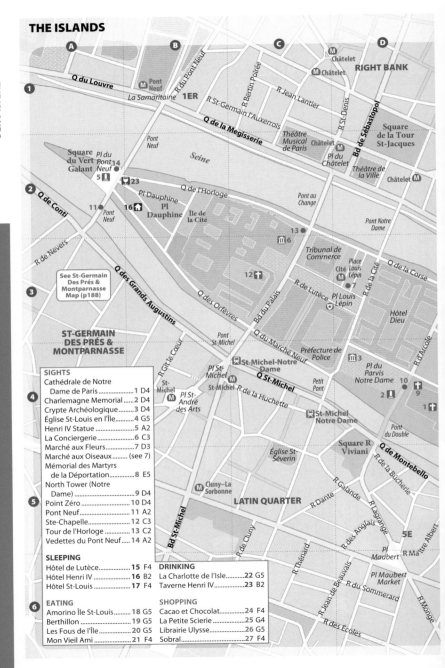

THE ISLANDS

SIGHTS

Cathédrale de Notre Dame de Paris	1 D4
Charlemagne Memorial	2 D4
Crypte Archéologique	3 D4
Église St-Louis en l'Île	4 G5
Henri IV Statue	5 A2
La Conciergerie	6 C3
Marché aux Fleurs	7 D3
Marché aux Oiseaux	(see 7)
Mémorial des Martyrs de la Déportation	8 E5
North Tower (Notre Dame)	9 D4
Point Zéro	10 D4
Pont Neuf	11 A2
Ste-Chapelle	12 C3
Tour de l'Horloge	13 C2
Vedettes du Pont Neuf	14 A2

SLEEPING

Hôtel de Lutèce	15 F4
Hôtel Henri IV	16 B2
Hôtel St-Louis	17 F4

EATING

Amorino Île St-Louis	18 G5
Berthillon	19 G5
Les Fous de l'Île	20 G5
Mon Vieil Ami	21 F4

DRINKING

La Charlotte de l'Isle	22 G5
Taverne Henri IV	23 B2

SHOPPING

Cacao et Chocolat	24 F4
La Petite Scierie	25 G4
Librairie Ulysse	26 G5
Sobral	27 F4

See St-Germain Des Prés & Montparnasse Map (p188)

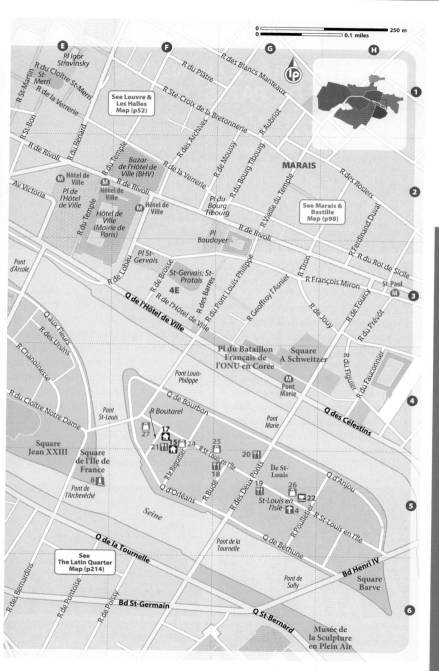

0   250 m
0   0.1 miles

E

Pl Igor
Stravinsky

R du Cloître St-Merri
R St-
Merri

R St-Martin

R de la Verrerie

R St-Bon

R du Renard

R de Rivoli

R du Temple

**See Louvre &
Les Halles
Map (p52)**

R des Blancs Manteaux

R du Plâtre

R Ste-Croix de la Bretonnerie

R des Archives

R de la Verrerie

R de Moussy

R Aubriot

R du Bourg Tibourg

R Vieille du Temple

MARAIS

R des Rosiers

**See Marais &
Bastille
Map (p98)**

R Ferdinand Duval

R du Roi de Sicile

F

G

H

1

2

Av Victoria

Pont
d'Arcole

M Hôtel de
Ville

Pl de
l'Hôtel
de Ville

Hôtel de
Ville

Bazar
de l'Hôtel de
Ville (BHV)

R de Rivoli

R du Temple

Hôtel de
Ville
(Mairie de
Paris)

M Hôtel de
Ville

Pl St-
Gervais

R de Lobau

R de Brosse

R des Barres

R du Pont Louis-Philippe

St-Gervais; St-
Protais

4E

R de l'Hôtel de Ville

Pl du
Bourg
Tibourg

R de Rivoli

Pl
Baudoyer

R François Miron

R Geoffroy l'Asnier

R de Jouy

R Tiron

R de Fourcy

R du Prévôt

St-Paul

M

3

Q aux Fleurs

R des Ursins

R Chanoinesse

R du Cloître Notre Dame

Q de l'Hôtel de Ville

Pont
St-Louis

Square
Jean XXIII

Square
de l'Île de
France

Pont de
l'Archevêché

Pl du Bataillon
Français de
l'ONU en Corée

Pont Louis-
Philippe

Q de Bourbon

R Boutarel

27

17

21

15

24

R le Regrattier

R Budé

25

R St-Louis en l'Île

18

20

8

Q d'Orléans

R des Deux Ponts

Île St-
Louis

19

St-Louis en
l'Isle

R Poulletier

26

R St-Louis en l'Île

22

4

Square
A Schweitzer

M
Pont
Marie

Pont
Marie

Q des Célestins

R du Figuier

R du Fauconnier

Q d'Anjou

4

5

Seine

Q de la Tournelle

**See
The Latin Quarter
Map (p214)**

R des Bernardins

R de Pontoise

R de Poissy

Bd St-Germain

Pont de la
Tournelle

Q de Béthune

Pont de
Sully

Q St-Bernard

Bd Henri IV

Square
Barye

Musée de
la Sculpture
en Plein Air

6

THE ISLANDS

HIGHLIGHTS

1 CATHÉDRALE DE NOTRE DAME DE PARIS

Cathédrale de Notre Dame de Paris is the most-visited non-ticketed site in Paris. Upwards of 14 million people cross its threshold every year for a reason. It's not just a masterpiece of French Gothic architecture; it has also been the focus of Catholic Paris for seven centuries. We love it for the silhouette of its majestic shape, its angry gargoyles, its stained-glass rosettes and the religious and historic symbolism haunting every corner.

HIGHLIGHTS

↘ OUR DON'T MISS LIST

❶ WESTERN FACADE
Climb the 422 spiralling steps to the top of the **western facade**, where you'll find yourself face-to-face with the cathedral's most frightening gargoyles, from goblins to birds and scowling devil-men. You'll also encounter the 13-tonne bell **Emmanuel** (all of the cathedral's bells are named) in the **South Tower** and, last but not least, a sweeping view of Paris from the **Galerie des Chimères** (Dreams Gallery).

❷ VIEW FROM THE SQUARE
Head to Square Jean XXIII, the pretty little park behind the cathedral, for one of the best views of Notre Dame. This is where you'll want to go snap-happy – you can really appreciate the forest of ornate **flying buttresses** that encircle the chancel and support the cathedral's walls and roof.

❸ ROSE WINDOWS
Inside, make a beeline for the three spectacular **rose windows**, the circular

Clockwise from top: Stained-glass windows and ceiling detail; Rooftop gargoyles; North rose stained-glass window; Southern aspect illuminated at night; St Denis, surrounded by angels, on the Portal of the Virgin

THE ISLANDS

HIGHLIGHTS

wheels of stained glass. The enormous, 10m-wide west window, over the western facade, represents human life – its features symbolise scenes such as the Zodiac and Labors of the Months. It's set above the 7800-pipe organ and is partially blocked, but is still a visual masterpiece. We also love the south window, whose central medallion shows **Christ of the Apocalypse** – a sword protrudes out of Christ's mouth symbolising that his word separates error from truth. Underneath, the heavenly court is represented by **16 prophets**. Late afternoon is the best time to see light streaming through the coloured glass.

❹ PORTALS

Examine the shapes of the elaborately sculpted 13th-century portals. Its statues were once brightly coloured to make them more effective as a *Biblia pauperum* – a 'Bible of the poor' to help the illiterate faithful understand Old Testament stories, the Passion of the Christ and the lives of the saints.

⤵ THINGS YOU NEED TO KNOW

Getting in Enter through the North Tower **Free Tours** Guided tours are led by highly informative staff happy to answer an array of questions. **See p89 for more information.**

HIGHLIGHTS

2

↘ STE-CHAPELLE

A masterpiece of delicacy, with a curtain of glazing across the 1st floor of richly coloured stained glass (marvel at that incredible, pungent blue), **Ste-Chapelle** (p92) is the most exceptional of Paris' Gothic buildings. It's best to hit it on a sunny day when the glass flickers in a glorious rainbow of colours.

3

↘ LA CONCIERGERIE

Explore where Marie-Antoinette and thousands of others spent their final days before losing their heads, at **La Conciergerie** (p90). Admire the city's best example of the Rayonnant Gothic style in its 14th-century Cavalrymen's Hall, the largest surviving medieval hall in Europe, and the adjacent Tour de l'Horloge (Clock Tower) - built in 1353, it's held a public clock aloft since 1370.

THE ISLANDS

HIGHLIGHTS

4

↘ PONT NEUF

Pont Neuf (p91), the oldest 'New Bridge' in town and an architectural delight, boasts some of the most fantastic views of the Seine, day and night. It's a prime example of the Italian renaissance period – its style was meant to reflect Paris as the capital of a powerful centralised state.

5

↘ BERTHILLON

It's largely undisputed that Paris' best ice cream comes from **Berthillon** (p94). Grab a scoop of fresh-fruit sorbet, creamy coffee, *nougat au miel* (honey nougat) or luscious *noisette* (hazelnut) and wander with your treat - along the Seine or rue St-Louis en l'Île – or grab a pew on Pont St-Louis and watch the buskers perform.

6

↘ ÎLE ST-LOUIS

Head to the smaller of the two islands, Île St-Louis, for a little quiet and respite from the bustle of its bigger brother, Île de la Cité. It boasts little in the way of sights, but take some time to ponder its French baroque **Église St-Louis en l'Île** (p93) and relax.

2 GLENN BEANLAND; 3 BRUCE BI; 4 JEAN-BERNARD CARILLET; 5 OSB70/ALAMY; 6 JOHN ELK III

2 Inside Ste-Chapelle (p92); 3 Salle des Gens d'Arms, La Conciergerie (p90); 4 Pont Neuf (p91); 5 Berthillon ice-creamery (p94); 6 Apartment building, Île St-Louis

THE ISLANDS

BEST...

BEST...

↘ THINGS FOR FREE

- **Pont Neuf** (p91) Paris' oldest bridge.
- **Marché aux Fleurs** (p91) Admire the colourful petals at the bountiful Flower Market.
- **Cathédrale de Notre Dame de Paris** (opposite) The city's iconic cathedral.

↘ VIEWS

- **Square Jean XXIII** (p84) See the back of the stunning Cathédrale de Notre Dame de Paris.
- **Pont Neuf** (p91) Stellar views of a parade of bridges and the island.
- **Square du Vert Galant** (p93) The tip of the Île de la Cité boasts water views and the expanse of the left and right banks.

↘ DETAILS

- **Gargoyles** (opposite) The Cathédrale de Notre Dame de Paris' stone devils and birds of prey seem so real.
- **Stained Glass** (p92) Ste-Chapelle's is Paris' oldest and most dazzling.
- **Tomb of the Unknown Deportee** (p91) Glass lit from behind, it features inscriptions by renowned writers and poets.

↘ PLACES TO RELAX

- **Île St-Louis** (p92) The island oasis away from the cathedral's hordes.
- **La Charlotte en Île** (p95) An exceptional tea room where you can sip and unwind.
- **Mon Vieil Ami** (p94) This restaurant's name means 'my old friend' – its calm, comforting surrounds will remind you of just that.

OLIVIER CIRENDINI

Mémorial des Martyrs de la Déportation (p91)

DISCOVER THE ISLANDS

Paris' pair of islands could not be more different. With its quaint car-free lanes, legendary ice-cream maker and bijou portfolio of street plaques celebrating famous residents of the past, Île St-Louis is a joy. Its boutiques lining the central street might not be worth the trip in itself, but browse and there's no saying what gem you might find.

At the island's western end, the area around Pont St-Louis and Pont Louis-Philippe is one of the city's most romantic spots. After nightfall, the Seine dances with the watery reflections of streetlights, headlamps, stop signals and the dim glow of curtained windows.

Stand on the square in front of Notre Dame on big-brother Île de la Cité and there is no doubt where you are: dodging snap-happy tourists, street sellers pushing Eiffel Tower key rings and backpackers guarding piles of packs while their mates check out the cathedral is a taste of the best and worst of Paris. Sensibly, not very many Parisians live on this island.

SIGHTS

CATHÉDRALE DE NOTRE DAME DE PARIS

☎ 01 42 34 56 10; www.cathedraledeparis.com; 6 place du Parvis Notre Dame, 4e; audioguide €5; ☽ 8am-6.45pm Mon-Fri, to 7.15pm Sat & Sun, information desk 9.30am-6pm Mon-Sat, 9am-6pm Sun; Ⓜ Cité

This is the heart of Paris – so much so that distances from Paris to every part of metropolitan France are measured from **place du Parvis Notre Dame**, the square in front of the Cathedral of Our Lady of Paris. A bronze star across the street from the cathedral's main entrance marks the exact location of *point zéro des routes de France*. To the west, Charlemagne (AD 742–814), emperor of the Franks, rides his steed under the trees.

Built on a site occupied by earlier churches and, a millennium before that, a Gallo-Roman temple, it was begun in 1163 according to the design of Bishop Maurice de Sully and largely completed by the early 14th century. The cathedral was badly damaged during the Revolution; architect Eugène Emmanuel Viollet-le-Duc carried out extensive renovations between 1845 and 1864. The cathedral is on a very grand scale; the interior alone is 130m long, 48m wide and 35m high and can accommodate more than 6000 worshippers.

Notre Dame is known for its sublime balance, though if you look closely you'll see all sorts of minor asymmetrical elements introduced to avoid monotony, in accordance with standard Gothic practice. These include the slightly different shapes of each of the three main **portals**.

Inside, exceptional features include three spectacular **rose windows** and the window on the northern side of the transept, which has remained virtually unchanged since the 13th century. The central choir, with its carved wooden stalls and statues representing the Passion of the Christ, is also noteworthy. There are free 1½-hour **guided tours** (☽ 2pm Wed & Thu, 2.30pm Sat) of the cathedral, given in English.

The **trésor** (treasury; adult/student/3-12yr €3/2/1; ☽ 9.30am-6pm Mon-Fri, 9.30am-6.30pm

THE ISLANDS

DISCOVER THE ISLANDS

THE ISLANDS

SIGHTS

Sat, 1.30-6.30pm Sun) in the southeastern transept contains artwork, liturgical objects, a church plate and first-class relics, some of them of questionable origin. Among these is the **Ste-Couronne**, the 'Holy Crown', which is purportedly the wreath of thorns placed on Jesus' head before he was crucified, and was brought here in the mid-13th century. It is exhibited between 3pm and 4pm on the first Friday of each month, 3pm to 4pm every Friday during Lent, and 10am to 5pm on Good Friday.

The entrance to the **Tours de Notre Dame** (Towers of Notre Dame; ☎ 01 53 10 07 00; www.monuments-nationaux.fr; rue du Cloître Notre Dame; adult/18-25yr €8/5, free for EU resident under 26yr & everyone under 18yr, 1st Sun of month Nov-Mar free for all; ☉ 10am-6.30pm Mon-Fri, 10am-11pm Sat & Sun Jul & Aug, 10am-6.30pm daily Apr, May & Sep, to 5.30pm daily Jan-Mar & Oct-Dec) is from the **North Tower**.

LA CONCIERGERIE
☎ 01 53 40 60 97; www.monuments-nationaux.fr; 2 bd du Palais, 1er; adult/18-25yr €7/4.50, free for EU resident under 26yr & everyone under 18yr, 1st Sun of month Nov-Mar free for all; ☉ 9.30am-6pm Mar-Oct, 9am-5pm Nov-Feb; Ⓜ Cité

The Conciergerie was built as a royal palace in the 14th century for the concierge of the Palais de la Cité, but later lost favour with the kings of France and became a prison and torture chamber. During the Reign of Terror (1793–94) it was used to incarcerate alleged enemies of the Revolution before they were brought before the Revolutionary Tribunal, which met next door in the Palais de Justice. Among the almost 2800 prisoners held in the dungeons here (in various 'classes' of cells, no less) before being sent in tumbrels to the guillotine were Queen Marie-Antoinette (see a reproduction of her cell) and, as the Revolution began to turn on its own, the radicals Danton, Robespierre and, finally, the judges of the Tribunal themselves.

A joint ticket with **Ste-Chapelle** (p92) costs adult/18-25yr/EU resident under 26yr & everyone under 18yr €11/7.50/free.

GAB/IMAGEBROKER

La Conciergerie

Flower stall, Marché aux Fleurs

KRZYSZTOF DYDYNSKI

⬊ MARCHÉ AUX FLEURS

The Île de la Cité's flower market has brightened up this square since 1808. On Sundays it becomes a **Marché aux Oiseaux** (bird market).

Things you need to know: Marché aux Fleurs (place Louis Lépin, 4e; ⊙ 8am-7.30pm Mon-Sat; Ⓜ Cité); **Marché aux Oiseaux** (⊙ 9am-7pm Sun)

CRYPTE ARCHÉOLOGIQUE

☎ 01 55 42 50 10; www.paris.fr; 1 place du Parvis Notre Dame, 4e; adult/14-26yr €4/3; ⊙ 10am-6pm Tue-Sun; Ⓜ Cité

The Archaeological Crypt is under the square in front of Notre Dame. The 117m-long and 28m-wide area displays *in situ* the remains of structures built on this site during the Gallo-Roman period, a 4th-century enclosure wall, the foundations of the medieval foundlings hospice and a few of the original sewers sunk by Haussman.

MÉMORIAL DES MARTYRS DE LA DÉPORTATION

square de l'Île de France, 4e; ⊙ 10am-noon & 2-7pm Apr-Sep, to 5pm Oct-Mar; Ⓜ St-Michel Notre Dame

The Memorial to the Victims of the Deportation, erected in 1962, is a haunting monument to the 160,000 residents of France – including 76,000 Jews (of which 11,000 were children) – deported to and murdered in Nazi concentration camps during WWII. A single barred 'window' separates the bleak, rough concrete courtyard from the waters of the Seine. Inside the **Tomb of the Unknown Deportee** is flanked by hundreds of thousands of bits of back-lit glass, and the walls are etched with inscriptions from celebrated writers and poets.

PONT NEUF

Ⓜ Pont Neuf

The sparkling white spans of Paris' oldest bridge, ironically called 'New Bridge', have linked the western end of the Île de la Cité with both river banks since 1607 when the king inaugurated it by crossing it on a white stallion. The occasion is commemorated by an equestrian **statue of**

THE ISLANDS

JEAN-BERNARD CARILLET

Square du Vert Galant

SIGHTS

⬎ IF YOU LIKE...

If you like chilling out in **Square du Vert Galant** (see the boxed text, opposite), head to the Seine-hugging **Quai St-Bernard** (Map p214) facing the Île St-Louis across the Pont de la Tournelle. On this street opposite the Jardin des Plantes, you'll find the **Musée de la Sculpture en Plein Air** (Open-Air Sculpture Museum; Map p214; ☎ 01 43 26 91 90; square Tino Rossi, 5e; admission free; ☽ 24hr; Ⓜ Quai de la Rapée), which flanks the river and has a brilliant view of the islands. A salad beneath a César or a baguette beside a Brancusi is a pretty classy way to see the Seine up close.

Henri IV, who was known to his subjects as the Vert Galant ('jolly rogue' or 'dirty old man', depending on your perspective). View the bridge's seven arches, decorated with humorous and grotesque figures of barbers, dentists, pickpockets, loiterers etc, from a spot along the river or a boat.

STE-CHAPELLE

☎ 01 53 40 60 97; www.monuments-nationaux. fr; 4 blvd du Palais, 1er; adult/18-25yr €8/5, free for EU resident under 26yr & everyone under 18yr, 1st Sun of the month Nov-Mar free for all; ☽ 9.30am-6pm Mar-Oct, 9am-5pm Nov-Feb; Ⓜ Cité

This is the place to visit on a sunny day! Security checks make it long and snail-slow to get into this gemlike Holy Chapel, the most exquisite of Paris' Gothic monu-ments, tucked away within the walls of the **Palais de Justice** (Law Courts). But once in, be dazzled by Paris' oldest and finest stained glass.

Built in just under three years (compared with nearly 200 for Notre Dame), Ste-Chapelle was consecrated in 1248. The chapel was conceived by Louis IX to house his personal collection of holy relics (including the Holy Crown now kept in the treasury at Notre Dame).

ÎLE ST-LOUIS

Downstream from Île de la Cité and en-tirely in the 4e arrondissement, St-Louis was actually two uninhabited islets called Île Notre Dame (Our Lady Isle) and Île aux Vaches (Cows Island) in the early 17th cen-tury. That was until a building contractor called Christophe Marie and two financiers worked out a deal with Louis XIII to create one island and build two stone bridges to the mainland. In exchange they could subdivide and sell the newly created real estate. This they did with great success, and by 1664 the entire island was covered with fine, airy, grey-stone houses facing the quays and water.

The only sight as such, French Baroque **Église St-Louis en l'Île** (☎ 01 46 34 11 60; 19bis rue St-Louis en l'Île, 4e; ☽ 9am-1pm & 2-7.30pm Tue-Sat, to 7pm Sun; Ⓜ Pont Marie) was built between 1664 and 1726.

SLEEPING

The smaller of the two islands in the middle of the Seine, the Île St-Louis, is by far the more romantic and has a string of excellent top-end hotels. It's an easy walk from central Paris. Oddly enough, the only hotel of any sort on the Île de la Cité is a budget one – at least for now.

HÔTEL DE LUTÈCE   Hotel €€€
☎ 01 43 26 23 52; www.paris-hotel-lutece.com; 65 rue St-Louis en l'Île, 4e; s/d/tr €155/195/230; Ⓜ Pont Marie; ✵ ⚟

An exquisite 23-room hotel, the Lutèce has an enviable spot on delightful Île St-Louis. The lobby/salon, with its ancient fireplace,

wood panelling, antique furnishings and terracotta tiles, sets the inviting tone of the whole place; the comfortable rooms are tastefully decorated and the location is one of the most desirable in the city.

HÔTEL ST-LOUIS   Hotel €€
☎ 01 46 34 04 80; www.hotel-saint-louis.com; 75 rue St-Louis en l'Île, 4e; s & d €140-220, tr €270; Ⓜ Pont Marie; ✵ ⚟ ⚟

One of several hotels lining posh rue St-Louis en l'Île, this 19-room hotel is getting a facelift that will have reached the nether regions by the time you arrive; check out room 52 at the top with its beams and balcony. The public areas, including the basement breakfast room dating from the early 17th century, have always been lovely and the welcome nothing short of passionate.

HÔTEL HENRI IV   Hotel €
☎ 01 43 54 44 53; www.henri4hotel.fr; 25 place Dauphine, 1er; s €42-69, d €52-76, tr €79-81; Ⓜ Pont Neuf or Cité; ⚟

This place, known for its 15 worn and very cheap rooms, has always been popular for its location, location and – above all else – location on the tip of the Île de la Cité. It would be impossible to find a hotel more romantically located at such a price in all of Paris – much less the Île de la Cité. Book well in advance.

SEINE-FUL PURSUITS

The Seine is more than just Paris' dustless highway or the line dividing the Right Bank from the Left. The river's award-winning role comes in July and August, when some 5km of its banks are transformed into **Paris Plages** (p48), 'beaches' with real sand, water fountains and sprays. The banks between the **Pont Alexandre III** (Map p150) and the **Pont d'Austerlitz** (Map p98) have been listed as a Unesco World Heritage Site since 1991, but the choicest spot for sunning, picnicking and maybe even a little romancing is the delightful **Square du Vert Gallant** (Ⓜ Pont Neuf), the little park at the tip of the Île de la Cité named after that rake Henri IV (see p92).

THE ISLANDS

EATING

EATING

Famed more for its ice cream than dining options, Île St-Louis is a pricey place to eat, although there are a couple of fine places worth a brunch or lunchtime munch with, depending on which you choose and where you sit, some great street entertainment thrown in for free. As for Île de la Cité, forget it – recommended eating spots are almost nonexistent.

MON VIEIL AMI   French, Alsatian €€€
☎ 01 40 46 01 35; www.mon-vieil-ami.com; 69 rue St-Louis en l'Île, 4e; starters/mains/dessert €11/22/8, menu €41; ⌚ lunch & dinner to 10.15pm Wed-Sun; Ⓜ Pont Marie

You're treated like an old friend – thus the name – from the minute you enter this sleek black bistro in one of Paris' most sought-after neighbourhoods. The pâté in pastry crust is a fabulous starter and any of the Alsatian *plats du jours* (€13) are worth exploring. The chocolate tart is the pick of the desserts.

LES FOUS DE L'ÎLE   French, Brasserie €€
☎ 01 43 25 76 67; www.lesfousdelile.com; 33 rue des Deux Ponts, 4e; 2-/3-course menus from €23/26; ⌚ 10am-2am; Ⓜ Pont Marie

No longer the arty café-cum-*salon de thé* that served somewhat uneven dishes and hung artwork of varying degrees of ability, this place has re-invented itself as a somewhat genteel brasserie, retaining the open kitchen and adding a cockerel theme (we don't know either) throughout. Try any of their Spanish-inspired tapas or the 'real' (their claim, not ours) *cassoulet* (hearty casserole or stew with beans and meat).

BERTHILLON   Ice Cream €
☎ 01 43 54 31 61; 31 rue St-Louis en l'Île, 4e; ice creams €2.10-5.40; ⌚ 10am-8pm Wed-Sun; Ⓜ Pont Marie

Berthillon is to ice cream what Château Lafite Rothschild is to wine and Valhrona is to chocolate. And with nigh on 70 flavours to choose from, you'll be spoiled for choice. While the fruit-flavoured sorbets (eg cassis, blackberry etc) produced by

KRZYSZTOF DYDYNSKI

Remains of Gallo-Roman Paris in Crypte Archéologique (p91)

La Charlotte de l'Isle

WILL SALTER

this celebrated *glacier* (ice-cream maker) are renowned, the chocolate, coffee, *marrons glacés* (candied chestnuts), Agenaise (Armagnac and prunes), *noisette* (hazelnut) and *nougat au miel* (honey nougat) are richer.

DRINKING

Drinking venues on the islands are as scarce as hens' teeth. They do exist but use them as a starting point as very few places stay open after the bewitching hour of midnight.

TAVERNE HENRI IV   Bar
☎ 01 43 54 27 90; 13 place du Pont Neuf, Île de la Cité, 1er; ⏱ 11.30am-10pm Mon-Fri, noon-6pm Sat; Ⓜ Pont Neuf
One of the very few places to drink on the Île de la Cité, this is a serious wine bar dating back to 1885 and a decent place for a nibble, with a choice of inexpensive *tartines* (€4.40 to €8.80), *charcuterie* (cold cooked meats; €9 to €13), cheese

and quiche. This place attracts lots of legal types from the nearby Palais de Justice and has become something of an institution.

LA CHARLOTTE DE L'ISLE   Tearoom
☎ 01 43 54 25 83; 24 rue St-Louis en l'Île, Île St-Louis, 4e; ⏱ 2-8pm Thu-Sun; Ⓜ Pont Marie
This tiny place is one of the loveliest *salons de thé* (tearooms) in all of Paris and definitely worth crossing the bridge for. The fairy-tale theme adds flavour (as if any was needed) to the chocolate and pastries, and the dozens of teas on offer are superbly chosen. Marionette shows usually take place on Wednesday. Pass by to get the latest flyer.

SHOPPING

Despite their small size, the islands (particularly the Île St-Louis) are a shopper's delight. The Île de la Cité is best for souvenirs and other tourist kitsch.

THE ISLANDS

DRINKING

THE ISLANDS

SHOPPING

LIBRAIRIE ULYSSE   Books & Comics
☎ 01 43 25 17 35; www.ulysse.fr, in French;
26 rue St-Louis en l'Île, 4e; ⏰ 2-8pm Tue-Fri;
Ⓜ Pont Marie

A delightful shop on historic Île St-Louis
counting some 20,000 travel guides,
magazines and maps. Count on sage
advice from well-travelled staff. They'll
open Saturday morning if you phone in
advance.

SOBRAL   Fashion & Accessories
☎ 01 43 25 80 10; www.sobraldesign.com; 79
rue St-Louis en l'Île, 4e; ⏰ 11am-7.30pm Mon-
Sat, to 7pm Sun; Ⓜ Pont Marie

Brighten up your life with a bangle, pen-
dant, pair of earrings or other costume
jewellery pieces made from recycled resin
by Brazilian jeweller Carlos Sobral. Yes, he
makes toilet seats and Eiffel Towers, too.

LA PETITE SCIERIE   Food & Drink
☎ 01 55 42 14 88; www.lapetitescierie.fr; 60
rue St-Louis en l'Île, 4e; ⏰ 11am-7pm Thu-Mon;
Ⓜ Pont Marie

This hole-in-the-wall shop called the
'Little Sawmill' sells every permutation of
duck edibles with the emphasis – *naturel-
lement* – on foie gras. The products come
direct from the shop's own farm with no
intermediary involved, so you can be as-
sured of the highest quality.

CACAO ET CHOCOLAT   Food & Drink
☎ 01 46 33 77 63; www.cacaoetchocolat.com;
29 rue du Buci, 6e; ⏰ 10.30am-7.30pm;
Ⓜ Mabillon

You haven't tasted chocolate till you've
had a hot chocolate (€3.50) spiced with
cinnamon, ginger or cayenne pepper at
this exotic shop showcasing cocoa beans
in every guise. Citrus, spice and chilli are
among the flavoured bars to buy here.

MARAIS & BASTILLE

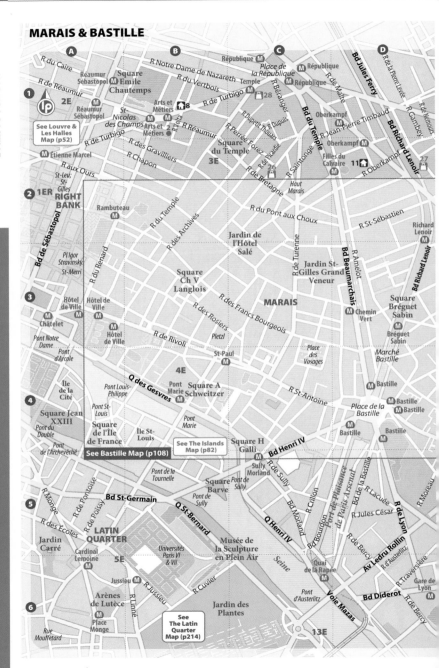

MARAIS & BASTILLE

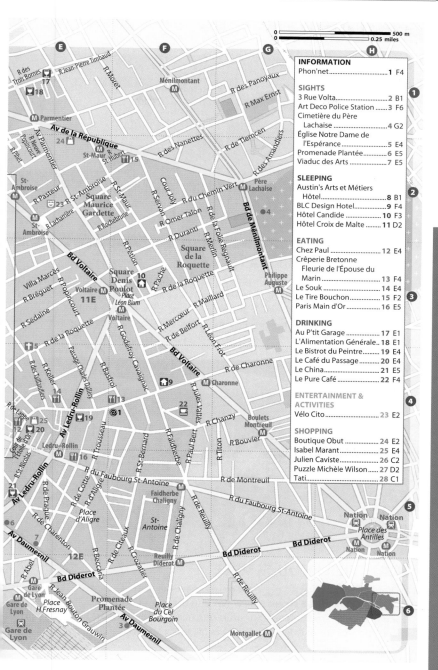

MARAIS & BASTILLE

INFORMATION
Phon'net 1 F4

SIGHTS
3 Rue Volta 2 B1
Art Deco Police Station 3 F6
Cimetière du Père
Lachaise 4 G2
Église Notre Dame de
l'Espérance 5 E4
Promenade Plantée 6 E5
Viaduc des Arts 7 E5

SLEEPING
Austin's Arts et Métiers
Hôtel 8 B1
BLC Design Hotel 9 F4
Hôtel Candide 10 F3
Hôtel Croix de Malte 11 D2

EATING
Chez Paul 12 E4
Crêperie Bretonne
Fleurie de l'Épouse du
Marin 13 F4
Le Souk 14 E4
Le Tire Bouchon 15 F2
Paris Main d'Or 16 E5

DRINKING
Au P'tit Garage 17 E1
L'Alimentation Générale ... 18 E1
Le Bistrot du Peintre 19 E4
Le Café du Passage 20 E4
Le China 21 E5
Le Pure Café 22 F4

**ENTERTAINMENT &
ACTIVITIES**
Vélo Cito 23 E2

SHOPPING
Boutique Obut 24 E2
Isabel Marant 25 E4
Julien Caviste 26 C2
Puzzle Michèle Wilson 27 D2
Tati 28 C1

HIGHLIGHTS

↘ OPÉRA DE PARIS BASTILLE

Never as visually spectacular or palatial as the Palais Garnier, this **opera house** (p110) is still the main opera venue in the capital. It features a 2700-seat au-ditorium with perfect acoustics and hosts some of the most ambitious opera productions in the city. Designed by the Uruguayan architect Carlos Ott, it was inaugurated on 14 July 1989, the 200th anniversary of the storming of the Bastille.

↘ RUE VIEILLE DU TEMPLE

No street screams 'Party!' more than this one. Smack in the centre of the Marais district, this **bar-lined street** (p120) has one big, continuous drinking fest taking place in its bars and cafés, serving up intoxicating cocktails and hopping vibes in eclectic surrounds such as 1930s zinc and contemporary design.

3

↘ CIMETIÈRE DU PÈRE LACHAISE

Gravestones in the world's most opulent cemetery (p107) read like a Who's Who of French history and the arts: 800,000 deceased call this enormous necropolis home, including urchin sparrow Édith Piaf, rock legend Jim Morrison, writer Oscar Wilde and painter Eugene Delacroix.

4

↘ PLACE DE LA BASTILLE

The site where the notorious prison stormed at the start of the Revolution once stood is now a large, busy traffic roundabout (p110). The Colonne de Juillet in its centre honours those killed in the 1830 July Revolution, when a group of revolutionaries seized the Hôtel de Ville. Those honoured are buried in vaults underneath.

5

↘ PLACE DES VOSGES

One of the city's most vibrant, this fabulous square (p105) and street market takes punters, shopping basket in hand, on a trip around Africa and the Middle East.

1 JEAN-BERNARD CARILLET; 2 WILL SALTER; 3 HUW JONES; 4 GARDEL BERTRAND/HEMIS/ALAMY; 5 BRUCE BI

1 Opéra de Paris Bastille (p110); 2 Street life on rue Vieille du Temple (p120); 3 Oscar Wilde's headstone covered in lipstick kisses, Cimetière du Père Lachaise (p107); 4 Colonne de Juillet, Place de Bastille (p110); 5 Place des Vosges (p105)

MARAIS & BASTILLE

MEDIEVAL MEANDERINGS IN THE MARAIS

MEDIEVAL MEANDERINGS IN THE MARAIS

The *hôtels particuliers* (private mansions) so characteristic of the Marais district are among the most beautiful Renaissance structures in the city. This walk, starting north of Metro St-Paul, covers roughly 1km and takes about 45 minutes to one hour.

❶ HÔTEL LAMOIGNON

The late-Renaissance Hôtel Lamoignon at 24 Rue Pavée (the first cobbled road in Paris) was built (1585–1612) for Diane de France (1538–1619), duchess of Angoulême and legitimised daughter of Henri II.

❷ HÔTEL CARNAVALET

Walk north along rue Payenne. At No 2 you'll see the back of the mid-16th-century Hôtel Carnavalet, built between 1548 and 1654 and once home to the letter-writer Madame de Sévigné (1626–96).

❸ HÔTEL LE PELETIER DE ST-FARGEAU

Further north is the Hôtel Le Peletier de St-Fargeau, which dates from the late 17th century. With the attached Hôtel Carnavalet, it now contains the **Musée Carnavalet** (p106).

❹ CHAPELLE DE L'HUMANITÉ

At No 5 is a Chapelle de l'Humanité, a Revolutionary-era 'Temple of Reason'; the quote on the facade reads: 'Love as the principal, order as the base, progress as the goal'. It's occasionally open to the public.

❺ HÔTEL DONON

From the grille just past the Chapelle de l'Humanité, you can see the rear of Hôtel Donon, built in 1598. It has a lovely geometric garden.

❻ HÔTEL DE MARLE

At 11 rue Payenne is Hôtel de Marle, built in the late 16th century and now containing the Institut Culturel Suédois (Swedish Cultural Institute) and its lovely Café Suédois.

❼ SQUARE GEORGE CAIN

Opposite Hôtel de Marle, square George Cain contains the remains of an old Hôtel de Ville on the south wall, with a relief of Judgement Day and a one-handed clock on the tympanum (beneath the roof).

❽ RUE DU PARC ROYAL

Heading east you'll pass two buildings dating from about 1620 that do civic duty as archives and historical libraries: Hôtel de Vigny at No 10

MEDIEVAL MEANDERINGS IN THE MARAIS

and the lovely pinkish-brick Hôtel Duret de Chevry at No 8, which now houses the Deutsches Historisches Institut (German Historic Institute).

❾ PLACE DES VOSGES

Walk south down rue de Sévigné, then follow rue des Francs Bourgeois eastwards to the **place des Vosges** (p105), with its four symmetrical fountains and an 1829 copy of a 1639 mounted statue of Louis XIII.

❿ HÔTEL DE SULLY

In the southwestern corner of place des Vosges is the back entrance to **Hôtel de Sully** (p105), a restored aristocratic mansion at 62 rue St-Antoine built in 1625. Behind the hôtel are two beautifully decorated, late-Renaissance courtyards, both of which are festooned with allegorical reliefs of the seasons and the elements.

MARAIS & BASTILLE

BEST...

BEST...

⬂ EAT STREETS

- **Rue du Vielle du temple** (p120) Nosh your way around the world from Africa to Eastern Europe.
- **Rue des Rosiers** (p114) Kosher specialties in every shape and form.
- **Around République** (p114) Ethnic eateries and noodle shops.

⬂ MUSEUMS

- **Musée d'Art et d'Histoire du Judaïsme** (p108) The Museum of the Art and History of Judaism traces Judaism in France and worldwide.
- **Maison Européenne de la Photographie** (p109) Edgy exhibits and photos related to France.
- **Musée Carnavalet** (p106) The history of Paris through artefacts and exhibits.

⬂ THINGS FOR FREE

- **Hôtel de Ville** (opposite) Admire the luxurious neo-Renaissance style of the capital's city hall.
- **Hôtel de Sully** (opposite) Ponder the posh 17th-century mansion and its gorgeous Renaissance courtyards.
- **Window shopping along rue des Francs Bourgeois** (p122) The best established boutiques in town reside here – you don't have to, but window shopping is distinctly French.

⬂ DRINKING SPOTS

- **Au P'tit Garage** (p119) One of the last neighbourhood bars in the area.
- **Café des Phares** (p120) The city's original *philocafé* (philosophers café).
- **Le Pure Café** (p120) Such a typical local café it's appeared in numerous films as the quintessential Parisian café.

WILL SALTER

Fashion boutiques along rue des Francs Bourgeois (p122)

DISCOVER MARAIS & BASTILLE

Though the Marais has become a coveted trendy address in recent years, it remains home to a long-established Jewish community. In the historic Jewish quarter – the so-called Pletzl (from the Yiddish for 'little square') – you'll find expensive boutiques sitting side-by-side with Jewish bookshops and stores selling religious goods, *cacher* (kosher) grocery shops and restaurants.

Once a run-down immigrant neighbourhood notorious for its high crime rate, the Bastille area has undergone a fair degree of gentrification, which started with the advent of the Opéra de Paris Bastille more than two decades ago. Once home to artisans and labourers, the area buzzed with the sound of cabinet makers, joiners, gilders and the like at work. Today most of that's gone, replaced with artists and their lofts. But the old spirit lives on in some hidden parts; the areas to the east of place de la Bastille in particular retain their lively atmosphere and ethnicity.

This area is where Paris pulsates after dark. It's not a hard-and-fast rule, but the Marais is largely a gay and lesbian playground.

SIGHTS

HÔTEL DE VILLE Map p108

☎ 39 75; www.paris.fr; place de l'Hôtel de Ville, 4e; Ⓜ Hôtel de Ville

After having been gutted during the 1871 Paris Commune, Paris' city hall was re-built in neo-Renaissance style from 1874 to 1882. The ornate facade is decorated with 108 statues of noteworthy Parisians. There's a **Salon d'Accueil** (Reception Hall; 29 rue de Rivoli, 4e; ☺ 10am-7pm Mon-Sat), which dispenses information and brochures and is used for temporary (and very popular) exhibitions, usually with a Paris theme. Some exhibitions take place in the **Salle St-Jean** (5 rue Lobau, 4e), which is entered from the eastern side of the building.

PLACE DES VOSGES Map p108

Ⓜ St-Paul or Bastille

Inaugurated in 1612 as place Royale and thus the oldest square in Paris, place des Vosges (4e) is an ensemble of 36 symmetrical houses with ground-floor arcades, steep slate roofs and large dormer windows arranged around a large and leafy square.

The author Victor Hugo lived in an apartment on the 3rd floor of the square's Hôtel de Rohan-Guéménée from 1832 to 1848. He moved here a year after the publication of *Notre Dame de Paris* (The Hunchback of Notre Dame) and completed *Ruy Blas* while living here. The **Maison de Victor Hugo** (Victor Hugo House; Map p108; ☎ 01 42 72 10 16; www.musee-hugo.paris.fr; 6 place des Vosges, 4e; permanent collections free, temporary exhibits adult/14-26yr/senior & student €7/3.50/5; ☺ 10am-6pm Tue-Sun) is now a municipal museum devoted to the life and times of the celebrated novelist and poet.

HÔTEL DE SULLY Map p108

62 rue St-Antoine, 4e; Ⓜ St-Paul

This aristocratic mansion dating from the early 17th century houses the HQ of the **Centre des Monuments Nationaux** (☎ 01 44 61 20 00; www.monuments-nationaux.fr;

MARAIS & BASTILLE

SIGHTS

Hôtel de Ville (p105) at dusk

IZZET KERIBAR

⬏ IF YOU LIKE...

If you like the **Hôtel de Ville** and **Hôtel de Sully** (p105), then head to the **Faubourg St-Germain area** east of the **Musée Rodin** (p178). In the 18th century, this formal world of exquisite ironwork, gold leaf, Seine-side art galleries and conventional manners was Paris' most fashionable neighbourhood. Elegant *hôtels particuliers* (private mansions) ran riot on rue de Lille, rue de Grenelle and rue de Varenne, now home to embassies, cultural centres and government ministries. Framing all this Parisian refinement is the Eiffel Tower in the skyline, the graceful curve of the Seine at eye level and, underfoot, the lawns of Les Invalides where it always feels like Sunday. Don't miss:

- **Hôtel Matignon** (Map p164) No 57 rue de Varenne has been the official residence of the French prime minister since the start of the Fifth Republic (1958).
- **53 rue de Varenne** (Map p172) It was to this stylish pad that Edith Wharton moved in 1910 to write *Le Temps de l'Innocence* (The Age of Innocence).
- **5bis rue Verneuil** (Map p164) The quarter's finest example of timeless extravagance is the house where Parisian singer, sexpot and *provocateur* Serge Gainsbourg lived from 1969 until his death in 1991. Neighbours have long since given up scrubbing off the reappearing graffiti and messages from fans.

⊗ 9am-12.45pm & 2-6pm Mon-Thu, 9am-12.45pm & 2-5pm Fri), the body responsible for many of France's historical monuments; there are brochures and information available on sites nationwide. The Hôtel de Sully **bookshop** (p123) is excellent for 'Parisiana', and the two Renaissance-style courtyards are worth the trip alone.

MUSÉE CARNAVALET Map p108

☎ 01 44 59 58 58; www.carnavalet.paris.fr, in French; 23 rue de Sévigné, 3e; permanent collections free, temporary exhibits adult/14-26yr/senior & student €7/3.50/5; ⊗ 10am-6pm Tue-Sun; Ⓜ St-Paul or Chemin Vert

The artefacts on display in the museum's sublime rooms chart the history of Paris from the Gallo-Roman period in the former Orangerie to modern times on the 1st floor and fill more than 100 rooms. Some of the nation's most important documents, paintings and other objects from the French Revolution are here (rooms 101 to 113), as is Fouquet's stunning art nouveau jewellery shop from the rue Royale (room 142) and Marcel Proust's cork-lined bedroom from his apartment on blvd Haussmann (room 147), where he wrote most of the 7350-page literary cycle *À la Recherche du Temps Perdu* (Remembrance of Things Past).

MUSÉE PICASSO Map p108

☎ 01 42 71 25 21; www.musee-picasso.fr, in French; 5 rue de Thorigny, 3e; ⏱ 9.30am-6pm Wed-Mon Apr-Sep, 9.30am-5.30pm Wed-Mon Oct-Mar; Ⓜ St-Paul or Chemin Vert

The Picasso Museum, housed in the stunning mid-17th-century Hôtel Salé, forms one of Paris' best-loved art collections. Unfortunately it was undergoing a massive renovation at the time of writing and will not reopen until 2012. Its collection includes more than 3500 drawings, engravings, paintings, ceramic works and sculptures from the *grand maître* (great master), Pablo Picasso (1881–1973), which his heirs donated to the French government in lieu of paying inheritance taxes.

CIMETIÈRE DU PÈRE LACHAISE Map p98

☎ 01 55 25 82 10; www.pere-lachaise.com; ⏱ 8am-6pm Mon-Fri, 8.30am-6pm Sat, 9am-6pm Sun mid-Mar–early Nov, 8am-5.30pm Mon-Fri, 8.30am-5.30pm Sat, 9am-5.30pm Sun early Nov–mid-Mar; Ⓜ Philippe Auguste, Gambetta or Père Lachaise

The world's most visited cemetery, Père Lachaise (named after a confessor of Louis XIV) opened its one-way doors in 1804. Its 69,000 ornate, even ostentatious, tombs

of the rich and/or famous form a verdant, 44-hectare sculpture garden. Among the 800,000 people buried here are: the composer Chopin; the playwright Molière; the poet Apollinaire; writers Balzac, Proust, Gertrude Stein and Colette; the actors Simone Signoret, Sarah Bernhardt and Yves Montand; the painters Pissarro, Seurat, Modigliani and Delacroix; the *chanteuse* (singer) Édith Piaf; the dancer Isadora Duncan; and even those immortal 12th-century lovers, Abélard and Héloïse, whose remains were disinterred and reburied here together in 1817 beneath a neo-Gothic tombstone.

Particularly visited graves are those of Oscar Wilde, interred in Division 89 in 1900, and 1960s rock star Jim Morrison, who died in a flat at 17-19 rue Beautreillis in the Marais in 1971 and is buried in Division 6.

On 27 May 1871, the last of the Communard insurgents, cornered by government forces, fought a hopeless, all-night battle among the tombstones. In the morning, the 147 survivors were lined up against the **Mur des Fédérés** (Wall of the Federalists), shot and buried where they fell in a mass grave. It is in the southeastern section of the cemetery.

Père Lachaise has five entrances, two of which are on bd de Ménilmontant. Maps indicating the location of noteworthy graves are available for free from the **conservation office** (☎ 01 55 25 82 10; 16 rue du Repos, 20e) in the southwestern corner of the cemetery.

MUSÉE COGNACQ-JAY Map p108

☎ 01 40 27 07 21; www.cognacq-jay.paris.fr, in French; 8 rue Elzévir, 3e; permanent collections free; ⏱ 10am-6pm Tue-Sun; Ⓜ St-Paul or Chemin Vert

This museum in the Hôtel de Donon brings together oil paintings, pastels,

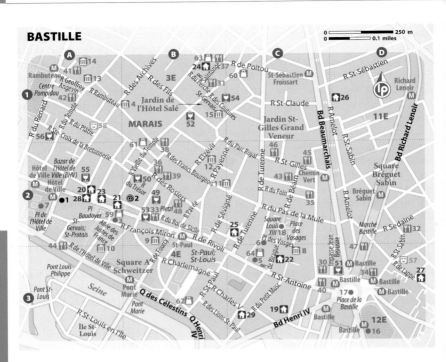

sculpture, *objets d'art,* jewellery, porcelain and furniture from the 18th century assembled by Ernest Cognacq (1839–1928), founder of La Samaritaine department store (now undergoing a protracted overhaul) and his wife Louise Jay. Although Cognacq appreciated little of his collection, boasting to all who would listen that he had never visited the Louvre and was only acquiring collections for the status, the artwork and *objets d'art* give a pretty good idea of upper-class tastes during the Age of Enlightenment.

ARCHIVES NATIONALES Map p108

☎ 01 40 27 60 96; www.archivesnationales. culture.gouv.fr, in French; 60 rue des Francs Bourgeois, 3e; Ⓜ Rambuteau or St-Paul
France's National Archives are housed in the Soubise wing of the impressive, early 18th-century Hôtel de Rohan-

Soubise, which also contains the **Musée de l'Histoire de France** (Museum of French History; ☎ 01 40 27 60 96; www.archivesnation ales.culture.gouv.fr/chan, in French; adult/senior & 18-25yr €3/2.30; 🕓 10am-12.30pm & 2-5.30pm Mon & Wed-Fri, 2-5.30pm Sat & Sun; Ⓜ Rambuteau or St-Paul). The museum contains antique furniture and 18th-century paintings but primarily documents – everything from medieval incunabula and letters written by Joan of Arc to the wills of Louis XIV and Napoleon.

MUSÉE D'ART ET D'HISTOIRE DU JUDAÏSME Map p108

☎ 01 53 01 86 60; www.mahj.org; 71 rue du Temple, 3e; permanent collection adult/ EU resident under 26yr & everyone under 18yr €6.80/free, temporary exhibit adult/18-25yr €7/4.50; 🕓 11am-6pm Mon-Fri, 10am-6pm Sun; Ⓜ Rambuteau

BASTILLE

The Museum of the Art & History of Judaism, housed in the sumptuous Hôtel de St-Aignan (1650), traces the evolution of Jewish communities from the Middle Ages to the present, with particular emphasis on the history of Jews in France but also that of communities in other parts of Europe and North Africa. Highlights include works by Chagall, Modigliani and Soutine.

MUSÉE DE LA POUPÉE Map p108
☎ 01 42 72 73 11; www.museedelapoupee paris.com; impasse Berthaud, 3e; adult/3-11yr/ senior & 12-25yr €8/3/5, under 12yr free Sun, free for all 2nd Fri; ◷ 10am-6pm Tue-Sun; Ⓜ Rambuteau

Frightening to some – all those beady little eyes and silent screams – the Doll Museum is more for adults than for children. There are around 500 of the lifeless creatures here, dating back to 1800, all arranged in scenes representing Paris through the centuries.

MÉMORIAL DE LA SHOAH Map p108
☎ 01 42 77 44 72; www.memorialdelashoah. org, in French; 17 rue Geoffroy-l'Asnier, 4e; admission free; ◷ 10am-6pm Sun-Wed & Fri, to 10pm Thu; Ⓜ St-Paul

Established in 1956, the Memorial to the Unknown Jewish Martyr has metamorphosed into the Memorial of the Holocaust and an important documentation centre. The permanent collection and temporary exhibits relate to the Holocaust and the German occupation of parts of France and Paris during WWII.

MAISON EUROPÉENNE DE LA PHOTOGRAPHIE Map p108
☎ 01 44 78 75 00; www.mep-fr.org; 5-7 rue de Fourcy, 4e; adult/senior & 8-25yr €6.50/3.50, 5-8pm Wed free; ◷ 11am-8pm Wed-Sun; Ⓜ St-Paul or Pont Marie

The European House of Photography, housed in the overly renovated Hôtel Hénault de Cantorbe (dating – believe it

MARAIS & BASTILLE

SIGHTS

JEAN-BERNARD CARILLET

Opéra de Paris Bastille

◥ OPÉRA DE PARIS BASTILLE

Paris' giant 'second' opera house, but in fact its main one nowadays, was designed by the Uruguayan architect Carlos Ott and inaugurated on 14 July 1989, the 200th anniversary of the storming of the Bastille. It has three theatres, including the main auditorium with around 2700 seats, all of which have an unrestricted view of the stage. There are 1¼-hour guided tours of the building, which depart at wildly different times depending on the week and the season.

Things you need to know: Map p108; ☎ 0 892 899 090, tours 01 40 01 19 70; www.opera -de-paris.fr; 2-6 place de la Bastille, 12e; guided tours adult/under 10yr/senior, student & 10-25yr €11/6/9; Ⓜ Bastille

or not – from the early 18th century), has cutting-edge temporary exhibits (usually retrospectives on single photographers), as well as an enormous permanent collection on the history of photography and its connections with France. There are frequent showings of short films and documentaries on weekend afternoons. The Japanese garden at the entrance is a delight.

PLACE DE LA BASTILLE Map p108
Ⓜ Bastille
The Bastille, the quintessential symbol of royal despotism, was demolished shortly

after a mob stormed it on 14 July 1789. The site where it once stood, place de la Bastille (11e and 12e), is now a very large and very busy traffic roundabout.

In the centre of the square is the 52m-high **Colonne de Juillet** (July Column), whose shaft of greenish bronze is topped by a gilded and winged figure of Liberty. It was erected in 1833 as a memorial to those killed in the street battles that accompanied the July Revolution of 1830 – they are buried in vaults under the column – and was later consecrated as a memorial to the victims of the February Revolution of 1848.

SLEEPING

HÔTEL LES JARDINS DU MARAIS
Map p108   Hotel €€€

☎ 01 40 21 20 00; www.lesjardinsdumarais.com; 74 rue Amelot, 11e; r €350-455, ste from €600; Ⓜ Chemin Vert; ✖ 🛜 ♿

You'd never know you were in Paris after walking through the door of this 263-room hotel housed in nine separate buildings designed by Gustave Eiffel and surrounding an enormous courtyard of cobblestones and gardens. Rooms have an art deco feel – lots of blacks, whites, purples and straight lines – and the outlets are always bursting at the seams. It's a delight but way to big to call itself a boutique hotel.

HÔTEL DU PETIT MOULIN
Map p108   Boutique Hotel €€€

☎ 01 42 74 10 10; www.hoteldupetitmoulin.com; 29-31 rue du Poitou, 3e; r €190-290, ste €350; Ⓜ Filles du Calvaire; ✖ 🛜 ♿

This scrumptious boutique hotel (OK, we're impressed that it was a bakery at the time of Henri IV) was designed from top to bottom by Christian Lacroix and features 17 completely different rooms. You can choose from medieval and rococo Marais sporting exposed beams and dressed in toile de Jouy wallpaper, to more modern surrounds with contemporary murals and heart-shaped mirrors just this side of kitsch. 'The Little Mill' is still one of our favourite hostelries in the Marais.

BLC DESIGN HOTEL
Map p98   Boutique hotel €€€

☎ 01 40 09 60 16; www.blcdesign-hotel-paris.com; 4 rue Richard Lenoir, 11e; s €95-180, d €180-230; Ⓜ Charonne; ✖ 🛜 ♿

Cobbled from what was a very ordinary one-star hotel, this 'symphony in white' has raised the bar on hotel standards east of the Bastille. Its 29 rooms, as comfort-able as they are 'Zen' stylish, are spread over six floors and we love the intimate little bar in the lobby. More rock star than royal, maybe, but it's on a roll.

HÔTEL CANDIDE Map p98   Hotel €€

☎ 01 43 79 02 33; www.new-hotel.com; 3 rue Pétion, 11e; s/d/tr €115/160/190; Ⓜ Voltaire; 🖳

This 48-room hotel within easy striking distance of the Bastille and the Marais offers relatively good value and is very convenient to the **Marché Bastille** (p257) on bd Richard Lenoir. It's on a very quiet street and we've always been impressed by the friendly, helpful service.

AUSTIN'S ARTS ET MÉTIERS HÔTEL Map p98   Hotel €€

☎ 01 42 77 17 61; www.hotelaustins.com; 6 rue Montgolfier, 3e; s/d €114/158; Ⓜ Arts et Métiers; ✖ 🛜

This three-star hotel southwest of place de la République and facing the **Musée**

IF WALLS COULD TALK

Centuries of history are inscribed on the facades and pediments of the 4e arrondissement and in the narrow streets, alleys, porches and courtyards; today the Marais is one of the few neighbourhoods of Paris that still has much of its pre-revolutionary architecture intact. These include the house at **3 rue Volta** (Map p98) in the 3e arrondissement, parts of which date back to 1292; the one at **51 rue de Montmorency**, also in the 3e and dating back to 1407 which is now a restaurant called **Auberge Nicolas Flamel** (p75); and the half-timbered 16th-century building at **11 and 13 rue François Miron** (Map p108) in the 4e.

des Arts et Métiers (p69) stands out primarily for its warm welcome and excellent service. The 29 rooms are minimally furnished but attractively done up in yellows, blues and reds. The brighter rooms face the street, while the larger ones overlook the inner courtyard. Choose room 12 if, like us, you like a bathroom with a window.

CASTEX HÔTEL Map p108   Hotel €€
☎ 01 42 72 31 52; www.castexhotel.com; 5 rue Castex, 4e; s/d €125/155, ste €220; Ⓜ Bastille; ⧉ 🛜

Equidistant from the Bastille and the Marais, the 30-room Castex has been modernised but manages to retain some of its 17th-century elements, including a vaulted stone cellar used as a breakfast room, terracotta tiles on the floor and toile de Jouy wallpaper. Try to get one of the independent rooms (1 and 2) off the lovely patio; No 3 is a two-room suite or family room.

HÔTEL CARON DE BEAUMARCHAIS
Map p108   Boutique Hotel €€
☎ 01 42 72 34 12; www.carondebeaumarchais.com; 12 rue Vieille du Temple, 4e; r €130-185; Ⓜ St-Paul; ⧉ 🛜

Decorated like an 18th-century private house contemporary with Beaumarchais, who wrote *Le Mariage de Figaro* (The Marriage of Figaro) at No 47 on this street, this award-winning themed hotel has to be seen to be believed. The small, museum-quality lobby, with its prized 18th-century pianoforte, gaming tables, chandeliers and original Beaumarchais manuscripts, sets the tone of the place. The 19 rooms aren't huge but are positively dripping in brocade, furniture decorated with tracery, and ormolu-framed mirrors. An experience like few others.

HÔTEL ST-LOUIS MARAIS
Map p108   Hotel €€
☎ 01 48 87 87 04; www.saintlouismarais.com; 1 rue Charles V, 4e; s €99, d & tw €115-140, tr €150, ste €160; Ⓜ Sully Morland; 🛜

This especially charming hotel built within a converted 17th-century convent is more Bastille than Marais, but still within easy walking distance of the latter. Wooden beams, terracotta tiles and heavy brocade drapes tend to darken the 19 renovated rooms, but certainly add to the atmosphere. Be aware that this four-floor hotel has no lift. Wi-fi costs €5.

HÔTEL DE NICE Map p108   Hotel €€
☎ 01 42 78 55 29; www.hoteldenice.com; 42bis rue de Rivoli, 4e; s €80-95, d €110-120, tr €135-145; Ⓜ Hôtel de Ville; 🛜

This is an especially warm, family-run place with 23 comfortable rooms. Some have balconies high above busy rue de Rivoli. Reception is on the 1st floor. Every square inch of wall space is used to display old prints, and public areas and bedrooms are full of Second Empire–style furniture, Oriental carpets and lamps with fringed shades.

HÔTEL JEANNE D'ARC
Map p108   Hotel €€
☎ 01 48 87 62 11; www.hoteljeannedarc.com; 3 rue de Jarente, 4e; s €62-90, d & tw €90-116, tr €146, q €160; Ⓜ St-Paul; 🛜 ♿

This cosy 35-room hotel near lovely place du Marché Ste-Catherine is a great little base for your peregrinations among the museums, bars and restaurants of the Marais, and almost has a country feel to it. About the only thing wrong with this place is that everyone knows about it, so you'll have to book well in advance. Check out the fantastic mirror in the breakfast room.

MARAIS & BASTILLE

SLEEPING

Gardens, Hôtel de Sully (p105)

HÔTEL DE LA PLACE DES VOSGES
Map p108   Hotel €€

☎ 01 42 72 60 46; www.hotelplacedesvosges.
com; 12 rue de Birague, 4e; s & d €90-95, ste
€150; Ⓜ St-Paul; 🛜

This superbly situated 17-room hotel is an
oasis of tranquillity due south of sublime
place des Vosges. The public areas are impressive and the rooms warm and cosy. A
tiny lift serves the 1st to 4th floors but it's
stairs only from the ground floor and to
the 5th floor. The suite on the top floor has
choice views and can accommodate up to
four people comfortably.

GRAND HÔTEL DU LOIRET
Map p108   Hotel €

☎ 01 48 87 77 00; www.hotel-loiret.fr; 8 rue
des Mauvais Garçons, 4e; s €50-80, d €70-90, tr/q
€110; Ⓜ Hôtel de Ville or St-Paul; 🖳

This 27-room budget hotel in the heart
of gay Marais is very popular with young
male travellers, not just because it is
within easy walking distance of just about
everything after dark, but because it sits
on the 'Street of the Bad Boys'. A few of

the singles have neither private shower
nor bath or toilet but share facilities off
the corridors. Those rooms are a steal at
€50. Internet access costs extra here.

HÔTEL LES SANS CULOTTES
Map p108   Hotel €

☎ 0 877 952 230, 01 48 05 42 92; www.lessan
sculottesfr.com; 27 rue de Lappe, 11e; s/d from
€60/75; Ⓜ Bastille

The nine rooms of this hotel above a nice
little bistro of the same name are on the
small side but are clean, tidy and decorated in bright colours and floral patterns.
Best of all, the place is very central to restaurants and nightlife of the Bastille. Be
warned that there is no lift here, though.

HÔTEL CROIX DE MALTE
Map p98   Hotel €

☎ 01 48 05 09 36; www.hotelcroixdemalte
-paris.com; 5 rue de Malte, 11e; s €60-90, d €65-
97; Ⓜ Oberkampf; 🛜

This cheery hotel will have you thinking
you're in the tropics. The breakfast room
just off the lobby is bathed in light and

MARAIS & BASTILLE

EATING

Salon Bleu Louis XVI, Musée Carnavalet (p106)

looks out onto a tiny glassed-in courtyard with greenery and a giant jungle mural; Walasse Ting jungle prints complete the picture. The 36 rooms are in two buildings, only one of which has a lift.

HÔTEL RIVOLI Map p108   Hotel €
☎ 01 42 72 08 41; 44 rue de Rivoli & 2 rue des Mauvais Garçons, 4e; s €35-55, d €44-55, tr €70; Ⓜ Hôtel de Ville

Long a Lonely Planet favourite, the Rivoli is forever cheap and cheery, with 20 basic, somewhat noisy rooms. The cheaper singles and doubles have washbasins only, but use of the shower room in the hallway is free. Annoyingly – given that it is in the heart of the Marais nightlife area – the front door is locked from 2am to 7am. Reception is on the 1st floor.

EATING

The Marais, filled with small restaurants of every imaginable type, is one of Paris' premier neighbourhoods for eating out. Towards République there's a decent selection of ethnic places. The Jewish restaurants (not all kosher) along **rue des Rosiers** (Map p108), the so-called Pletzl area, serve specialities from Central Europe, North Africa and Israel.

Bastille is another area chock-a-block with restaurants, some of which have added a star or two to their epaulettes in recent years. Narrow rue de Lappe and rue de la Roquette (11e), just east of place de la Bastille, may not be as hip as they were a dozen years ago, but they remain popular streets for nightlife and attract a young, alternative crowd.

LE DÔME BASTILLE
Map p108   French, Seafood €€€
☎ 01 48 04 88 44; 2 rue de la Bastille, 4e; starters €8.50-16.50, mains €20-31; ☾ lunch & dinner to 11pm; Ⓜ Bastille

This lovely restaurant, little sister to the more established (and touristy) Dôme in Montparnasse, specialises in superbly prepared fish and seafood dishes. The blackboard menu changes daily. Wines are a uniform €23.90 per bottle.

BOFINGER Map p108   French, Brasserie €€€

☎ 01 42 72 87 82; www.bofingerparis.com; 5-7 rue de la Bastille, 4e; starters €9-18.50, mains €16.90-35, 2-/3-course menus €25/30; ☽ lunch & dinner to midnight or 12.30am; Ⓜ Bastille

Founded in 1864, Bofinger is reputedly the oldest brasserie in Paris, though its polished art nouveau brass, glass and mirrors throughout flag a redecoration a few decades later. As at most Parisian brasseries, specialities include Alsatian-inspired dishes such as *choucroute* (sauerkraut with assorted meats; €19.80 to €21), and seafood dishes. Ask for a seat downstairs and under the *coupole* (stained-glass dome); it's the prettiest part of the restaurant. Just opposite **Le Petit Bofinger** (☎ 01 42 72 05 23; 6 rue de la Bastille, 4e; starters €6.20-19.30, mains €14.90-25.80, menus with wine €18 & €25.50; ☽ lunch & dinner to midnight daily; Ⓜ Bastille) is the brasserie's less brash (and cheaper) little sister.

LE PETIT MARCHÉ
Map p108   French, Bistro €€

☎ 01 42 72 06 67; 9 rue de Béarn, 3e; starters €9.50-15, mains €16-24, menu €12.50 (lunch only); ☽ lunch & dinner to midnight; Ⓜ Chemin Vert

This great little bistro just up from the place des Vosges fills up at lunch and again in the evening with a mixed crowd who come for the hearty cooking and friendly service. The salad starters are popular, as is the *selle d'agneau au basilique* (saddle of lamb with basil). The open kitchen also offers a fair few vege choices.

CHEZ NÉNESSE Map p108   French, Bistro €€

☎ 01 42 78 46 49; 17 rue de Saintonge, 3e; starters €8-16, mains €17-18; ☽ lunch & dinner to 10.30pm Mon-Fri; Ⓜ Filles du Calvaire

The atmosphere at this bistro is very 'old Parisian café' and unpretentious. Fresh, high-quality ingredients are used to make the dishes, such as *salade de canard au vinaigre d'hydromel* (duck salad with honey vinegar) and *fricassée de volaille aux morilles* (poultry fricassee with morel mushrooms). The lunchtime starters are €4 and *plats du jour* are € 9.50 or €10.

LE HANGAR Map p108   French, Bistro €€

☎ 01 42 74 55 44; 12 Impasse Berthaud, 3e; starters €9-10, mains €16-20; ☽ lunch & dinner to 11pm Tue-Sat; Ⓜ Les Halles

Unusual for big mouths like us, we almost balk at revealing this perfect little restaurant tucked away just south of the **Musée de la Poupée** (p109). It serves all the bistro favourites – rillettes, foie gras, steak tartare – in relaxing, quiet surrounds. The terrace is a delight in fine weather and the service professional and personal.

LE SOUK Map p98   North African €€

☎ 01 49 29 05 08; www.lesoukfr.com, in French; 1 rue Keller, 11e; starters €7-15, mains €15-20, menus €19.50 & €26.50; ☽ lunch & dinner to 11.30pm Tue-Sat; Ⓜ Ledru Rollin

We like coming here almost as much for the decor as the food – from the clay pots overflowing with spices on the outside to the exuberant (but never kitsch) Moroccan interior. And the food? As authentic as the decoration, notably the duck *tajine*, the pigeon pastilla and vegetarian couscous. Be warned: mains are enormous, so this might have to be a one-dish meal.

CHEZ JANOU
Map p108   French, Provencal Bistro €€

☎ 01 42 72 28 41; www.chezjanou.com; 2 rue Roger Verlomme, 3e; starters €9.50-11, mains €14.50-19, menu €12.50 (lunch only); ☽ lunch & dinner to midnight; Ⓜ Chemin Vert

Not exactly 'French bistro' as ordered by Central Casting but close to it, this lovely little spot just east of place des Vosges attracts celebs (last seen: John Malkovich) and hangers on with its inspired Provençal cooking, 80 different types of pastis and excellent service. Try the superb ratatouille with anchovy and black olive dips and the spelt risotto with scallops.

MAI THAI Map p108   Thai €€

☎ 01 42 72 18 77; www.maithai.fr, in French; 24bis rue St-Gilles, 3e; starters €9-11, mains €13-20, menu €13.50 (lunch only); ✆ lunch & dinner to 11pm daily; Ⓜ Chemin Vert

This stylish place, done up in warm tones of orange, red and yellow with Buddha figures, the *sine qua non* of Thai restaurants, throughout, has a loyal clientele; you should book in advance for dinner. Among *les classiques de la cuisine du Siam* (classics of the cuisine of Siam) on offer is chicken cooked with sacred basil (€15) and the unusual spicy Thai sausages (€13).

LES CAVES ST-GILLES

Map p108   Spanish €€

☎ 01 48 87 22 62; www.caves-saint-gilles.fr; 4 rue St-Gilles, 3e; tapas €5.50-26, mains €12-18; ✆ lunch & dinner to 11.30pm daily; Ⓜ Chemin Vert

This Spanish wine bar a short distance northeast of place des Vosges is the most authentic place on the Right Bank for tapas, paella (at the weekend only; €19) and sangria (€28 for 1.4cL).

LE TIRE BOUCHON Map p98   French €€

☎ 01 47 00 43 50; 5 rue Guillaume Bertrand, 11e; starters €7.50-14, mains €15-18, menus €12 & €15 (lunch only), €26.50; ✆ lunch & dinner to 11pm Mon-Sat; Ⓜ St-Maur

This mock old-style bistro close to the flashy rue Oberkampf has a dozen tables with gingham tablecloths arranged around a polished wooden bar. Add a few old photographs of the *quartier*, a touch of greenery and some decent bottles of wine and *voilà*: 'The Corkscrew'. The *cassoulet* (casserole or stew with beans and meat) and

the fillet of sea bream in a lobster sauce will tickle your taste buds. Expect friendly, attentive service but book in advance.

CAFFÉ BOBOLI Map p108   Italian €€

☎ 01 42 77 89 27; www.caffeboboli.com; 13 rue du Roi de Sicile, 4e; starters €8.90-12.50, mains €13.60-17.80; ✆ lunch Tue-Sun, dinner to 11pm Mon-Sat; Ⓜ St-Paul

Affordable Italian fare in the heart of the Marais? Not as preposterous a notion as you might think with this small restaurant run by two young Florentines. The food is very wholesome and based on vegetables, cheese and *charcuterie* like Parma ham and beef carpaccio. On the walls are original paintings and photographs that are changed every few months.

LE PETIT DAKAR

Map p108   African, Senegalese €€

☎ 01 44 59 34 74; 6 rue Elzévir, 3e; starters €6-8, mains €14-16, menu €15 (lunch only); ✆ lunch Tue-Sat, dinner to 11pm Tue-Sun; Ⓜ St-Paul

Some people think this is the most authentic Senegalese restaurant in Paris; the *tiéboudienne* (rice, fish and vegetables) is particularly well received.

LE TRUMILOU Map p108   French, Bistro €€

☎ 01 42 77 63 98; www.letrumilou.com; 84 quai de l'Hôtel de Ville, 4e; starters €4-14, mains €15-22, 2-/3-course menu €16.50/19.50; ✆ lunch & dinner to 11pm; Ⓜ Hôtel de Ville

This no-frills bistro just round the corner from the Hôtel de Ville and facing the posh Île de St-Louis square is a Parisian institution in situ for over a century. If you're looking for an authentic menu from the early 20th century and prices (well, almost) to match, you won't do better than this. Specialities of the house include *canard aux pruneaux* (duck with prunes; €17) and *ris de veau grand-mère* (veal sweetbreads in mushroom cream sauce; €22).

Musée Cognacq-Jay (p107)

OLIVIER CIRENDINI

CHEZ PAUL Map p98   French, Bistro €€
☎ 01 47 00 34 57; www.chezpaul.com, in French; 13 rue de Charonne, 11e; starters €5.60-17, mains €15-23; ☻ lunch & dinner to 12.30am; Ⓜ Ledru Rollin

When they put up a 'French restaurant' film set in Hollywood, this ever-expanding bistro is what it must look like. An extremely popular bistro, it has traditional French main courses handwritten on a yellowing menu and brusque service – Paris in true form! Stick with the simplest of dishes – the steak or foie gras with lentils – and make sure you've booked ahead.

PARIS MAIN D'OR
Map p98   French, Corsican €€
☎ 01 44 68 04 68; 133 rue du Faubourg St-Antoine, 11e; starters €7.50-15, mains €14-20, menu €13; ☻ lunch & dinner to 11pm Mon-Sat; Ⓜ Ledru Rollin

The unprepossessing, cafélike 'Paris Golden Hand' serves authentic Corsican dishes to an appreciative audience, many of them coppers (traditionally the preferred form of employment among

Corsicans in the capital). *Sturza preti* (spinach and fine *brocciu* cheese; €9) and traditional omelette with *brocciu* and *jambon sec* (dried ham, matured for two years) are some of the appetisers on the menu. For mains, favourites include the *tian d'agneau aux olives* (lamb ragout with olives; €18) and the *caprettu arrustini* (roast kid; €21). Pasta dishes come in at about €11, the *plat du jour* is €9.50.

CAFÉ DE L'INDUSTRIE
Map p108   French, Café €
☎ 01 47 00 13 53; 16 & 17 rue St-Sabin, 11e; starters €4.40-8, mains €8-16, menu €10.50 (lunch only); ☻ 9am-2am; Ⓜ Bastille

This popular café-restaurant with neocolonial decor has two locations directly opposite one another. It's a pleasant space and the perfect spot to meet a friend instead of at one of the crowded cafés or bars in Bastille. Food is competitively priced but not always up to scratch; to avoid disappointment stick with the simple entrées or just graze off the fabulous

MARAIS & BASTILLE

EATING

OLIVIER CIRENDINI

Courtyard, Archives Nationales (p108)

dessert table (€4 to €6). The *plats du jours* are between €9 and €11.50.

CHEZ HEANG Map p108   Korean €

☎ 01 48 07 80 98; 5 rue de la Roquette, 11e; barbecue €8.50-17.50, menus €8.80 (lunch only) & €12-23.80; ☾ lunch & dinner to midnight; Ⓜ Bastille

Also known as 'Barbecue de Seoul', this tiny place is where you cook your food on a grill in the middle of your table and eat little side dishes known as *banchan* that include the Korean staple *kimchi* (spicy-hot pickled cabbage). The *fondue maison*, a kind of spicy hotpot in which you dip and cook your food, costs €28 per person (minimum two).

GEORGET (ROBERT ET LOUISE)

Map p108   French €€

☎ 01 42 78 55 89; 64 rue Vieille du Temple, 3e; starters €5.20-15.80, mains €11.40-18, menu €12 (lunch only); ☾ lunch Wed-Sun, dinner to 11pm daily; Ⓜ St-Sébastien Froissart

This 'country inn', complete with its red gingham curtains, offers delightful, sim-ple and inexpensive French food, including *côte de bœuf* (side of beef; €40), which is cooked on an open fire and prepared by the original owners' daughter, Georget, and her husband. If you arrive early, choose to sit at the farmhouse table, right next to the fireplace. It's a jolly, truly Rabelaisian evening. The *plat du jour* is a snip at €12.

CHEZ MARIANNE

Map p108   Jewish €

☎ 01 42 72 18 86; 2 rue des Hospitalières St-Gervais, 4e; dishes €4.60-21; ☾ noon-midnight; Ⓜ St-Paul

This is a Sephardic alternative to the Ashkenazi fare usually available at Pletzl eateries. Platters containing four to 10 different meze (such as falafel, hummus, purées of aubergine and chickpeas) cost from €12 to €26. The takeaway window sells falafel in pita for €5 and there's also a bakery attached. Chez Marianne's set *menus* include a number of vegetarian options but note that food served here is not Beth Din kosher.

BREIZH CAFÉ Map p108 French, Breton €

☎ 01 42 72 13 77; www.breizhcafe.com; 109 rue Vieille du Temple, 4e; crêpes & galettes €3.80-10.50; ✆ lunch & dinner to 11pm Wed-Sun; Ⓜ St-Sébastien Froissart

It may use a minority language in its name (*breizh* is 'Breton' in Breton), but we doubt you'll hear much of that Celtic tongue spoken here. Concentrate instead on the sound of Cancale oysters being sucked, crêpes of organic flour prepared on a grill *autrement* (in a different way) and any of the 20 types of ciders on offer being uncorked. This is definitely a cut-above *crêperie*.

L'AS DE FELAFEL

Map p108 Jewish, Kosher €

☎ 01 48 87 63 60; 34 rue des Rosiers, 4e; dishes €5-7; ✆ noon-midnight Sun-Thu, to 5pm Fri; Ⓜ St-Paul

This has always been our favourite place for those deep-fried balls of chickpeas and herbs (€5) and serves turkey and lamb shwarma sandwiches (€7) too. It's always packed, particularly at weekday lunch, so avoid that time if possible.

CRÊPERIE BRETONNE FLEURIE DE L'ÉPOUSE DU MARIN

Map p98 French, Breton €

☎ 01 43 55 62 29; 67 rue de Charonne, 12e; starters €4-8.50, crêpes & galettes €2.40-8.50; ✆ lunch Mon-Fri, dinner to 11.30pm Mon-Sat; Ⓜ Charonne

Head to the 'Sailor's Wife' if you fancy savoury buckwheat *galettes* – try the ham, cheese and egg *complète* – or a sweet crêpe and wash it down with dry *cidre de Rance* (Rance cider; €6.50 for 50cL) served in a teacup (as is traditional). The Breton paraphernalia and B&W photos will keep you occupied if there's a lull in the chatter.

DRINKING

The Marais is an excellent spot for a night out. It's a lively mix of gay-friendly (and gay-only) café society and bourgeois arty spots, with an interesting sprinkling of eclectic bars and relatively raucous pubs.

Bastille has become increasingly *démodé* (unfashionable) and even crass over the years, but it invariably draws a crowd, particularly to heaving rue de Lappe. Things get quieter – and better – as you go further up rue de la Roquette and rue de Charonne.

AU PETIT FER À CHEVAL Map p108 Bar

☎ 01 42 72 07 27; 30 rue Vieille du Temple, 4e; ✆ 8am-2am; Ⓜ Hôtel de Ville or St-Paul; 🛜

The original (1903) horseshoe-shaped zinc bar leaves little room for much else, but nobody seems to mind at this genial place. It overflows with friendly regulars enjoying a drink or a sandwich (simple meals are served from noon to 1.15am). The stainless-steel toilets are straight out of a Flash Gordon film even after all this time.

AU P'TIT GARAGE Map p98 Bar

☎ 01 48 07 08 12; 63 rue Jean-Pierre Timbaud, 11e; ✆ 6pm-2am; Ⓜ Parmentier

Just about the last 'neighbourhood' bar in the *quartier*, the 'Little Garage' attracts local custom with its rock 'n' roll, laid-back staff and rough-and-ready decor.

LA PERLE Map p108 Bar

☎ 01 42 72 69 93; 78 rue Vieille du Temple, 3e; ✆ 6am-2am Mon-Fri, 8am-2am Sat & Sun; Ⓜ St-Paul or Chemin Vert

This is where *bobos* (bohemian bourgeois) come to slum it over *un rouge* (glass of red wine) until the DJ arrives and things liven up. We like the (for real) distressed look of the place and the model locomotive over the bar.

BAR-HOPPING STREETS

Prime drinking spots in Paris, perfect for evening meandering to soak up the scene.

Rue Vieille du Temple & surrounding streets, 4e (Map p108; Ⓜ St-Paul) Marais cocktail of gay bars and chic cafés.

Rue Oberkampf & rue Jean-Pierre Timbaud, 11e (Map p98; Ⓜ Oberkampf) Hip bars, bohemian hang-outs and atmospheric cafés.

Rue de la Roquette, rue Keller & rue de Lappe, 11e (Map p98; Ⓜ Voltaire, Ledru-Rollin) Whatever you fancy; Bastille has the lot.

L'ALIMENTATION GÉNÉRALE

Map p98   Bar

☎ 01 43 55 42 50; 64 rue Jean-Pierre Timbaud, 11e; ⏲ 5pm-2am Wed, Thu & Sun, 5pm-4am Fri & Sat; Ⓜ Parmentier

Another rue JPT stalwart, 'The Grocery Store' is a massive space, with crazy retro decor and outrageous toilets. Music is a big deal here. DJs play on weekends; expect to pay €10 with a drink for big names.

CAFÉ DES PHARES Map p108   Café

☎ 01 42 72 04 70; 7 place de la Bastille, 4e; ⏲ 7.30am-3am Sun-Thu, to 4am Fri & Sat; Ⓜ Bastille

'The Beacons Café' is best known as the city's original *philocafé* (philosophers' café). For two-hour debates on such topics as 'What is a fact?' and 'Can people communicate?', head for this place at 11am on Sunday. It may sound posy, but this is Paris.

L'APPAREMMENT CAFÉ Map p108   Café

☎ 01 48 87 12 22; 18 rue des Coutures St-Gervais, 3e; ⏲ noon-2am Mon-Sat, to midnight Sun; Ⓜ St-Sébastien Froissart

A tasteful haven tucked behind the Musée Picasso at a merciful distance from the madding crowds of the Marais, this place is a bit like a private living room, with wood panelling, sofas, scattered parlour games, dog-eared books – and Parisians languidly studying their 'lounch' (their word, not ours) and (Sunday till 6pm) their brunch – or is that 'brounch'? – menus.

LE PURE CAFÉ Map p98   Café

☎ 01 43 71 47 22; 14 rue Jean Macé, 11e; ⏲ 7am-2am; Ⓜ Charonne

This old café, which should be declared a national monument (if it already hasn't been), moonlights as a restaurant with a modern kitchen and some dishes that veer toward 'world' food (mains €17.50 to €21). But we like it as it was intended to be, especially over a *grand crème* (large white coffee) and the papers on Sunday morning. It has appeared as Central Casting's 'typical French café' in a number of films, including the 2004 British film *Before Sunset*.

LE CHINA Map p98   Cocktail Bar

☎ 01 43 46 08 09; 50 rue de Charenton, 12e; ⏲ 7pm-2am; Ⓜ Ledru-Rollin or Bastille

The much loved (and missed) China Club, with its Asian gentleman's club feel, huge bar and high ceilings, has metamorphosed into 'The China' and who can tell the difference? There's still jazz in the basement that harkens back to the Shanghai of the 1930s and a well-reputed menu with dim sum between €8 and €12.

LA TARTINE Map p108   Wine Bar

☎ 01 42 72 76 85; 24 rue de Rivoli & 17 rue du Roi de Sicile, 4e; ⏲ 8am-2am; Ⓜ St-Paul

A wine bar where little has changed since the days of gas lighting (some of the fixtures are still in place), this place offers 15 selected reds, whites and rosés by the *pot* (46cL). There's not much to eat except lots of *tartines* (open-faced sandwiches).

LE BISTROT DU PEINTRE

Map p98   Wine Bar

☎ 01 47 00 34 39; 116 av Ledru-Rollin, 11e;
🕑 7am-2am Mon-Sat, 8am-2am Sun;
Ⓜ Bastille; 📶

This lovely belle époque bistro and wine bar should really count more as a restaurant than a drinking place; after all, the food is great. But the 1902 art nouveau bar, elegant terrace and spot-on service put this place on our apéritif A-list – and that of local artists, *bobos* and local celebs.

LE CAFÉ DU PASSAGE

Map p98   Wine Bar

☎ 01 49 29 97 64; 12 rue de Charonne, 11e;
🕑 6pm-2am; Ⓜ Ledru-Rollin

This is the destination of choice for wine buffs, who relax in armchairs while sampling vintages from the excellent range on offer. 'The Arcade Café' has hundreds of wines available, including many by the glass (from €4.80).

ENTERTAINMENT & ACTIVITIES

LE BALAJO Map p108   Clubbing

☎ 01 47 00 07 87; www.balajo.fr; 9 rue de Lappe, 11e; admission from €12; 🕑 10pm-2am Tue & Thu, 11pm-5am Fri & Sat, 3-7.30pm Sun; Ⓜ Bastille

A mainstay of Parisian nightlife since 1936, this ancient ballroom is devoted to salsa classes and Latino music during the week. Weekends see DJs spinning a mixed bag of rock, disco, funk, R 'n' B and house. While a bit lower-shelf these days, it scores a mention for its historical value and its old-fashioned *musette* (accordion music) gigs on Sundays.

OPÉRA DE PARIS BASTILLE

Map p108   Opera

☎ 0 892 899 090, 01 72 29 35 35; www.opera -de-paris.fr, in French; 2-6 place de la Bastille, 12e; opera €5-172, ballet €5-87, concerts €5-49; Ⓜ Bastille

Despite some initial resistance to this 3400-seat venue, the capital's main opera

Bofinger (p115)

OLIVER STREWE

house is now performing superbly. While less alluring than the **Palais Garnier** (p150), at least all seats in the main hall have an unrestricted view of the stage. Ticket sales begin with different opening dates for bookings by telephone, online or from the **box office** (Map p108; 130 rue de Lyon, 11e; ☎ 10.30am-6.30pm Mon-Sat). The cheapest opera seats are €7 and sold only from the box office. On the first day they are released, box office tickets can be bought only from the opera house at which the performance is to be held. At Bastille, standing-only tickets for €5 are available 1½ hours before performances begin. Occasionally, 15 minutes before the curtain goes up, last-minute seats at reduced rates (usually €20 for opera and ballet performances) are released to people aged under 28 or over 60.

↘ GAY & LESBIAN NIGHTLIFE

- **3w Kafé** (Map p108; ☎ 01 48 87 39 26; 8 rue des Écouffes, 4e; ☎ 5.30pm-2am; Ⓜ St-Paul) The name of this flagship cocktail bar/pub on a street with several dyke bars means 'Women with Women' so it can't be any clearer.

- **Le Quetzal** (Map p108; ☎ 01 48 87 99 07; 10 rue de la Verrerie, 4e; ☎ 5pm-2am; Ⓜ Hôtel de Ville) Perennial favourite gay bar – one of the first in the Marais.

- **Raidd Bar** (Map p108; ☎ 01 42 77 05 13; www.raiddbar.com; 23 rue du Temple, 4e; ☎ 5pm-4am; Ⓜ Hôtel de Ville) This is a club-bar that takes its cue from Splash in New York, with showering go-go boys behind glass and a terrace on which to cool off.

LES BAINS DU MARAIS

Map p108   Hammams & Spas

☎ 01 44 61 02 02; www.lesbainsdumarais.com, in French; 31-33 rue des Blancs Manteaux, 4e; massage from €70; ☎ 10am-8pm Mon, Fri & Sat, 10am-11pm Sun, Tue-Thu; Ⓜ Rambuteau or Hôtel de Ville

Luxury personified, this hammam (€35) combines classical with modern – Levantine decor and mint tea with as many pampering treatments as you'd care to name. The hammam is reserved for men and for women on different days; 'mixed days', where bathing suits are obligatory, are Wednesday evening and all day Saturday and Sunday.

VÉLO CITO Map p98   Bicycle Hire

☎ 01 43 38 47 19; www.velocito.fr, in French; 7 rue St-Ambroise, 11e; per day €25; ☎ 10am-7pm Mon-Sat; Ⓜ St-Ambroise

Smart electric bicycles for cruising around the city are available from this outlet located between Bastille and République; rental is by the day only and you need to leave your passport as a deposit. It distributes an excellent free map (1:53:000) detailing some lovely *pistes cyclables* starting at RER stations around Paris.

SHOPPING

The Marais boasts some excellent speciality stores and an ever-expanding fashion presence. Rue des Francs Bourgeois and, towards the other side of rue de Rivoli, rue François Mirron have well-established boutique shopping for clothing, home furnishings and stationery. Place des Vosges is lined with high-end art and antique galleries.

The neighbourhoods around Bastille in the 11e also have some interesting shops, including rue Keller, where you'll find young designers, records and manga/

Chez Marianne (p118)
WILL SALTER

comics shops; and rue de Charonne, known for its cut-rate clothes shops.

LIBRAIRIE DE L'HÔTEL DE SULLY
Map p108   Books & Comics
☎ 01 44 61 21 75; www.editions.monuments -nationaux.fr; 62 rue St-Antoine, 4e; ☺ 10am-7pm; Ⓜ St-Paul
This early-17th-century aristocratic mansion housing the Centre des Monuments Nationaux (Monum), the body responsible for many of France's historical monuments, has one of the best bookshops in town for titles related to Paris. From historical texts and biographies to picture books and atlases, it's all here.

FRAGONARD Map p108   Cosmetics
☎ 01 44 78 01 32; www.fragonard.com; 51 rue des Francs Bourgeois, 4e; ☺ 10.30am-7.30pm Mon-Sat, noon-7pm Sun; Ⓜ St-Paul
This Parisian perfume maker has alluring natural scents in elegant bottles as well as candles, essential oils and soaps. In addition to the splendid smells, there's a small, expensive and very tasteful selection of

clothing, hand-stitched linen tablecloths and napkins, as well as jewellery. There's also a **St-Germain branch** (☎ 01 42 84 12 12; 196 bd St-Germain, 6e; Ⓜ St-Germain des Prés), and Fragonard runs the **Musée du Parfum** (p153), which has its own shop.

APC Map p108   Fashion & Accessories
☎ 01 42 78 18 02; www.apc.fr; 112 rue Vieille du Temple, 3e; ☺ 11.30am-8pm; Ⓜ Chemin Vert
The hip streetwear of the Atelier de Production et Création (Production and Creation Workshop) is very popular with those young Parisian guys with pop-rock haircuts, white sneakers and jeans. The focus is on simple lines and straight cuts, though some pieces are more adventurous. It also has women's clothes.

ISABEL MARANT
Map p98   Fashion & Accessories
☎ 01 43 26 04 12; www.isabelmarant.tm.fr; 16 rue de Charonne, 11e; ☺ 10.30am-7.30pm Mon-Sat; Ⓜ Bastille
Great cardigans and trousers, interesting accessories, beautiful fabrics and ethnic

influences: just a few reasons Isabel Marant has become the *chouchou* (darling) of Paris fashion. Bohemian and stylish, these are clothes that people look good in.

L'HABILLEUR

Map p108   Fashion & Accessories

☎ 01 48 87 77 12; 44 rue de Poitou, 3e; ☺ noon-7.30pm Mon-Sat; Ⓜ St-Sébastien Froissart

For 15 years this shop has been known for its discount designer wear – offering 50% to 70% off original prices. It generally stocks last season's collections including Paul & Joe, Giorgio Brato and Belle Rose. The men's selection is quite extensive.

À L'OLIVIER Map p108   Food & Drink

☎ 01 48 04 86 59; www.alolivier.com; 23 rue de Rivoli, 4e; ☺ 2-7pm Mon, 9.30am-7pm Tue-Sat; Ⓜ St-Paul

'At the Olive Tree' has been *the* place for oil, from olive and walnut to soy and sesame, since 1822; buy it from one of the stainless vats on display. It also offers olive-oil tastings and olive-oil beauty products, as well as vinegars, jams and honeys.

JULIEN CAVISTE Map p98   Food & Drink

☎ 01 42 72 00 94; 50 rue Charlot, 3e; ☺ 10am-1.30pm & 3.30-8pm Tue-Sat, 10am-1.30pm Sun; Ⓜ Filles du Calvaire

This independent wine shop at the southern end of rue Charlot focuses on small, independent producers and organic wines. There's a unique selection of Rhône, Languedoc and Loire vintages and exceptional sparkling wines. The enthusiastic merchant will locate and explain wine for you, whatever your budget.

BOUTIQUE OBUT

Map p98   Games & Hobbies

☎ 01 47 00 91 38; www.labouleobut.com; 60 av de la République, 11e; ☺ 10am-noon & 12.30-6.30pm Tue-Sat; Ⓜ Parmentier

This is the Parisian mecca for fans of *pétanque* or the similar (though more formal) game of boules, a form of bowls played with heavy steel balls wherever a bit of flat and shady ground can be found. It will kit you out with all the equipment necessary to get a game going and even has team uniforms. Three-ball sets start at €24.

PUZZLE MICHÈLE WILSON

Map p98   Games & Hobbies

☎ 01 47 00 12 57; www.puzzles-et-jeux.com; 39 rue de la Folie Méricourt, 11e; ☺ 10am-6pm Tue-Fri, 2-7pm Sat; Ⓜ St-Ambroise

Puzzleurs and *puzzleuses* will love the selection of hand-cut wooden jigsaw puzzles available in this shop. Ranging in size (and degree of difficulty) from 80 to – wait for it – 5000 pieces, the puzzles depict for the most part major works of art; everyone from Millet and Bosch to the impressionists is represented. The ones of medieval stained glass and 18th-century fans are particularly fine. There are two other outlets, including a **15e branch** (Map p188; ☎ 01 45 75 35 28; 97 av Émile Zola, 15e; ☺ 9am-7pm Mon-Fri, 10am-7pm Sat; Ⓜ Charles Michels).

LA BOUTIQUE DES INVENTIONS

Map p108   Gifts & Souvenirs

☎ 01 42 71 44 19; www.la-boutique-des-inventions.com; 13 rue St-Paul, 4e; ☺ 11am-7pm Wed-Sun; Ⓜ St-Paul

This unique shop in the heart of Village St-Paul, a delightful little shopping square with boutiques and galleries, is a forum for inventors and their inventions. Be the first on the block to own a shaker that sprinkles its own salt, a pepper grinder that twists itself or a miraculous filter that turns water into wine. Lots of wacky designs, too.

⬂ MONTMARTRE & PIGALLE

MONTMARTRE & PIGALLE

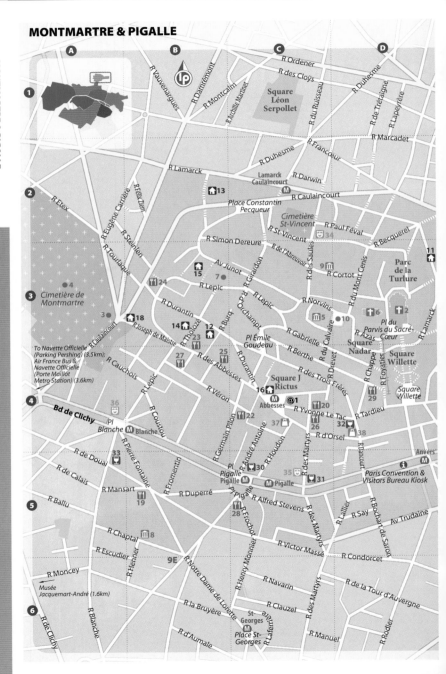

0 250 m
0 0.1 miles

INFORMATION
Taxiphone Internet..........................**1** C4

SIGHTS
Basilique du Sacré Cœur................**2** D3
Cimetière de Montmarte
  Entrance..**3** A3
Cimetière de Montmartre...............**4** A3
Dalí Espace Montmartre..................**5** C3
Église St-Pierre de Montmartre......**6** D3
Moulin de la Galette........................**7** B3
Musée de la Vie Romantique.........**8** B5
Musée de Montmartre......................**9** C3
Place du Tertre..............................**10** D3

SLEEPING
Ermitage Hôtel..............................**11** D3
Hôtel Bonséjour Montmartre......**12** B3
Hotel Caulaincourt Square...........**13** B2
Hôtel des Arts..............................**14** B3
Hôtel Particulier Montmartre.......**15** B3
Hôtel Regyn's Montmartre...........**16** B4
Kube Hôtel..................................**17** H3
Terrass Hôtel................................**18** B3

EATING
À La Cloche d'Or..........................**19** B5
Au Petit Budapest........................**20** C4

Aux Négociants............................**21** E2
Chez Toinette...............................**22** C4
La Mascotte..................................**23** B3
Le Café Qui Parle.........................**24** B3
Le Grenier à Pain.........................**25** B4
Le Miroir......................................**26** C4
Le Mono......................................**27** B4
Marché des Gastronomes............**28** C5
Michelangelo...............................**29** D4

DRINKING
Chào Bà Café..............................**30** C5
Ice Kube.................................(see 17)
La Fourmi....................................**31** C5
Le Progrès...................................**32** D4
O P'tit Douai................................**33** A5

**ENTERTAINMENT &
ACTIVITIES**
Au Lapin Agile.............................**34** C2
La Cigale.................................(see 31)
Le Divan du Monde......................**35** C5
Moulin Rouge..............................**36** A4

SHOPPING
Ets Lion......................................**37** C4
La Citadelle.................................**38** D4
Tati..**39** F4

HIGHLIGHTS

⇲ BASILIQUE DU SACRÉ CŒUR

On the Butte de Montmartre (Montmartre Hill), spiral 234 steps to the top of the steps of this very Parisian icon (p133) that took more than four decades to complete – on a clear day the view is spectacular. Inside the basilica, the glittering mosaics and chapel-lined crypt are also worth a look.

⇲ CIMETIÈRE DE MONTMARTRE

Writers, composers, artists, film directors and dancers (including Émile Zola, Stendhal and Degas) lay at rest in this lovely necropolis (p134), the most famous in Paris after Père Lachaise. It's a magnificent, contemplative sanctuary in this popular neighbourhood, and more than worth a slow afternoon stroll when the rest of the area gets busy.

MONTMARTRE & PIGALLE

HIGHLIGHTS

3

⤵ CLOS MONTMARTRE

Quel surprise! Wine in the middle of the capital city? The 2000 vines in this 1930s vineyard (p130; originally planted to thwart real-estate development), the only one existing in central Paris, produce an average 800 bottles of wine a year, which are auctioned off for charity.

4

⤵ PLACE DU TERTRE

The pinnacle of touristy Paris, this crowded, but quintessentially picturesque, Montmartre square (p133) is a relentless fiesta of packed café terraces, postcard-toting gift shops, street performers and over-zealous portrait artists just dying to sketch a caricature of your face – a fun and memorable keepsake from your Parisian tour.

5

⤵ MOULIN ROUGE

While the red, 19th-century windmill of Paris' most-famous cabaret (p141) burnt down, its 1925 replacement is just as impressive – and the show is full of life and fun. More recently, the windmill and its surrounding neighbourhood have provided the inspiration for numerous films, such as the 2001 *Moulin Rouge*.

1 GLENN BEANLAND; 3 OLIVIER CIRENDINI; 4 WILL SALTER; 5 CHRISTOPHER GROENHOUT; 6 BRUCE BI

1 Basilique du Sacré Cœur (p133); 2 Cimetière de Montmartre (p134); 3 Clos Montmartre (p130); 4 Artist painting a portrait in Place du Tertre (p133); 5 Moulin Rouge (p141)

MONTMARTRE ART AMBLE

When Montmartre was incorporated into the capital in 1860, its picturesque charm and low rents attracted painters and writers. The late 19th and early 20th centuries were Montmartre's heyday, when Picasso and Braque introduced the world to cubism. The walk starts at the neighbourhood's two windmills and ends at Basilique du Sacré Cœur. It covers roughly 1km and takes about one hour.

❶ MOULIN BLUTE-FIN & MOULIN DE LA GALETTE

In the 17th and 18th centuries, Montmartre was dotted with windmills, used to grind wheat into flour. Today only two remain, the Moulin Blute-Fin and (about 100m east) the Moulin de la Galette, also called Moulin Radet. *Galette* was the name of the rye bread that the Drebays sold to Parisians, accompanied with a glass of milk.

❷ PASSE-MURAILLE STATUE

Crossing through place Marcel Aymé, you'll see a curious statue of a man emerging from a stone wall. It portrays Dutilleul, the hero of Marcel Aymé's short story *Le Passe-Muraille* (The Walker through Walls), who finally became trapped halfway inside a wall. Aymé lived in the adjacent apartment building from 1902 to 1967.

❸ CIMETIÈRE ST-VINCENT

Head north up rue Girardon, and pass the Allée des Brouillards (Fog Alley) where several artists squatted in the late 19th century – Renoir lived at No 8. Descend the stairs from place Dalida into rue St-Vincent; on the other side of the wall is Cimetière St-Vincent, final resting place of Maurice Utrillo (1883–1955), the 'painter of Montmartre'.

❹ AU LAPIN AGILE

Just over rue des Saules is the celebrated cabaret Au Lapin Agile, whose name comes from *Le Lapin à Gill,* a mural of a rabbit jumping out of a cooking pot by caricaturist André Gill, which can still be seen on the western exterior wall. Poet Guillaume Apollinaire, great proponent of cubism, was a regular here.

❺ CLOS MONTMARTRE

Turn right (south) onto rue des Saules. Just opposite is the Clos Montmartre, a small vineyard dating from 1933 (originally planted to thwart real estate development), whose 2000 vines produce an average of 800 bottles of wine each October. Just opposite is the Maison Rose, the famous subject of an Utrillo painting and now a restaurant.

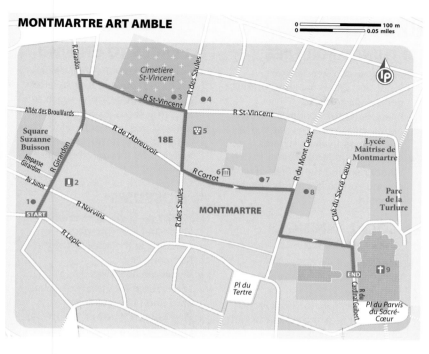

MONTMARTRE ART AMBLE

❻ MUSÉE DE MONTMARTRE

The Musée de Montmartre (p134) is on rue Cortot (at No 12–14), the first street on the left after the vineyard. The museum is housed in Montmartre's oldest building – a manor house built in the 17th century – and was the one-time home to painters Renoir, Utrillo and Raoul Dufy.

❼ ERIC SATIE'S HOUSE

The celebrated composer lived from 1890 to 1898 in the house at 6 rue Cortot.

❽ WATER TOWER

At the end of rue Cortot turn right (south) onto rue du Mont Cenis – the attractive water tower just opposite dates from the early 20th century. Turn left onto (tiny) rue de Chevalier de la Barre and then right onto rue du Cardinal Guibert.

❾ BASILIQUE DU SACRÉ CŒUR

The entrance to the Basilique du Sacré Cœur (p133) and the stunning vista over Paris from its steps are just to the south.

MONTMARTRE & PIGALLE

BEST...

BEST...

⬈ THINGS FOR FREE

- **Basilique du Sacré Cœur** (opposite) Climb the steps of this domed masterpiece.
- **Place du Tertre** (opposite) Watch people get their faces painted at one of Paris' liveliest squares.
- **Cimetière de Montmartre** (p134) Wander among the graves of writers and composers in this peaceful cemetery.

⬈ LOCAL DINING FAVOURITES

- **Chez Toinette** (p139) Dine on superbly cooked, uncomplicated French fare.
- **Aux Négociants** (p139) A French bistro that feels more like the Paris of six decades ago.
- **La Mascotte** (p138) French seafood dishes in a simple, convivial setting.

⬈ PLACES TO UNWIND

- **Le Progrès** (p140) A real neighbourhood café in a touristy area.
- **Chào Bà Café** (p140) A touch of feng shui seems to pervade this relaxing café with oriental touches.
- **Cimetière de Montmartre** (p134) Take a stroll through this tranquil cemetery.

⬈ MUSEUMS

- **Musée de la vie Romantique** (opposite) Even the garden is romantic at the Museum of the Romantic Life.
- **Musée de Montmartre** (p134) Learn about Montmartre's rebellious and bohemian past.
- **Dalí Espace Montmartre** (p134) Like a 3-D film on canvas, Dalí's work is as eye-catching as ever in this museum dedicated to the surrealist master.

DENNIS JOHNSON

Place du Tertre, Montmartre

DISCOVER MONTMARTRE & PIGALLE

A wellspring of Parisian myth, Montmartre has always stood apart. From its days as a simple village on the hill to the bohemian lifestyle that Toulouse-Lautrec and other artists immortalised in the late 19th and early 20th centuries, the area has repeatedly woven itself into the city's collective imagination.

Today, of course, the area thrives on busloads of tourists, who come to climb the cascading steps up to Sacré Cœur and wander through its alluring narrow hillside lanes. But even with the all the souvenir kitsch and milling crowds, it's hard not to appreciate the views looking out over Paris, or find some romance relaxing in a backstreet café.

Back down at the foot of the hill is the rough-and-ready charm of the city's red-light district, a mix of erotica shops, striptease parlours, trendy nightspots and cabarets. If you take the time to wander you'll find some unusual, less-touristy areas.

SIGHTS

BASILIQUE DU SACRÉ CŒUR

☎ 01 53 41 89 00; www.sacre-coeur-montmartre.com; 35 rue du Chevalier de la Barre, 18e; ☯ 6am-10.30pm; Ⓜ Anvers

Sacred Heart Basilica, perched at the very top of Butte de Montmartre, was built from contributions pledged by Parisian Catholics as an act of contrition after the humiliating Franco-Prussian War of 1870–71. Construction began in 1876, but the basilica was not consecrated until 1919. In a way, atonement here has never stopped; a perpetual prayer 'cycle' that began at the consecration of the basilica continues round the clock to this day.

Some 234 spiralling steps lead you to the basilica's dome (admission €5, cash only; ☯ 9am-7pm Apr-Sep, to 5.30pm Oct-Mar), which affords one of Paris' most spectacular panoramas; they say you can see for 30km on a clear day. Weighing in at 19 tonnes, the bell called La Savoyarde in the tower above is the largest in France. The chapel-lined crypt, visited in conjunction with the dome, is huge but not very interesting. If you don't want to walk the hill, you can use a regular metro ticket to take the funicular (☯ 6am-midnight).

PLACE DU TERTRE

Ⓜ Abbesses

Half a block west of Église St-Pierre de Montmartre, which once formed part of a 12th-century Benedictine abbey, is what was once the main square of the village of Montmartre. These days it's filled with cafés, restaurants, tourists and rather obstinate portrait artists and caricaturists, who will gladly do your likeness. Whether it looks even remotely like you is another matter.

MUSÉE DE LA VIE ROMANTIQUE

☎ 01 55 31 95 67; www.vie-romantique.paris.fr, in French; 16 rue Chaptal, 9e; temporary exhibitions adult/14-26yr €7.50/5, permanent collection free; ☯ 10am-6pm Tue-Sun; Ⓜ Blanche or St-Georges

One of our favourite small museums in Paris, the Museum of the Romantic Life is in a splendid location at the lovely Hôtel Scheffer-Renan in the centre of the district once known as 'New Athens'. The

MONTMARTRE & PIGALLE

SIGHTS

OLIVIER CIRENDINI

Cimetière de Montmartre

⬎ CIMETIÈRE DE MONTMARTRE

Established in 1798, this 11-hectare cemetery is perhaps the most celebrated necropolis in Paris after Père Lachaise. It contains the graves of writers Émile Zola (whose ashes are now in the Panthéon), Alexandre Dumas (fils) and Stendhal, composers Jacques Offenbach and Hector Berlioz, artist Edgar Degas, film director François Truffaut and dancer Vaslav Nijinsky – among others.

Maps showing the location of the tombs are available free from the conservation office at the cemetery's entrance.

Things you need to know: ☎ 01 53 42 36 30; 20 av Rachel, 18e; ⏰ 8am-6pm Mon-Fri, 8.30am-6pm Sat, 9am-6pm Sun mid-Mar–early Nov, 8am-5.30pm Mon-Fri, 8.30am-5.30pm Sat, 9am-5.30pm Sun early Nov–mid-Mar; Ⓜ Place de Clichy

museum, at the end of a film-worthy cobbled lane, is devoted to the life and work of Amandine Aurore Lucile Dupin Baronne (1804–76) – better known to the world as George Sand – and her intellectual circle of friends, and is full of paintings, *objets d'art* and personal effects. Don't miss the tiny but delightful garden.

MUSÉE DE MONTMARTRE
☎ 01 49 25 89 39; www.museedemontmartre. fr, in French; 12 rue Cortot, 18e; adult/senior, student & 10-25yr €7/5.50; ⏰ 11am-6pm Tue-Sun; Ⓜ Lamarck Caulaincourt

The Montmartre Museum displays paintings, lithographs and documents mostly relating to the area's rebellious and bohemian/artistic past. It is located in a 17th-century manor house, which is the oldest structure in the *quartier,* and also stages exhibitions of artists who are still living in the *quartier.*

DALÍ ESPACE MONTMARTRE
☎ 01 42 64 40 10; www.daliparis.com; 11 rue Poulbot, 18e; adult/student & 8-26yr/senior €10/6/7; ⏰ 10am-6.30pm; Ⓜ Abbesses
More than 300 works by Salvador Dalí (1904–89), the flamboyant Catalan sur-

realist printmaker, painter, sculptor and self-promoter, are on display at this surrealist-style basement museum located just west of place du Tertre.

SLEEPING

Montmartre, encompassing the 18e and the northern part of the 9e, is one of the most charming neighbourhoods in Paris and a good place to base yourself in. There is a lot of variety here, from boutique to bohemian and *hôtels particuliers* (private mansions) to hostels. Many of the hotels here have views of some kind – whether of the streets of Montmartre and Sacré Coeur or the Paris skyline stretching away to the south – and top-floor availability is a good factor to take into account when choosing your room.

HÔTEL PARTICULIER
MONTMARTRE Boutique Hotel €€€
☎ 01 53 41 81 40; http://hotel-particulier
-montmartre.com; 23 av Junot, 18e; ste €390-
590; Ⓜ Lamarck Caulaincourt; ✷ 🛜
An 18ᵗʰ-century mansion hidden down a private alleyway in Montmartre, this jewel sparkles from every angle. Much more than an exclusive hotel, it's the equivalent of staying in a modern art collector's personal residence, with rotating exhibitions from around the world, five imaginative suites designed by top French artists (Philippe Mayaux, Natacha Lesueur), and a lush garden landscaped by Louis Benech of Jardin des Tuileries fame. Non-guests can stop by for evening cocktails (☺ 5pm-midnight); reservations required.

KUBE HÔTEL Boutique Hotel €€€
☎ 01 42 05 20 00; www.muranoresort.com;
1-5 passage Ruelle, 18e; s €250, d €300-400, ste
€500-750; Ⓜ La Chapelle; ✷ 🖥 🛜

The easternmost edge of the 18e, virtually the lap of Gare du Nord, is the last place in Paris you'd expect to find an über-trendy boutique hotel, but this 41-room hostelry manages to pull it off. The theme here is, of course, three dimensional square – from the glassed-in reception box in the entrance courtyard to the cube-shaped furnishings in the 41 guestrooms to the ice in the cocktails at the celebrated **Ice Kube** (p140) bar. The offspring of the stylish Murano Urban Resort the Kube might have been less open-handed with the florescent reds and *faux* fur, but if that's what it takes to get guests to trek all the way to La Chapelle, so be it.

BRUCE BI
Montmartre street scene at night

MONTMARTRE & PIGALLE

SLEEPING

BRUCE B[

Musée Jacquemart-André

⤳ IF YOU LIKE...

If you like the Musée de Montmartre (p134) and its historic structure, head to Musée Jacquemart-André (☎ 01 45 62 11 59; www.musee-jacquemart-andre.com; 158 blvd Haussmann, 8e; adult/7-17yr & student incl audioguide €11/8.50, under 7yr free; ☥ 10am-6pm; Ⓜ Miromesnil). The Jacquemart-André Museum, founded by collector Édouard André and his portraitist wife Nélie Jacquemart, is in an opulent mid-19ᵗʰ-century residence on one of Paris' posher avenues. It has furniture, tapestries and enamels, but is most noted for its paintings by Rembrandt and Van Dyck and Italian Renaissance works by Bernini, Botticelli, Carpaccio, Donatello, Mantegna, Tintoretto, Titian and Uccello. Don't miss the Jardin d'Hiver (Winter Garden), with its marble statuary, tropical plants and double-helix marble staircase. Just off it is the delightful *fumoir* (the erstwhile smoking room) filled with exotic objects collected by Jacquemart during her travels. The salon de thé (tearoom; ☥ 11.45am-5.45pm) is one of the most beautiful in the city.

TERRASS HÔTEL
Hotel €€€

☎ 01 46 06 72 85; www.terrass-hotel.com; 12 rue Joseph de Maistre, 18e; s & d €280-340, ste €385-415; Ⓜ Blanche; ✺ ▢ ☞

This very sedate, stylish hotel at the southeastern corner of the Montmartre Cemetery and due east of the Butte de Montmartre (Montmartre Hill) has 92 spacious and well-designed rooms and suites, an excellent restaurant and bar, and quite simply the best views in town. For the ultimate Parisian experience, choose double room 608 for stunning views of the Eiffel Tower and Panthéon or room 802, which boasts its own private terrace. Some of the rooms on floors 4, 5 and 6 were designed by Kenzo.

HÔTEL DES ARTS
Hotel €€

☎ 01 46 06 30 52; www.arts-hotel-paris.com; 5 rue Tholozé, 18e; s €95, d & tw €140-165; Ⓜ Abbesses or Blanche; ▢ ☞

This friendly, attractive 50-room hotel is convenient to both Pigalle and Montmartre. Its comfortable midrange rooms are done up in traditional style (lots of floral motifs); consider spending an extra €25 for a superior room, which have nicer views and are a tad larger. Just up the street is the old-style windmill **Moulin de la Galette** (p130) – how's that for location?

HÔTEL REGYN'S MONTMARTRE
Hotel €€

☎ 01 42 54 45 21; www.hotel-regyns-paris.com; 18 place des Abbesses, 18e; s €79-99, d & tw €91-120; Ⓜ Abbesses; 🖥 📶
This 22-room hotel is a good choice if you want to stay in old Montmartre and not break the bank. It's just opposite the Abbesses metro station, which has one of the best-preserved Hector Guimard art nouveau entrance canopies (see p72), and outside the hotel is a lovely old plane tree. Some of the rooms have views out over Paris. Wi-fi costs extra.

ERMITAGE HÔTEL
Hotel €€

☎ 01 42 64 79 22; www.ermitagesacrecoeur.fr; 24 rue Lamarck, 18e; s €82-85, d €96-100, tr €120, q €145; Ⓜ Lamarck Caulaincourt; 🖥
Located in a 19th-century townhouse, the family-run Ermitage is a quaint 12-room

bed and breakfast in the shadow of Sacré Cœur. The traditional-style rooms are simple but attractive, with floral-patterned walls and antique furnishings. Like many hotels in this area, the upper floors have better views.

HOTEL CAULAINCOURT SQUARE
Hotel, Hostel €

☎ 01 46 06 46 06; www.caulaincourt.com; 2 square Caulaincourt, 18e; dm €25, s €50-60, d & tw €63-76, tr €89; Ⓜ Lamarck Caulaincourt; 🖥 📶
This budget hotel is perched on the back side of Montmartre, beyond the tourist hoopla, in a real Parisian neighbourhood. The rooms are in decent condition, with parquet floors and a funky interior design, though there is no lift; beware if you have a lot of luggage. It also has dorm rooms.

HÔTEL BONSÉJOUR MONTMARTRE
Hotel €

☎ 01 42 54 22 53; www.hotel-bonsejour-montmartre.fr; 11 rue Burq, 18e; s €33-69, d €56-69; Ⓜ Abbesses; 🖥
At the top of a quiet street in Montmartre, this is a perennial budget favourite. It's a

MONTMARTRE & PIGALLE

SLEEPING

OLIVIER CIRENDINI

Musée de Montmartre (p134)

simple place to stay – no lift or parquet floors – but welcoming, comfortable and very clean. Some rooms (eg Nos 14, 23, 33, 43 and 53) have little balconies attached – these are the ones to go for – and at least one room (No 55) offers a fleeting glimpse of Sacré Cœur. Communal showers cost €2.

EATING

The 18e arrondissement, where you'll find Montmartre and the northern boundary of Pigalle, thrives on crowds and little else. As a general rule, the lower down the hill you go, the better the options. Note that in Montmartre many restaurants are open for dinner only.

LA MASCOTTE   French, Seafood €€
☎ 01 46 06 28 15; www.la-mascotte-mont martre.com; 52 rue des Abbesses, 18e; starters €9-12, mains €20-30, menu €20 (lunch only) & €38; ☺ lunch & dinner to midnight;
Ⓜ Abbesses
La Mascotte is a small, unassuming spot much frequented by regulars who can't

get enough of its seafood and regional cuisine. In winter, don't hesitate to sample the wide variety of seafood, especially the shellfish. In summer sit on the terrace and savour the delicious *fricassée de pétoncles* (fricassee of queen scallops). Meat lovers won't be disappointed with various regional delicacies, including Auvergne sausage and Troyes *andouillette* (veal tripe sausage).

À LA CLOCHE D'OR   French €€
☎ 01 48 74 48 88; www.alaclochedor.com, in French; 3 rue Mansart, 9e; starters €7-14, mains €18-30; menus €18.50 (lunch only), €29.50 & €32; ☺ lunch Mon-Fri, dinner to 5am Mon-Sat;
Ⓜ Blanche or Pigalle
At the foot of the Butte Montmartre, operating since 1928 and once the property of actress Jeanne Moreau's parents, 'The Gold Bell' is the antithesis of trendy. Decorated in 'old bistro' style with photos of stars of stage (mostly) and screen (some) plastering the walls, it serves up favourites like steak tartare (its signature dish), massive steaks and fish of the day.

KRZYSZTOF DYDYNSKI

Musée de la Vie Romantique (p133)

CHEZ TOINETTE   French €€

☎ 01 42 54 44 36; 20 rue Germain Pilon, 18e; starters €7-13, mains €17-22; ⏲ dinner to 11.15pm Mon-Sat; Ⓜ Abbesses

The atmosphere of this convivial restaurant is rivalled only by its fine cuisine. In the heart of one of the capital's most touristy neighbourhoods, Chez Toinette has kept alive the tradition of old Montmartre with its simplicity and culinary expertise. Game lovers won't be disappointed; *perdreau* (partridge), *biche* (doe), *chevreuil* (roebuck) and the famous *filet de canard à la sauge et au miel* (fillet of duck with sage and honey) are the house specialities and go well with a glass of Bordeaux.

LE MIROIR   French €€

☎ 01 46 06 50 73; 94 rue des Martyrs, 18e; starters €9, mains €17, menus €18 (lunch only) & €25 & €32; ⏲ lunch Tue-Sun, dinner Tue-Sat; Ⓜ Abbesses

This unassuming modern bistro is smack bang in the middle of the Montmartre tourist trail, yet it remains a local favourite. There are lots of delightful pâtés and rillettes to start off with, including guinea hen with dates, duck with mushrooms, haddock and lemon, followed by well-prepared standards such as stuffed veal shoulder.

MICHELANGELO   Italian €€

☎ 01 42 23 10 77; 3 rue André-Barsacq, 18e; menu around €25; ⏲ dinner Tue-Sat; Ⓜ Anvers or Abbesses

A one-man show, chef Michelangelo does it all – the shopping, the chopping, the table-waiting, the cooking, the sitting down with guests for a glass of wine while the pasta is boiling…it is, in fact, the equivalent of being invited over to a Sicilian chef's house for dinner. Reservations are mandatory.

LE CAFÉ QUI PARLE   French €€

☎ 01 46 06 06 88; www.lecafequiparle.com; 24 rue Caulaincourt, 18e; starters €8-14, mains €15-26; menus €12.50 & €17; ⏲ closed Sun dinner; Ⓜ Lamarck Caulaincourt or Blanche; 📶

'The Talking Café' is a fine example of where modern-day eateries are headed in Paris. It offers inventive, reasonably priced dishes prepared by owner-chef Damian Moeuf amid comfortable surroundings. We love the art on the walls and the ancient safes down below (the building was once a bank).

AU PETIT BUDAPEST   Hungarian €€

☎ 01 46 06 10 34; 96 rue des Martyrs, 18e; starters €7.50-17.50, mains €14.50-22, menu €19.50; ⏲ lunch Sat & Sun, dinner Tue-Sun; Ⓜ Abbesses

With old etchings and the requisite Gypsy music, this little eatery does a reasonable job of recreating the atmosphere of a late-19th-century Hungarian *csárda* (traditional inn). From the chicken paprika to the *crêpe à la Hortobagy* (crêpe with meat and crème fraîche; €10.50), these are refined versions of popular Hungarian dishes.

AUX NÉGOCIANTS   French €

☎ 01 46 06 15 11; 27 rue Lambert, 18e; starters €5.30-6.80, mains €12-14.50; ⏲ lunch & dinner to 10.30pm Mon-Fri; Ⓜ Château Rouge

This old-style wine bar and bistro is far enough from the madding crowds of Montmartre to attract a faithful local clientele. Pâtés, terrines, traditional mains like *bœuf bourguignon,* and wine paid for according to consumption – it all feels like the Paris of the 1950s (or even earlier).

LE MONO   African, Togolese €

☎ 01 46 06 99 20; 40 rue Véron, 18e; starters €4-6.50, mains €11-14.50; ⏲ dinner to 1am Thu-Tue; Ⓜ Abbesses or Blanche

Le Mono, run by a cheery Togolese family, offers West African specialities, including *lélé* (flat, steamed cakes of white beans and shrimp; €6.50), *azidessi* (beef or chicken with peanut sauce; €12), *gbekui* (goulash with spinach, onions, beef, fish and shrimp; €13) and *djenkoumé* (grilled chicken with semolina noodles; €12).

SELF-CATERING

For picnic supplies you can also head to the **Marché des Gastronomes** (9 place Pigalle; ☺ 10am-9pm Tue-Sat, 10am-7pm Sun, 5pm-9pm Mon; Ⓜ Pigalle), a supermarket with all sorts of French specialties. The bakery **Le Grenier à Pain** (38 rue des Abbesses, 18e; ☺ 7.30am-8pm Thu-Mon; Ⓜ Abbesses) is not one to miss, with delicious *fougasses* and a *baguette à la tradition* that won the best baguette in Paris award in 2010.

DRINKING

Crowded around the hill side of Montmartre you'll find an eclectic selection of places to drink.

LA FOURMI   Bar
☎ 01 42 64 70 35; 74 rue des Martyrs, 18e; ☺ 8am-2am Mon-Thu, to 4am Fri & Sat, 10am-2am Sun; Ⓜ Pigalle

A Pigalle stayer, 'The Ant' hits the mark with its lively yet unpretentious atmosphere. The decor is hip but not overwhelming, the zinc bar is long and inviting and the people are laid-back. The music is mostly rock – quality, well-known tunes that get you going while leaving space in the airways for the rise and fall of unbridled conversation.

CHÀO BÀ CAFÉ   Café
☎ 01 46 06 72 90; 22 blvd de Clichy, 18e; ☺ 8.30am-2am Sun-Wed, to 4am Thu, to 5am Fri & Sat; Ⓜ Pigalle; ☲

This comfortable café-restaurant on two levels is decorated in colonial Asian style

with huge plants, ceiling fans and bamboo chairs. It serves great cocktails (from €9.50) in goldfish bowl–sized glasses, and somewhat bland Franco-Vietnamese fusion food. And by the way: *chào bà* means *bonjour madame* in Vietnamese.

LE PROGRÈS   Café
☎ 01 42 64 07 37; 7 rue des Trois Frères, 18e; ☺ 9am-2am; Ⓜ Abbesses

A real live *café du quartier* perched in the heart of Abbesses, 'The Progress' occupies a corner site with huge windows and simple seating and attracts a relaxed mix of local artists, shop staff, writers and hangers-on. It's great for convivial evenings, with DJs and bands some nights, but it's also a good place to come for inexpensive meals and daytime coffees.

O P'TIT DOUAI   Café
☎ 01 53 21 91 35; 92 rue Blanche, 9e; ☺ 8am-2am; Ⓜ Blanche

This colourful neighbourhood café is just down the street from the Moulin Rouge, but it might as well be light years away. Trade in the mayhem for some tranquillity over coffee, wines by the glass (from €2.50) or some traditional Parisian fare at mealtimes.

ICE KUBE   Cocktail Bar
☎ 01 42 05 20 00; 1-5 passage Ruelle, 18e; ☺ 7pm-1.30am Wed-Sat, 2-11pm Sun; Ⓜ La Chapelle

Every city worth its, err, salt, has got to have an ice bar nowadays, and this *temple de glace* (ice temple) on the 1st floor of the *très boutique* **Kube Hôtel** (p135) is the French capital's first. The temperature is set at -5°C, there are down jackets on loan and the bar is a shimmering block of carved ice. For €38 you get four vodka cocktails and 30 minutes of chill time.

Dalí Espace Montmartre (p134)

ESPACE DALÍ

ENTERTAINMENT & ACTIVITIES

MOULIN ROUGE
Cabaret

☎ 01 53 09 82 82; www.moulinrouge.fr; 82 bd de Clichy, 18e; Ⓜ Blanche

Ooh la la… What is probably Paris' most celebrated cabaret was founded in 1889 and its dancers appeared in the celebrated posters by Toulouse-Lautrec. It sits under its trademark red windmill (actually a 1925 replica of the 19th-century original) and attracts viewers and voyeurs by the busload.

LE DIVAN DU MONDE
Cultural Venue

☎ 01 40 05 06 99; www.divandumonde.com; 75 rue des Martyrs, 18e; admission €10-15; ⏱ 11pm-5am Fri & Sat; Ⓜ Pigalle

Take some cinematographic events, Gypsy gatherings, nouvelles chansons françaises (new French songs). Add in soul/funk fiestas, air-guitar face-offs and rock parties of the Arctic Monkeys/Killers/Libertines persuasion and stir with an Amy Winehouse swizzle stick. You may now be getting some idea of the inventive, open-minded approach at this excellent cross-cultural venue in Pigalle.

LA CIGALE
Music Hall

☎ 01 49 25 81 75; www.lacigale.fr; 120 bd de Rochechouart, 18e; admission €25-60; Ⓜ Anvers or Pigalle

Now classed as a historical monument, this music hall dates from 1887 but was redecorated 100 years later by Philippe Starck. Having welcomed artists from Jean Cocteau to Sheryl Crow, today it prides itself on its avant-garde program, with rock and jazz concerts by French and international acts.

AU LAPIN AGILE
Cabaret

☎ 01 46 06 85 87; www.au-lapin-agile.com; 22 rue des Saules, 18e; adult €24, student except Sat €17; ⏱ 9pm-2am Tue-Sun; Ⓜ Lamarck Caulaincourt

This rustic cabaret venue was favoured by artists and intellectuals in the early 20th century and chansons are still performed here. The four-hour show starts at 9.30pm and includes singing and po-etry. Some love it, others feel it's a bit of a trap. Admission includes one drink (€6 or €7 subsequently). It's named after *Le Lapin à Gill,* a mural of a rabbit jumping out of a cooking pot by caricaturist André Gill, which can still be seen on the western exterior wall.

SHOPPING

Montmartre is swimming in souvenirs, and yet there is much more here to dis-cover. The area around rues des Martyrs, Yvonne le Tac, Vieuville and Houdon constitutes a good stroll for the patient shopper.

TATI   Department Store
☎ 01 55 29 52 20; www.tati.fr, in French; 4 bd de Rochechouart, 18e; ☺ 10am-7pm Mon-Fri, 9.30-7pm Sat; Ⓜ Barbès Rochechouart
With its war cry of *les plus bas prix* (the lowest prices) – and quality to match, some would say – Tati has been Paris' great working-class department store for more than half a century. Don't be surprised to see trendy Parisians fighting for bargains hidden in the crammed bins and piled onto tables. There's a smaller **3e branch** (Map p98; ☎ 01 48 87 72 81; 172-174 rue du Temple, 3e; ☺ 9.30am-7.30pm Mon-Fri, 10am-7pm Sat; Ⓜ Temple or République) as well.

LA CITADELLE   Fashion & Accessories
☎ 01 42 52 21 56; 1 rue des Trois Frères, 18e; ☺ 11am-8pm Mon-Sat, to 7pm Sun; Ⓜ Abbesses
This designer discount shop hidden away in Montmartre has some real finds from new French, Italian and Japanese de-signers. Look out for labels such as Les Chemins Blancs and Yoshi Kondo.

ETS LION   Food & Drink
☎ 01 46 06 64 71; www.epicerie-lion.fr, in French; 7 rue des Abbesses, 18e; ☺ 10.30am-8pm Tue-Sat, 11am-7pm Sun; Ⓜ Abbesses
Another stop on the foodie trail is this gourmet and gardening shop, selling homemade jams, packaged *riz au lait* (rice pudding), multicoloured Eiffel Tower pasta and olive oils. They carry a good se-lection of organic products.

CHAMPS-ÉLYSÉES & GRANDS BOULEVARDS

INFORMATION
Canada Embassy **1** C5
Japanese Embassy **2** B3
Pharmacie des Champs...... **3** B4

SIGHTS
Arc de Triomphe.................. **4** A3
Louis Vuitton Espace
  Culturel............................(see 30)
Musée National Gustave
  Moreau **5** G2

SLEEPING
Hidden Hotel **6** A2
Hôtel Amour **7** G2
Hôtel Chopin........................ **8** H4
Hôtel Joyce.......................... **9** G2
Hôtel Langlois **10** G3
Hôtel Monte Carlo **11** H3

EATING
Bert's.................................. **12** B5
Chartier.............................. **13** H4
La Boule Rouge.................. **14** H3
Ladurée **15** B4
Le Hide **16** A3
Les Ailes **17** H3
Les Pâtes Vivantes............ **18** H3
Nouveau Paris-Dakar........ **19** H3
Spoon **20** C4

DRINKING
Au Général La Fayette...... **21** H3
Au Limonaire...................... **22** H4

ENTERTAINMENT &
ACTIVITIES
Crazy Horse **23** B5
Queen................................ **24** B4

SHOPPING
Chanel **25** C5
Christian Dior.................... **26** C5
Givenchy **27** B5
Guerlain **28** C4
Jean-Paul Gaultier **29** B4
Louis Vuitton **30** B4

TRANSPORT
Air France Buses................ **31** A3
Bateaux Mouches............ **32** C5

See Grands Boulevards Map (p150)

See Invalides &
Eiffel Tower
Map (p164)

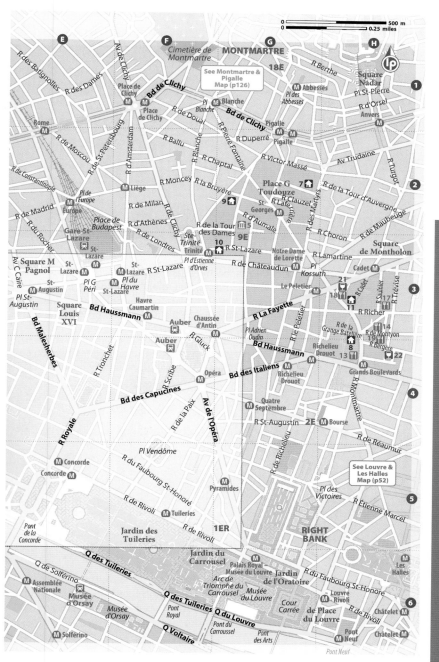

HIGHLIGHTS

⬥ PALAIS GARNIER

By day, take a tour – guided or DIY – of this classic example of opulent, Second-Empire architecture. By night it's all about ballet, theatre and dance in the original home of Parisian opera, the 19th-century **Palais Garnier** (p150). Ballets and classical music concerts performed by the ONP's (Opéra National de Paris) affiliated orchestra and ballet companies are staged here.

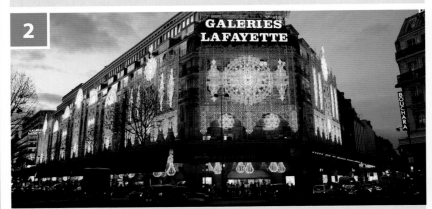

⬥ GALERIES LAFAYETTE

Get an overview of Parisian fashion while shopping at the capital's best-known **department store** (p161): its Friday-afternoon fashion shows and the panoramic views from its rooftop terrace will sweep you off your feet, as will its contemporary art gallery and a cocktail at its on-site bar.

◥ ARC DE TRIOMPHE

Climb to the top of Paris' signature arch (p149) and gasp: what a breathtaking, bird's eye view of the Axe Historique (Historic Axis), the western continuation of the Tuileries' east–west axis. Follow the av des Champs-Élysées to the Arc de Triomphe and, ultimately, all the way to the modern Grande Arche in the skyscraper district of La Défense further out of town.

◥ PLACE DE LA CONCORDE

Louis XVI and thousands more were guillotined in this enormous square (p150) during the Reign of Terror (1793–4). Linked to place de l'Étoile by the Champs-Élysées, and with a towering obelisk in its centre, the square was given its present name in the hope that it would become a place of peace and harmony.

◥ AVENUE DES CHAMPS-ÉLYSÉES

Over-the-top, grandiose and even kind of kitsch, you can't leave Paris without strolling the Av des Champs-Élysées (p149). A wide, overwhelming and bustling commercial artery full of enormous big-name shops and clogged traffic, it's anchored by the Arc de Triomphe at one end and Place de la Concorde at the other.

1 TPG/IMAGEBROKER; 2 BRUCE BI; 3 NEIL SETCHFIELD; 4 IZZET KERIBAR; 5 JONATHAN SMITH

1 Palais Garnier (p150); 2 Galeries Lafayette (p161) with Christmas lights; 3 Arc de Triomphe (p149); 4 Fountain of River Commerce and Navigation, Place de la Concorde (p150); 5 Av des Champs-Élysées from the Eiffel Tower (p149)

CHAMPS-ÉLYSÉES & GRANDS BOULEVARDS

BEST...

BEST...

🔽 SHOPPING

- **Av des Champs-Élysées** (opposite) Yes, it's littered with brands you can get anywhere, but it's *the* avenue, after all.
- **Triangle d'Or** (p162) Go on a *haute couture* treasure hunt in the triangle of fashion.
- **Galeries Lafayette** (p161) This quintessential department store has clothing and a dramatic cupola.
- **Place de la Madeleine** (p162) Gourmet food, fashion and art come together in the square surrounding the neoclassical Église de la Madeleine.

🔽 MUSEUMS

- **La Pinacothèque** (p151) A brilliant, small museum focusing primarily on 20th-century art.
- **Grand Palais** (p151) Some of the best temporary art exhibits in Paris are on display beneath the huge glass dome here.

- **Petit Palais** (p153) The exceptional Museum of Fine Arts houses medieval and Renaissance *objets d'art*.

🔽 THINGS FOR FREE

- **Musée du Parfum** (p153) Learn all about the history of perfume from Fragonard, one of France's premier perfume makers.
- **Louis Vuitton Espace Culturel** (p153) You never know what you'll find at this modern art exhibit hall above the designer's flagship store.
- **Place de la Concorde** (p150) Features a stunning 23m-high obelisk.

🔽 TRADITIONAL MEALS

- **Bistrot Du Sommelier** (p155) Hearty French bistro fare with an exceptional wine list.
- **Le Persil Fleur** (p157) Consistently satisfying staples in an old-world atmosphere.
- **Le Roi Du Pot Au Feu** (p158) A typical Parisian bistro, right down to the chequered tablecloths.

KRZYSZTOF DYDYNSKI

Spire and sculptures on the roof of the Grand Palais (p151)

DISCOVER CHAMPS-ÉLYSÉES & GRANDS BOULEVARDS

There is no Paris without the Eiffel Tower, the most iconic of city icons, but the Champs-Élysées, with its landmark Arc de Triomphe at one end and epicly proportioned place de la Concorde at the other, is a close second (though the offerings on the boulevard itself are now somewhat limited). The 12 avenues radiating out from the Arc de Triomphe – known as place de l'Étoile or place Charles de Gaulle – bathe in the glow of fame. The Grands Boulevards (wide boulevards) – with its beautiful, Haussmann-era buildings – is a commercial neighbourhood with oodles of luxury shops and reflects the way many visitors dream a Paris district should look like, architecturally.

Fans of haute couture should make for the so-called Golden Triangle just south of the Champs-Élysées. Those of more modest means but still with that urge to shop will head for the *grands magazines* (department stores) of the Grands Boulevards.

SIGHTS

ARC DE TRIOMPHE Map p144

☎ 01 55 37 73 77; www.monuments-nationaux. fr; viewing platform adult/18-26yr €9/5.50, EU resident under 26yr free, 1st Sun of month Nov-Mar free; ☉ 10am-11pm Apr-Sep, to 10.30pm Oct-Mar; Ⓜ Charles de Gaulle-Étoile

The Triumphal Arch is 2km northwest of place de la Concorde in the middle of place Charles de Gaulle (aka place de l'Étoile), the world's largest traffic round-about and the meeting point of 12 ave-nues (and three arrondissements). It was commissioned in 1806 by Napoleon to commemorate his imperial victories but remained unfinished when he started los-ing – at first battles and then whole wars. It was finally completed under Louis-Philippe in 1836. Among the armies to march triumphantly through the Arc de Triomphe were the Germans in 1871, the Allies in 1919, the Germans again in 1940 and the Allies again in 1944.

From the viewing platform on top of the arch (50m up via 284 steps and well worth the climb) you can see the dozen broad avenues – many of them named after Napoleonic victories and illustrious generals – radiating towards every com-pass point. Tickets to the viewing platform of the Arc de Triomphe are sold in the underground passageway that surfaces on the even-numbered side of av des Champs-Élysées. It is the only *sane* way to get to the base of the arch and is *not* linked to nearby metro tunnels.

AVENUE DES CHAMPS-ÉLYSÉES
Map p144

Ⓜ Charles de Gaulle-Étoile, George V, Franklin D Roosevelt or Champs-Élysées Clemenceau

Av des Champs-Élysées (the name refers to the 'Elysian Fields' where happy souls dwelt in the hereafter, according to Greek myth) links place de la Concorde with the Arc de Triomphe. The avenue has symbol-ised the style and *joie de vivre* of Paris since the mid-19th century and today is most popular with international brands looking to promote their prestige.

At the bottom of av des Champs-Élysées, on place Clemenceau, stands

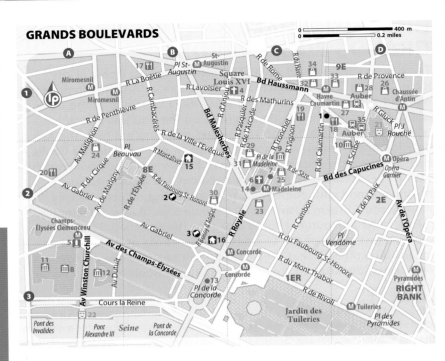

a 3.6m-tall bronze **Charles de Gaulle statue** (Map p150) in full military gear ready to march down the broad avenue to the Arc de Triomphe in a liberated Paris on 26 August 1944.

PALAIS GARNIER Map p150
www.operadeparis.fr, in French; place de l'Opéra, 9e; M **Opéra**

This renowned opera house was designed in 1860 by Charles Garnier to showcase the splendour of Napoleon III's France. Unfortunately, by the time it was completed – 15 years later – the Second Empire was but a distant memory and Napoleon III had been dead for two years. Still, this is one of the most impressive monuments erected in Paris during the 19th century; today it stages ballets, classical music concerts and, of course, opera (p160). You can visit it along with

a small museum (mostly temporary exhibits) on an **unguided tour** (adult/10-25yr €9/5; 10am-4.30pm). Alternatively, reserve a spot on an English-language **guided tour** (08 25 05 44 05; adult/10-25yr/senior €12/6/10; 11.30am & 2.30pm daily Jul & Aug, 11.30am & 2.30pm Wed, Sat & Sun Sep-Jun). You can get tickets for the guided tour at the door, however, staff advise showing up at least 30 minutes ahead of time. Check the website for the exact schedule.

PLACE DE LA CONCORDE Map p150
M **Concorde**

Place de la Concorde was laid out between 1755 and 1775. The 3300-year-old pink granite **obelisk** with the gilded top standing in the centre of the square was presented to France in 1831 by Muhammad Ali, viceroy and pasha of Egypt. Weighing 230 tonnes and tower-

GRANDS BOULEVARDS

ing 23m over the cobblestones, it once stood in the Temple of Ramses at Thebes (now Luxor). The eight **female statues** adorning the four corners of the square represent France's largest cities (at least in the second half of the 18th century).

GRAND PALAIS Map p150

☎ Information 01 44 13 17 17, ☎ bookings 08 92 700 840; www.grandpalais.fr, www.rmn.fr; 3 av du Général Eisenhower, 8e; with/without booking adult €12/11, student & 13-25yr €9/8, under 13yr free; ☼ 10am-10pm Fri-Mon & Wed, to 8pm Thu; Ⓜ Champs-Élysées Clemenceau
Erected for the 1900 Exposition Universelle, the Grand Palais now houses the **Galeries Nationales** beneath its huge 8.5-ton art nouveau glass roof. Some of Paris' biggest exhibitions (Renoir, Chagall) are held here, lasting three to four months. The **Nave**, in the same building, also stages special events (an impromptu Prince concert, holiday lightshows), which require a separate ticket. Booking in advance for either is strongly recommended. Ongoing renovations will expand the exhibit space.

LA PINACOTHÈQUE Map p150

☎ 01 42 68 02 01; www.pinacotheque.com; 28 place de la Madeleine, 8e; adult/12-25yr €10/8; ☼ 10.30am-6pm, to 9pm Wed; Ⓜ Madeleine
One of the best private museums in Paris, La Pinacothèque organises three to four major exhibits per year. The focus is primarily on 20th-century art (Pollock, Utrillo, Munch, Lichtenstein) but it has

LYCRA ON THE CHAMPS

Catching the final leg of the world's most prestigious cycling race, the three-week **Tour de France** (www.letour.fr), is a euphoric experience. If you're visiting Paris towards the end of July, join the tens of thousands of spectators along the av des Champs-Élysées. The race finishes sometime in the afternoon, but secure a spot at the barricades before noon to ensure you'll get a clear view of the cyclists. The final day varies from year to year but is usually the 3rd or 4th Sunday in July.

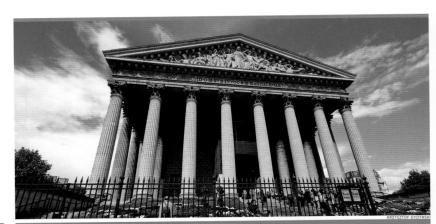

KRZYSZTOF DYDYNSKI

Église de Ste-Marie Madeleine

PLACE DE LA MADELEINE

Ringed by fine-food shops, place de la Madeleine is 350m north of place de la Concorde, at the end of rue Royale. The square is named after the 19th-century neoclassical church in its centre, the **Église de Ste-Marie Madeleine** (Church of St Mary Magdalene). Constructed in the style of a Greek temple, what is now simply called 'La Madeleine' was consecrated in 1842 after almost a century of design changes and construction delays.

The **monumental staircase** on the south side affords one of the city's most quintessential Parisian panoramas: down rue Royale to place de la Concorde and its obelisk and across the Seine to the Assemblée Nationale.

Paris' cheapest belle époque attraction is the **public toilet** on the east side of La Madeleine, which dates from 1905. There has been a **flower market** on the east side of the church since 1832.

Things you need to know: Map p150; Ⓜ Madeleine; Église de Ste-Marie Madeleine (☎ 01 44 51 69 00; www.eglise-lamadeleine.com, in French; place de la Madeleine, 8e; ⏰ 9.30am-7pm); **public toilet** (⏰ 10am-6.15pm); **flower market** (⏰ 8am-8pm)

also hosted China's terracotta army and a Dutch Masters retrospective.

PALAIS DE LA DÉCOUVERTE
Map p150

☎ 01 56 43 20 20; www.palais-decouverte.fr, in French; av Franklin D Roosevelt, 8e; adult/senior, student & 5-18yr €7/4.50; ⏰ 9.30am-6pm Tue-Sat, 10am-7pm Sun; Ⓜ Champs-Élysées Clemenceau

This children's science museum has excellent temporary exhibits (eg moving life-like dinosaurs) as well as a hands-on, interactive permanent collection focussing on astronomy, biology, physics and the like. The **planetarium** (admission €3.50) has four shows a day; there are also hourly science demonstrations (both in French).

PETIT PALAIS Map p150

☎ 01 53 43 40 00; www.petitpalais.paris.fr; av Winston Churchill, 8e; temporary exhibits adult/14-26yr/senior & student €9/4.50/6.50, permanent collections & under 14yr free; ☻ 10am-6pm Wed-Sun, to 8pm Thu (temporary exhibit only); Ⓜ Champs-Élysées Clemenceau

Like the Grand Palais opposite, this architectural stunner was also built for the 1900 Exposition Universelle, and is home to the Paris municipality's **Museum of Fine Arts**. It specialises in medieval and Renaissance *objets d'art* such as porcelain and clocks, tapestries, drawings and 19th-century French painting and sculpture. There are also some standout paintings here by Rembrandt, Colbert and Cézanne.

MUSÉE DU PARFUM Map p150

☎ 01 47 42 04 56; www.fragonard.com; 9 rue Scribe, 2e; admission free; ☻ 9am-6pm Mon-Sat; Ⓜ Opéra

If the art of perfume-making entices, stop by this collection of copper distillery vats and antique flacons and test your nose on a few basic scents (how many can you identify correctly?). It's run by the *perfumerie* Fragonard and located in a beautiful old *hôtel particulier*; free guided visits are available in multiple languages.

LOUIS VUITTON ESPACE CULTUREL Map p144

☎ 01 53 57 52 03; www.louisvuitton.com/espaceculturel; 60 rue de Bassano, 8e; admission free; ☻ noon-7pm Mon-Sat, 11am-7pm Sun; Ⓜ George V

At the top of Louis Vuitton's flagship store is this modern art gallery with changing exhibits throughout the year. The main entrance is off a side street (at the time of research it was via an art-installation elevator that had no lights or buttons), but you can also reach it via the mam-moth flagship store, which, of course, is something of a sight in itself.

SLEEPING

Like the 1er, the Champs-Élysées is home to deluxe palace hotels and global chains, though there are options here with more personality. Heading east the choices increase; the area between the Grands Boulevards and Pigalle is a beautiful neighbourhood and, being less touristy than the Champs-Élysées, a great place to immerse yourself in the city's charms and day-to-day life.

HÔTEL DE CRILLON Map p150 Hotel €€€

☎ 01 44 71 15 00; www.crillon.com; 10 place de la Concorde, 8e; s €750, d €750-930, ste from €1200; Ⓜ Concorde; ✂ ⌨ &

This colonnaded 200-year-old 'jewel in the heart of Paris', whose sparkling public areas (including **Les Ambassadeurs** restaurant, with new chef Christopher Hache at the helm) are sumptuously decorated with chandeliers, original sculptures, gilt mouldings, tapestries and inlaid furniture, is the epitome of French luxury. The 147 rooms are spacious with king-sized beds and have floor-to-ceiling marble bathrooms with separate shower and bath. And Le Crillon is not just a pretty face; in 1778 the treaty in which France recognised the independence of the new USA was signed here by Louis XVI and Benjamin Franklin.

HIDDEN HOTEL Map p144 Hotel €€€

☎ 01 40 55 03 57; www.hidden-hotel.com; 28 rue de l'Arc de Triomphe, 17e; s €245, d €285-485; Ⓜ Charles de Gaulle-Étoile; ✂ ⌨ ⚆

The Hidden is one of the Champs-Élysées' best secrets: an ecofriendly boutique hotel, it's serene, stylish, reasonably spacious, and it even sports green credentials.

Musée National Gustave Moreau

⤵ IF YOU LIKE...

If you like the tapestries at the **Petit Palais** (p153), head to the **Musée National Gustave Moreau** (Map p144; ☎ 01 48 74 38 50; www.musee-moreau.fr; 14 rue de La Rochefoucauld, 9e; adult/18-25yr €7.50/5.50, under 18yr free, 1st Sun of the month free, reduced admission with ticket from Palais Garnier or Musée d'Orsay; ☉ 10am-5.15pm Wed-Mon; Ⓜ Trinité). Dedicated to the eponymous symbolist painter's work, this museum is housed in what was once Moreau's studio. It's crammed with 4800 of his paintings, drawings and sketches. Many of Moreau's paintings are exceptional – we particularly like *La Licorne* (The Unicorn), inspired by *La Dame à la Licorne* (The Lady with the Unicorn) cycle of tapestries in the **Musée National du Moyen Age** (p224).

The earth-coloured tones are the result of natural pigments (there's no paint), and all rooms feature handmade wooden furniture, stone basins for sinks, and linen curtains surrounding Coco-mat beds. The Emotion rooms, which have a terrace, are among the most popular. Need we say that the breakfast is almost 100% organic?

HÔTEL AMOUR Map p144   Hotel €€
☎ 01 48 78 31 80; www.hotelamourparis.fr; 8 rue Navarin, 9e; s €100, d €150-280; Ⓜ St-Georges or Pigalle; 🛜
Planning a romantic escapade to Paris? Say no more. One of the 'in' hotels of the moment, the inimitable black-clad

Amour (formerly a love hotel by the hour) features original design and artwork in each of the rooms and is very much worthy of the hype – you won't find a more stylish place to lay your head in Paris at these prices. Of course, you have to be willing to forgo television (there isn't any) – but who needs TV when you're in love?

HÔTEL JOYCE Map p144   Hotel €€
☎ 01 55 07 00 01; www.astotel.com; 29 rue La Bruyère, 9e; s, d & tw €150-236, ste €399; Ⓜ St-Georges; 🔀 🖳 🛜
The Joyce is a new boutique hotel that's located in a lovely residential area in be-

tween Montmartre and l'Opéra. It's got all the modern design touches (iPod docks, a sky-lit breakfast room fitted out with old Range Rover seats) and even makes some ecofriendly claims – it relies on 50% renewable energy and uses organic products when available. Rates vary with the season; discounts are often available online.

HÔTEL LANGLOIS Map p144 Hotel €€
☎ 01 48 74 78 24; www.hotel-langlois.com; 63 rue St-Lazare, 9e; s €110-120, d & tw €140-150, ste €190; M Trinité; 🖾 🖳 🛜
If you're looking for a bit of belle époque Paris, the Langlois won't let you down. Built in 1870, this 27-room hotel has kept its charm, from the tiny caged elevator to sandstone fireplaces in many rooms (sadly decommissioned) as well as original bathroom fixtures and tiles. Room 64 has wonderful views of the rooftops of Montmartre.

HÔTEL ALISON Map p150 Hotel €€
☎ 01 42 65 54 00; www.hotelalison.com; 21 rue de Surène, 8e; s €86-98, d €120-194, tr €192; M Madeleine; 🖾 🖳 🛜
This excellent-value 34-room midrange hotel, just west of place de la Madeleine, attracts with the bold colours of its carpets and furnishings and modern art in the lobby. Prices depend on whether rooms have bath or shower and a view.

HÔTEL CHOPIN Map p144 Hotel €€
☎ 01 47 70 58 10; www.hotelchopin.fr; 46 passage Jouffroy & 10 blvd Montmartre, 9e; s €68-84, d €92-106, tr €125; M Grands Boulevards; 🛜
Dating back to 1846, the Chopin is down one of Paris' most delightful 19th-century passages couverts (covered shopping arcades) and a great deal for its location right off the Grands Boulevards (entrance at 10 bd Montmartre). The sprawling 36-room hotel may be a little faded, but it's

still enormously evocative of the belle époque. Wi-fi is only available in the lobby.

HÔTEL MONTE CARLO Map p144 Hotel €
☎ 01 47 70 36 75; www.hotelmontecarlo.fr; 44 rue du Faubourg Montmartre, 9e; s €55-105, d & tw €69-129, tr €119-149; M Le Peletier; 🛜
A unique budget hotel, the Monte Carlo is a steal, with colourful, personalised rooms and a great neighbourhood location. The owners go the extra mile and even provide a partly organic breakfast. The cheaper rooms come without bathroom or shower, but overall it outclasses many of the other choices in its price range. Rates vary with the season.

EATING
The 8e arrondissement around the Champs-Élysées is known for its big-name chefs (Alain Ducasse, Pierre Gagnaire, Guy Savoy) and culinary icons (Taillevent), but there are all sorts of under-the-radar restaurants scattered in the back streets, where the Parisians who live and work in the area actually dine. If you're just looking for a simple breakfast or lunch, head to rue de Ponthieu, which runs parallel to the Champs (to the north), where you'll find several bakeries, cafés, and pasta bars catering to the office workers in the area. Note most will be closed in the evenings and on weekends.

BISTROT DU SOMMELIER Map p150 French €€€
☎ 01 42 65 24 85; www.bistrotdusommelier. com; 97 blvd Haussmann, 8e; starters €13.50-22, mains €24-30, lunch menu €33, with wine €43, dinner menus €65-110; 🕑 lunch & dinner to 10.30pm Mon-Fri; M St-Augustin
This is the place to choose if you are as serious about wine as you are about food.

The whole point of this attractive eatery is to match wine with food, and owner Philippe Faure-Brac, one of the world's foremost sommeliers, is at hand to help. The best way to sample his wine-food pairings is on Friday, when a three-course tasting lunch with wine is €50 and a five-course dinner with wine is €75. The food, prepared by chef Jean-André Lallican, is hearty bistro fare and, surprisingly, not all the wines are French.

SPOON Map p144   Fusion €€€
☎ 01 40 76 34 44; www.spoon-restaurants.com; 14 rue de Marignan, 8e; starters €10-19, mains €19-36, menu €33 (lunch only) & €75; 🕑 lunch & dinner to 11pm Mon-Fri; Ⓜ Franklin D Roosevelt Diners at this Ducasse/Starck-inspired venue are invited to mix and match their own main courses and sauces – pan-seared red mullet, say, with a choice of barbecue, lemon or sesame sauces or duckling with peppers, lemon-parsley butter or crushed olives. There are a few vegetarian options on the menu, which have kept it popular with the stay-slim fashion crowd. It has an excellent selection of New World and non-French European wines.

MARKET Map p150   Fusion €€€
☎ 01 56 43 40 90; www.jean-georges.com; 15 av Matignon, 8e; starters €10-27, mains €18-39, two-dish tasting menu €34 (lunch and early dinner till 8.30pm); 🕑 lunch Mon-Fri, brunch noon-4.30pm Sat & Sun, dinner to 11.30pm daily; Ⓜ Franklin D Roosevelt Alsatian chef Jean-Georges Vongerichten's swish fusion restaurant focuses on fresh market produce delivered with his signature eclectic combinations and Asian leanings. For flavours that are going someplace unexpected, sample sea bream in a sweet-and-sour broth, duck filet with cocoa beans and fig chutney, or black truffle and fontina cheese pizza. Like his restaurants in Manhattan and Shanghai (among others), Market stands out in the crowd, though it's rare JG is actually in the kitchen. Lunch attracts a predominantly business crowd; dinner is a much sexier proposition.

Petit Palais (p153)

BRUCE BI

JEAN-BERNARD CARILLET

Meal served up at Market restaurant

LE PERSIL FLEUR Map p150   French €€

☎ 01 42 65 40 19; www.persilfleur.com; 8 rue Boudreau, 9e; starters €8-17, mains €17-26, menus €34 & €39; ⏲ lunch & dinner Mon-Fri; Ⓜ Auber or Havre Caumartin

Le Persil Fleur is the type of old-fashioned French restaurant where the patron welcomes customers, chats extensively with the regulars and personally checks on each table as meals progress. Don't be put off by the faded décor – this place remains popular because the food is consistently good. Expect French standards that depart from the usual sauces – lamb with cumin and mint, beef filet with cocoa or duck with caramelised onions.

LA BOULE ROUGE
Map p144   Jewish, Kosher €€

☎ 01 47 70 43 90; 1 rue de la Boule Rouge, 9e; starters €5-8, mains €15-28; menus €20 (lunch only) & €26-33; ⏲ lunch & dinner to midnight Mon-Sat; Ⓜ Cadet or Grands Boulevards

Though this Tunisian stalwart has been in situ for three decades, 'The Red Ball' has been getting a lot of press – good,

bad or otherwise – only since Monsieur Sarkozy was spotted dining here. It's a lovely space, with a wonderful caravan mural on the ceiling and photos of politicians and celebs on the walls. Some of the couscous dishes served here – mince with okra, spinach, spicy chicken with corn – are unusual and the three-course menu includes an excellent array of kemia (vegetarian meze) plus a drink.

LE HIDE Map p144   French €€

☎ 01 45 74 15 81; www.lehide.fr; 10 Rue du Général Lanrezac, 17e; starters €8.50, mains €16, menus €22 & 29; ⏲ lunch Mon-Fri, dinner to 11pm Mon-Sat; Ⓜ Charles de Gaulle-Étoile

A reader favourite, Le Hide is another tiny neighbourhood bistro (seating 33 people) serving scrumptious traditional French fare: snails, baked shoulder of lamb, monkfish in lemon butter. As at Aoki, the chef is Japanese, which in Paris is an indication of top quality – this place fills up faster than you can scurry down the steps at the nearby Arc de Triomphe. Reserve well in advance.

LE ROI DU POT AU FEU

Map p150   French €€

☎ 01 47 42 37 10; 34 rue Vignon, 9e; starters €4-7, pot-au-feu €17, menus €21 & 28; ⏱ noon-10.30pm Mon-Sat; Ⓜ Havre Caumartin

A typical Parisian bistro atmosphere, '30s décor and checked tablecloths all add to the charm of 'The King of Hotpots'. What you really want to come here for is a genuine pot-au-feu, a stockpot of beef, aromatic root vegetables and herbs stewed together, with the stock served as an entree and the meat and vegetables as the main course. You drink from an open bottle of wine and pay for what you've consumed. No reservations accepted.

LES AILES Map p144   Jewish, Kosher €€

☎ 01 47 70 62 53; www.lesailes.fr, in French; 34 rue Richer, 9e; mains €16-29; ⏱ lunch & dinner to 11.30pm; Ⓜ Cadet

With a delicatessen and bakery attached, 'Wings' is a kosher North African (Sephardic) place that has superb couscous with meat or fish (€18 to €24) and grills as well as light meals of salad and pasta (€11 to €19.50). Don't even consider a starter; you'll be inundated with little plates of salad, olives etc before you can say *shalom*. Sabbath meals (pre-ordered and prepaid) are also available.

NOUVEAU PARIS-DAKAR

Map p144   African, Senegalese €€

☎ 01 42 46 12 30; www.lenouveauparisdakar. com, in French; 11 rue de Montyon, 9e; starters €7-8, mains €14-22, menus €10.90 (lunch only) & €26-40; ⏱ lunch Mon-Thu, Sat & Sun, dinner to 1am daily; Ⓜ Grands Boulevards

This is a little bit of Senegal in Paris, with Mamadou still reigning as the 'King of Dakar'. Specialities here include *yassa* (chicken or fish marinated in lime juice and onion sauce; €14) and *maffé Cap Vert*

(lamb in peanut sauce; €14). There's live African music most nights.

CHARTIER Map p144   French, Bistro €

☎ 01 47 70 86 29; www.restaurant-chartier. com; 7 rue du Faubourg Montmartre, 9e; starters €2.20-6.80, mains €8.50-13.50, menu with wine €19.40; ⏱ lunch & dinner to 10pm; Ⓜ Grands Boulevards

Chartier, which started life as a *bouillon*, or soup kitchen, in 1896, is a real gem that is justifiably famous for its 330-seat belle époque dining room. It's no longer as good a deal as it once was, but for a taste of old-fashioned Paris, the atmosphere is definitely unbeatable. Note that reservations are not accepted and some readers have been turned away at the last minute on busy nights – if there's a long queue, head elsewhere.

LES PÂTES VIVANTES

Map p144   Chinese €

☎ 01 45 23 10 21; 46 du Faubourg Montmartre, 9e; noodles €9.50-12; ⏱ lunch & dinner Mon-Sat; Ⓜ Le Peletier

This is one of the few spots in Paris for hand-pulled noodles (*là miàn*) made to order in the age-old northern Chinese tradition. It packs in a crowd, so arrive early to stake out a table on the ground floor and watch as the nimble noodle maker works his magic. There's also a **St-Germain branch** (☎ 01 40 46 84 33; 22 blvd St-Germain, 5e; Ⓜ St-Germain des Prés).

BERT'S Map p144   Café €

☎ 01 47 23 43 37; www.berts.com; 4 av du Président Wilson, 8e; sandwiches €5.80-6.90, salads €5.90-8.40; ⏱ 8am-8pm Mon-Fri, 10.30am-8pm Sat, 11am-8pm Sun; Ⓜ Alma Marceau

Elsewhere this modern café chain with worn leather couches and comfy armchairs might not stand out, but in this part of town it's a good address to have on

Au Limonaire

JEAN-BERNARD CARILLET

hand – not least because it's open daily. Sandwiches are served on organic bread and there are plenty of veggie options available.

DRINKING

The Champs-Élysées is still a popular place for drinking but the vast majority of venues are terribly expensive and tend to be either tacky tourist traps or exceedingly pretentious lounges. As far as nightlife is concerned, this is a better area to come to for clubbing.

Haussmann's windswept boulevards have plenty of brasseries that are good for a coffee break or post-shopping drink, but for the most part, Paris' more atmospheric bars and cafés tend to be elsewhere.

AU GÉNÉRAL LA FAYETTE
Map p144   Café
☎ 01 47 70 59 08; 52 rue La Fayette, 9e;
☒ 10am-4am; Ⓜ Le Peletier
With its all-day menu, archetypal belle époque décor and special beers on offer,

this old-style brasserie is an excellent stop for an afternoon coffee, evening drink or typical French meal outside normal restaurant hours.

AU LIMONAIRE Map p144   Wine Bar
☎ 01 45 23 33 33; http://limonaire.free.fr; 18 cité Bergère, 9e; ☒ 7pm-midnight Mon, 6pm-midnight Tue-Sun; Ⓜ Grands Boulevards
This little wine bar is one of the best places to listen to traditional French *chansons* and local singer-songwriters. Performances begin at 7pm on Sunday and at 10pm Tuesday to Saturday. It's free entry, and simple meals are served for between €8.50 and €11. Reservations are recommended.

ENTERTAINMENT & ACTIVITIES

CRAZY HORSE Map p144   Cabaret
☎ 01 47 23 32 32; www.lecrazyhorseparis.com; 12 av George V, 8e; Ⓜ Alma Marceau
This popular cabaret, whose dressing (or, rather, undressing) rooms were featured

IZZET KERIBAR

Galeries Lafayette

in Woody Allen's film *What's New Pussycat?* (1965), now promotes fine art – abstract 1960s patterns as they appear superimposed on the female nude form.

QUEEN Map p144 Clubbing
☎ 01 53 89 08 90; www.queen.fr; 102 av des Champs-Élysées, 8e; admission €20; ⏰ 11.30pm-10am; Ⓜ George V

Once the king (as it were) of gay discos in Paris, Le Queen now reigns supreme with a very mixed crowd, though it still has a mostly gay Disco Queen night on Monday. While right on the Champs-Élysées, it's not as difficult to get into as it used to be – and not nearly as inaccessible as most of the nearby clubs. There's a festive atmosphere and mix of music with lots of house and electro.

SHOWCASE Map p150 Clubbing
☎ 01 45 61 25 43; www.showcase.fr; Port des Champs Élysées, under Pont Alexandre III, 8e; admission €15; ⏰ 11.30pm-dawn Fri & Sat; Ⓜ Invalides or Champs Élysées-Clemenceau

This gigantic electro club has solved the neighbour-versus-noise problem that haunts so many other Parisian nightlife spots: it's secreted away beneath a bridge alongside the Seine. Unlike many of the other exclusive backstreet clubs along the Champs, the Showcase can pack 'em in (up to 1500 clubbers) and is less stringent about its door policy, though you'll still want to look like a star.

PALAIS GARNIER Map p150 Opera
☎ 08 92 89 90 90; www.opera-de-paris.fr; place de l'Opéra, 9e; Ⓜ Opéra

The city's original opera house is smaller and more glamorous than its Bastille counterpart, and boasts perfect acoustics. Due to its odd shape, however, some seats have limited or no visibility. Ticket prices and conditions (including last-minute discounts) at the **box office** (cnr rues Scribe & Auber ⏰ 11am-6.30pm Mon-Sat) are identical to those at the **Opéra de Paris Bastille** (p110).

SHOPPING

Global chains line the Champs-Élysées, but it's the luxury fashion houses in the Triangle d'Or that make the area famous. For more on the wonderful window-shopping here, see the boxed text, p162.

The area around Opéra and the Grands Boulevards is where you'll find Paris' most popular *grands magasins*.

GUERLAIN Map p144 — Cosmetics

☎ 01 45 62 52 57; www.guerlain.com; 68 av des Champs-Élysées, 8e; ◷ 10.30am-8pm Mon-Sat, noon-7pm Sun; Ⓜ Franklin D Roosevelt

Guerlain is Paris' most famous parfumerie, and its shop (dating from 1912) is one of the most beautiful in the city. With its shimmering mirror and marble art-deco interior, it's a reminder of the former glory of the Champs-Élysées. For total indulgence, make an appointment at their decadent **spa** (☎ 01 45 62 11 21).

GALERIES LAFAYETTE

Map p150 — Department Store

☎ 01 42 82 36 40; www.galerieslafayette.com, in French; 40 bd Haussmann, 9e; ◷ 9.30am-8pm Mon-Wed, Fri & Sat, to 9pm Thu; Ⓜ Auber or Chaussée d'Antin

Probably the best known of the big Parisian department stores, Galeries Lafayette is spread across three buildings: the main store, the men's store (and Lafayette Gourmet) and the home-design store. Not counting the hours of shopping, there's quite a bit to do in the main store. You can check out modern art in the new **gallery** (1st fl; ◷ 11am-7pm Mon-Sat), take in a **fashion show** (☎ bookings 01 42 82 30 25; ◷ 3pm Fri Mar-Jul & Sep-Dec), or ascend to the rooftop for a windswept Parisian panorama (free). When your legs need a break, head up to the 6th floor Lafayette

Café, the **rooftop restaurant** (◷ May-Oct) or the 1st floor champagne bar.

LE PRINTEMPS

Map p150 — Department Store

☎ 01 42 82 57 87; www.printemps.com; 64 bd Haussmann, 9e; ◷ 9.35am-8pm Mon-Wed, Fri & Sat, to 10pm Thu; Ⓜ Havre Caumartin

This is actually three separate stores – **Le Printemps de la Mode** (women's fashion), **Le Printemps de l'Homme** (for men) and **Le Printemps de la Beauté et Maison** (for beauty and household goods) – offering a staggering display of perfume, cosmetics and accessories, as well as established and up-and-coming designer wear.

KRZYSZTOF DYDYNSKI

Louis Vuitton (p162) display, av des Champs-Élysées

HISTORIC HAUTE COUTURE

A stroll around the legendary Triangle d'Or (av Montaigne and av George V) and along rue du Faubourg St-Honoré, all in the 8e (Map p144; Ⓜ George V), constitutes the walk of fame of top French fashion. Rubbing shoulders with the world's top international designers are Paris' most influential French fashion houses:

Chanel (Map p144; ☎ 01 47 23 74 12; www.chanel.com; 42 av Montaigne, 8e) Box jackets and little black dresses, chic ever since their first appearance in the 1920s.

Christian Dior (Map p144; ☎ 01 40 73 73 73; www.dior.com; 30 av Montaigne, 8e) Post-WWII, Dior's creations dictated style, re-establishing Paris as the world fashion capital.

Christian Lacroix (Map p150; ☎ 01 42 68 79 04; www.christianlacroix.com; 73 rue du Faubourg St-Honoré, 8e) Taffeta and lace flirt with denim and knits in this designer's theatrical combinations.

Givenchy (Map p144; ☎ 01 44 31 51 25; www.givenchy.com; 3 av George V, 8e) The first to present a luxurious collection of women's prêt a porter.

Hermès (Map p150; ☎ 01 40 17 47 17; www.hermes.com; 24 rue du Faubourg St-Honoré, 8e) Founded in 1837 by a saddle-maker, Hermès' famous scarves are *the* fashion accessory.

Jean-Paul Gaultier (Map p144; ☎ 01 44 43 00 44; www.jeanpaulgaultier.com; 44 av George V, 8e) A shy kid from the Paris suburbs, JPG morphed into the *enfant terrible* of the fashion world with his granny's corsets, men dressed in skirts and Madonna's conical bra.

Louis Vuitton (Map p144; ☎ 01 53 57 52 00; www.vuitton.com; 101 av des Champs-Élysées, 8e) Take home a Real McCoy canvas bag with the 'LV' monogram.

HÉDIARD   Map p144   Food & Drink

☎ 01 43 12 88 88; www.hediard.fr; 21 place de la Madeleine, 8e; ☿ 9am-9pm Mon-Sat; Ⓜ Madeleine

This famous luxury food shop established in 1854 consists of two adjacent sections selling prepared dishes, teas, coffees, jams, wines, pastries, fruits, vegetables and so on.

PLACE DE LA MADELEINE

Map p150   Food & Drink

place de la Madeleine, 8e; Ⓜ Madeleine

Ultragourmet food shops are the treat here – if you feel your knees start to go all wobbly in front of a display window, you know you're in the right place. The most notable names include truffle dealers **La Maison de la Truffe** (☎ 01 42 65 53 22; www.maison-de-la-truffe.com, in French; 19 place de la Madeleine; ☿ 10am-10pm Mon-Sat); luxury food shop **Hédiard**; mustard specialist **Boutique Maille** (☎ 01 40 15 06 00; www.maille.com; 6 place de la Madeleine; ☿ 10am-7pm Mon-Sat); and Paris' most famous caterer, **Fauchon** (☎ 01 70 39 38 00; www.fauchon.fr; 26 & 30 place de la Madeleine; ☿ 8.30am-7pm Mon-Sat), selling incredibly mouth-watering delicacies, from foie gras to jams, chocolates and pastries.

INVALIDES & EIFFEL TOWER

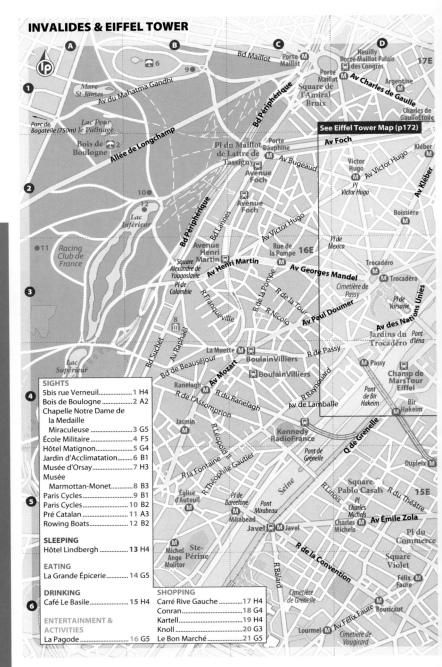

INVALIDES & EIFFEL TOWER

See Eiffel Tower Map (p172)

SIGHTS
5bis rue Verneuil 1 H4
Bois de Boulogne 2 A2
Chapelle Notre Dame de
 la Medaille
 Miraculeuse 3 G5
École Militaire 4 F5
Hôtel Matignon 5 G4
Jardin d'Acclimatation 6 B1
Musée d'Orsay 7 H3
Musée
 Marmottan-Monet 8 B3
Paris Cycles 9 B1
Paris Cycles 10 B2
Pré Catalan 11 A3
Rowing Boats 12 B2

SLEEPING
Hôtel Lindbergh 13 H4

EATING
La Grande Épicerie 14 G5

DRINKING
Café Le Basile 15 H4

ENTERTAINMENT &
ACTIVITIES
La Pagode 16 G5

SHOPPING
Carré Rive Gauche 17 H4
Conran 18 G4
Kartell 19 H4
Knoll 20 G3
Le Bon Marché 21 G5

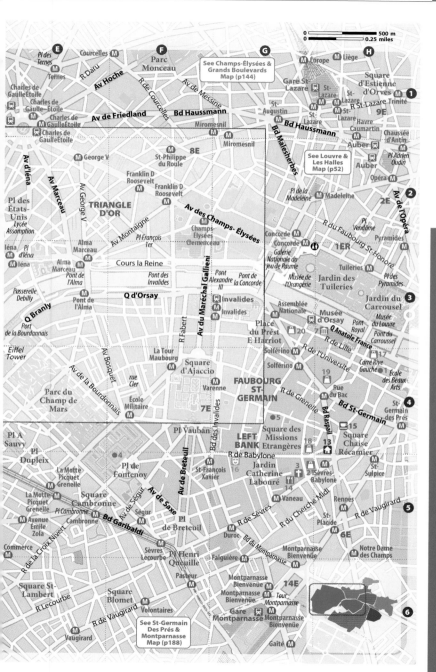

INVALIDES & EIFFEL TOWER

HIGHLIGHTS

HIGHLIGHTS

1 | THE SEINE

Sun-splashed ripples glistening, couples canoodling, dogs scampering and street musicians strumming melodies in the distance; the Seine lures you with its magnetic charms and makes you feel like nothing else matters. Lazily curving its way through town, it forces you to pause and unwind. Meander along its romantic quays or frolic on its dazzling beaches, serenely drift on its waters on a cruise or ramble across all its bridges – however you do it, it's Paris at its most enchanting.

↘ OUR DON'T MISS LIST

❶ TAKE A STROLL
You can stroll along the banks of the Seine on a slew of river-hugging pedestrian walkways, but our favourite stretches are the elevated strip between the **Musée d'Orsay** (p177) and the **Eiffel Tower** (p171) and the below-street-level section along the right bank's **Jardin des Tuileries** (p66).

❷ LOLL ON THE BEACH
Paris Plages (Paris Beaches) might only be around for a month each year (mid-July to mid-August; see p48), but oh, what a month it is. Urban dwellers flock as sophisticated hangouts featuring sand, pebbles and palm trees take over 1.5km of the riverbank. Sunbathing rules the day and waterside cocktails dominate the evening. It's relaxed beach and bar action, all in one.

❸ CROSS ITS BRIDGES
Over two dozen bridges crisscross the Seine in Paris, but our favourites are the ones linking the **Île de la Cité** (p89)

Clockwise from top: Cruiseboat on the Seine; *Bateau mouche* (passenger ferry) passing Notre Dame (p84); Pont Neuf (p91); Paris Plages (p48); The Seine and Île de la Cité (p89)

CLOCKWISE FROM TOP: GLENN BEANLAND; JEAN-BERNARD CARILLET; GLENN BEANLAND; WILL SALTER; JEAN-PIERRE LESCOURRET

with the left and right banks. Most notable are **Pont Neuf** (p91), between the island and the right bank, for its sweeping view of three further bridges (gloriously lit up at night); and **Pont au Double** and **Pont de l'Archeveché** – both boast fabulous glimpses of the **Cathédrale de Notre Dame** (p89).

❹ TAKE A RIVER CRUISE

Gliding along the river on one of Paris' boats at night, with all the riverbanks and majestic buildings ablaze in all their splendour, feels like a magical movie scene. In warmer months, take one of the open-topped boats – when you pass under bridges, it feels like you can almost reach up and touch them. See p273.

⬂ THINGS YOU NEED TO KNOW

Bring Layers It often gets breezy on those open-topped boats, even in the summer. **Pre-Dinner Drinks** Avoid the dinner and lunch cruises – you're better off just having a drink onboard and grabbing dinner elsewhere.

HIGHLIGHTS

2

⬊ ASCEND LA TOUR EIFFEL

Only the fact that it was a perfect platform for the transmitting antennas needed for the new science of radiotelegraphy saved the 'metal asparagus', as many Parisians in 1909 snidely called it, from being ripped down. A century on, 7 million visitors a year make their way to the top of this **iconic landmark** (p171), more Parisian than Paris itself.

3

⬊ INDIGENOUS ART

Like all good Paris museums, the collection of indigenous artwork at the **Musée du Quai Branly** (p172) is as controversial as it is innovative. Take in its 'vertical living garden', which gives a whole new meaning to the term 'growing' (it scales the exterior of the structure) before heading inside to contemplate anthropological artefacts from across the globe.

◢ FRENCH ARCHITECTURE & HERITAGE

The colossal 23,000 sq metre **Cité de l'Architecture et du Patrimoine** (p173) houses a monumental collection of elements of French architecture and heritage. It's an education and a delight, and the views of the Eiffel Tower from the windows are equally monumental.

◢ ASIAN SCULPTURE & ART

Contemplate Asian art and symbolism at the **Musée Guimet des Arts Asiatiques** (Guimet Museum of Asiatic Arts; p173). Its transcendent collection of paintings, statuary, sculptures, *objets d'art* and religious articles represents the art of over a dozen Asian countries, from Afghanistan and Nepal to Japan and China.

◢ FISHY MATTERS

Be awed by the quiet yet monstrous beasts cascading through their territory in the shark tunnel at 3500-sq-metre **Cinéaqua** (p175), one of Europe's newest and largest aquariums. Over 500 species of the underwater world wriggle their way around behind glass, and an interactive touchpool yields squeals and smiles all around.

2 CHRISTOPHER GROENHOUT; 3 WILL SALTER; 4 BRUCE BI; 5 BRUCE BI; 6 CLAUDE THIBAULT/ALAMY

2 City view from the Eiffel Tower (p171); 3 Musée du Quai Branly (p172); 4 Cité de l'Architecture et du Patrimoine (p173); 5 Musée Guimet des Arts Asiatiques (p173); 6 Cinéaqua (p175)

INVALIDES & EIFFEL TOWER

BEST...

BEST...

↘ PLACES FOR A STROLL

- **Esplanade des Invalides** (p178) A 500m-long expanse of lawn.
- **Banks of the Seine** Water and Eiffel Tower views.
- **Parc du Champ de Mars** (p172) The long swath of green extending from *the* tower.

↘ LESSER-KNOWN MUSEUMS

- **Musée Marmottan-Monet** (p174) The world's largest collection of works by impressionist painter Monet.
- **Musée Dapper** (p176) Sub-Saharan African and Caribbean art that influenced Picasso and Man Ray.
- **Musée du Vin** (p176) Wine, baby, wine. How it's made, plus a glass of the famous tipple.

↘ FRENCH FARE

- **58 Tour Eiffel** (p182) In the tower, with a to-die-for view over the city.
- **Café Constant** (p184) Innovative bistro fare mixed with dishes French grandmothers make at home.
- **Brasserie Thoumieux** (p183) A laid-back local institution.

↘ MAGNIFICENT MONUMENTS

- **Palais de Chaillot** (p173) Curved, colonnaded wings built for the 1937 Exposition Universelle and stellar views of the Seine and the tower.
- **Flamme de la Liberté** (p176) The Statue of Liberty's little sister.
- **Hôtel des Invalides** (p178) The stunning complex that provided housing for 4000 *invalides* (disabled war veterans).

BRUCE B?

Parc du Champ de Mars (p172) through the arches of the Eiffel Tower

DISCOVER INVALIDES & EIFFEL TOWER

With its hourly sparkles that illuminate the evening skyline, the Eiffel Tower needs no introduction. Ascending to its viewing platforms will offer you a panorama over the whole of Paris, with the prestigious neighbourhood of Passy (the 16e arrondissement) stretching out along the far banks of the Seine to the west.

Passy is home to some fabulous museums, including the Musée Marmottan-Monet, with the world's largest collection of Monet paintings, and the underrated Cité de l'Architecture et du Patrimoine, with captivating sculptures and murals. On the Left Bank is the prominent Musée du Quai Branly, introducing indigenous art and culture from outside Europe.

Moving east, in the neighbouring 7e arrondissement is Faubourg St-Germain, an elegant if staid *quartier* that graces the streets between the Seine and rue de Babylone, 1km south, with beautiful 18th-century mansions. The smooth lawns of Esplanade des Invalides map its western fringe green.

SIGHTS

EIFFEL TOWER Map p172

☎ 08 92 70 12 39; www.tour-eiffel.fr; to 2nd fl adult/12-24yr/4-12yr €8.10/6.40/4, to 3rd fl €13.10/11.50/9, stairs to 2nd fl €4.50/3.50/3; ☼ lifts & stairs 9am-midnight mid-Jun–Aug, lifts 9.30am-11pm, stairs 9.30am-6pm Sep–mid-Jun; Ⓜ Champ de Mars-Tour Eiffel or Bir Hakeim

There are many ways to experience the Eiffel Tower, from an evening ascent amid the lights to a meal in one of its two **restaurants** (p182), and even though some seven million people come annually, few would dispute the fact that each visit is unique. Like many Parisian icons (the Centre Pompidou or the Louvre's glass pyramid), it has gone from being roundly criticised by city residents to much loved – though the transformation didn't take place overnight.

Named after its designer, Gustave Eiffel, la Tour Eiffel was built for the 1889 Exposition Universelle (World Fair), marking the centenary of the French Revolution. At the time it faced massive opposition from Paris' artistic and literary elite, and the 'metal asparagus', as some Parisians snidely called it, was almost torn down in 1909 – spared because it proved an ideal platform for the transmitting antennas needed for the newfangled science of radiotelegraphy.

Today, the three levels are open to the public (entrance to the 1st level is included in all admission tickets), though the top level closes in heavy wind. You can take the lifts (in the east, west and north pillars), or, if you're feeling fit, the stairs in the south pillar up to the 2nd platform. Highly recommended is the **online booking system** (www.tour-eiffel.fr) that allows you to buy your tickets in advance, thus avoiding the monumental queues at the ticket office. You need to be able to print out your tickets to use this service or have your ticket on a smart-phone screen (eg Blackberry or iPhone) that can be read by the scanner at the entrance.

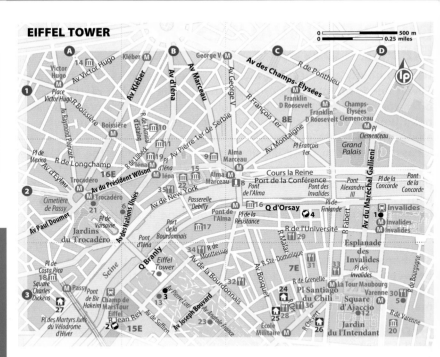

PARC DU CHAMP DE MARS Map p172

Ⓜ Champ de Mars-Tour Eiffel or École Militaire
Running southeast from the Eiffel Tower, the grassy Field of Mars (named after the Roman god of war) was originally used as a parade ground for the cadets of the 18th-century **École Militaire** (Military Academy; Map p164), the vast, French-classical building (1772) at the southeastern end of the park, which counts Napoleon Bonaparte among its graduates. The wonderful Wall for Peace memorial (2000; www.wallforpeace.com) facing the academy and the statue of Maréchal Joffre (1870–1931) are by Clara Halter.

The **Marionnettes du Champ de Mars** (Map p172; ☎ 01 48 56 01 44; allée du Général Margueritte, 7e; Ⓜ École Militaire) stages puppet shows (€3) in a covered and heated *salle* (hall) in the park at 3.15pm and 4.15pm on Wednesday, Saturday and Sunday.

MUSÉE DU QUAI BRANLY Map p172

☎ 01 56 61 70 00; www.quaibranly.fr; 37 quai Branly, 7e; adult/18-25yr & student €8.50/6, EU resident under 26yr free, 1st Sun of month free; ☽ 11am-7pm Tue, Wed & Sun, to 9pm Thu-Sat Ⓜ Pont de l'Alma or Alma-Marceau
Opened to great fanfare in mid-2006, the architecturally impressive Quai Branly Museum introduces the art and cultures of Africa, Oceania, Asia and the Americas through innovative displays, film and musical recordings. With *Là où dialoguent les cultures* (Where cultures communicate) as its motto, the museum is one of the most dynamic and forward-thinking in the world. The anthropological explanations are kept to a minimum; what is displayed here is meant to be viewed as art. A day pass allowing entry to the temporary exhibits as well as the permanent collection costs €10/7 per adult/concession.

EIFFEL TOWER

INFORMATION

Aérogare des Invalides	**1**	D2
Australian Embassy	**2**	A3
Fat Tire Bike Tours	**3**	B3
South African Embassy	**4**	C2

SIGHTS

53 Rue de Varenne	**5**	D3
Cinéaqua	**6**	B2
Eiffel Tower	**7**	B3
Flamme de la Liberté	**8**	C2
Fondation Pierre Bergé-Yves Saint Laurent	**9**	B2
Galerie-Musée Baccarat	**10**	B1
Galeries du Panthéon Bouddhique du Japon et de la Chine	**11**	B2
Hôtel des Invalides	**12**	D3
Marionettes de Champ de Mars	**13**	B3
Musée Dapper	**14**	A1
Musée d'Art Moderne de la Ville de Paris	**15**	B2
Musée des Égouts de Paris	**16**	C2
Musée du Quai Branly	**17**	B2
Musée du Vin	**18**	A3
Musée Guimet des Arts Asiatiques	**19**	B2
Musée Rodin	**20**	D3
Palais de Chaillot	**21**	A2
Palais de Tokyo	**22**	B2
Parc du Champ de Mars	**23**	B3

SLEEPING

Cadran Hôtel	**24**	C3
Hôtel du Champ-de-Mars	**25**	C3
Hôtel Muguet	**26**	C3
Hôtel Sezz	**27**	A3

EATING

58 Tour Eiffel	(see 7)
Amorino Cler	**28**	C3
Bellota Bellota	**29**	C2
Besnier	**30**	D3
Brasserie Thoumieux	**31**	C3
Café Constant	**32**	C3
Café de l'Esplanade	**33**	D3
Firmin Le Barbier	**34**	B3
La Cantine Russe	**35**	B2
Rue Cler	**36**	C3

ENTERTAINMENT & ACTIVITIES

Fat Tire Bike Tours	(see 3)

PALAIS DE CHAILLOT Map p172

place du Trocadéro et du 11 November, 16e; Ⓜ **Trocadéro**

The two curved, colonnaded wings of the Palais de Chaillot, built for the 1937 Exposition Universelle, and the terrace between them afford an exceptional panorama of the Jardins du Trocadéro, the Seine and the Eiffel Tower.

In the palace's eastern wing is the standout **Cité de l'Architecture et du Patrimoine** (☎ 01 58 51 52 00; www.citechaillot.fr; 1 place du Trocadéro et du 11 November, 16e; adult/18-25yr €8/5, EU resident under 26yr free; ⏱ 11am-7pm Mon, Wed & Fri-Sun, to 9pm Thu), a mammoth 23,000 sq metres of space spread over three floors and devoted to French architecture and heritage. While it may sound about as exciting as an academic textbook, it really is a fantastic museum. The highlight is the light-filled ground floor, which contains a beautiful collection of 350 plaster and wood casts *(moulages)* of cathedral portals, columns and gargoyles, and replicas of murals and stained glass originally created for the 1878 Exposition Universelle. The views of the Eiffel Tower from the windows are equally monumental.

MUSÉE GUIMET DES ARTS ASIATIQUES Map p172

☎ 01 56 52 53 00; www.museeguimet.fr; 6 place d'Iéna, 16e; permanent collection adult/senior & student €7.50/5.50, EU resident under 26yr & all under 18yr free; ⏱ 10am-6pm Wed-Mon; Ⓜ Iéna

The Guimet Museum of Asiatic Arts is France's foremost repository for Asian art

THE EIFFEL TOWER IN NUMBERS

- Height: 324m
- Distance seen from the 2nd level: 50 to 70km
- Number of steps: 1665
- Number of rivets: 2.5 million
- Number of 'sparkle' lights: 20,000
- Tonnes of iron: 7300
- Coats of paint since 1889: 19
- Length of time it takes a team of 25 to do one paint job: 18 months
- Distance tightrope-artist Philippe Petit traversed in 1989, from the Palais Chaillot (across the Seine) to the Tower's 2nd level: 700m

BRUCE BI

Musée Marmottan-Monet

↘ MUSÉE MARMOTTAN-MONET

This museum, situated two blocks east of the Bois de Boulogne between Porte de la Muette and Porte de Passy, has the world's largest collection of artworks by impressionist painter Claude Monet (1840–1926) – there are about 100 pieces in total – as well as paintings by the likes of Gauguin, Sisley, Pissarro, Renoir, Degas, Manet and Berthe Morisot. It also contains an important collection of French, English, Italian and Flemish miniatures from the 13th to the 16th centuries.

Things you need to know: Map p164; ☎ 01 44 96 50 33; www.marmottan.com; 2 rue Louis Boilly, 16e; adult/8-25yr €9/5; ⊙ 11am-9pm Tue, to 6pm Wed-Sun; Ⓜ La Muette

and has sculptures, paintings, *objets d'art* and religious articles from Afghanistan, India, Nepal, Pakistan, Tibet, Cambodia, China, Japan and Korea. Part of the collection, comprising Buddhist paintings and sculptures brought to Paris in 1876 by collector Émile Guimet, is housed in the **Galeries du Panthéon Bouddhique du Japon et de la Chine** (Buddhist Pantheon Galleries of Japan & China; ☎ 01 40 73 88 00; 19 av d'Iéna; admission free; ⊙ 9.45am-5.45pm Wed-Mon; Ⓜ Iéna) in the scrumptious Hôtel Heidelbach a short distance to the north. Don't miss the wonderful **Japanese garden** (⊙ 1-5pm Wed-Mon) here.

PALAIS DE TOKYO Map p172

☎ 01 7 23 54 01; www.palaisdetokyo.com; 13 av du Président Wilson, 16e; adult/senior & 18-26yr €6/4.50; ⊙ noon-midnight Tue-Sun; Ⓜ Iéna
The Tokyo Palace, created for the 1937 Exposition Universelle and now a contemporary art space, has no permanent collection. Instead its shell-like interior of polished concrete and steel is the stark backdrop for rotating, interactive art installations (the rooftop, for example, has been the setting for attention-getting projects like the transient Hotel Everland and the see-through restaurant Nomiya).

CINÉAQUA Map p172

☎ 01 40 69 23 23; www.cineaqua.com; 2 av des Nations Unies, 16e; adult/13-17yr/3-12yr €19.50/15.50/12.50; ⏱ 10am-7pm Apr-Sep, 10am-6pm Oct-Mar

On the eastern side of the Jardins du Trocadéro is Paris' largest aquarium. It's not the best you'll ever see, but it's a decent rainy-day destination for families, with a shark tank and some 500 species of fish on display. There are also, somewhat oddly, three cinemas inside (only one of which shows ocean-related films), though non-French-speaking kids will need to be old enough to read subtitles, as almost everything is dubbed into French.

MUSÉE D'ART MODERNE DE LA VILLE DE PARIS Map p172

☎ 01 53 67 40 00; www.mam.paris.fr, in French; 11 av du Président Wilson, 16e; temporary exhibits from adult €5-9, 13-25yr, senior & student €2.50-5.50, under 13yr & permanent collections free; ⏱ 10am-6pm Tue-Sun, to 10pm Thu; Ⓜ Iéna

The permanent collection at the city's modern art museum displays works representative of just about every major artistic movement of the 20th and nascent 21st centuries: Fauvism, Cubism, Dadaism, and so on up through video installations. While it merits a peek – you'll find works by Modigliani, Matisse, Braque and Soutine here – the permanent collection is nowhere near the level of the Centre Pompidou. There is one jewel of a room though, containing several gorgeous canvases from Dufy and Bonnard.

GALERIE-MUSÉE BACCARAT Map p172

☎ 01 40 22 11 00; www.baccarat.com; 11 place des États-Unis, 16e; adult/student & 18-25yr €5/3.50; ⏱ 10am-6.30pm Mon & Wed-Sat; Ⓜ Boissière or Kléber

Showcasing 1000 stunning pieces of crystal, many of them custom-made for princes and dictators of desperately poor former colonies, this flashy museum is at home in its striking new rococo-style

Parc du Champ de Mars (p172) and the Eiffel Tower (p171)

BRUCE BI

premises designed by Philippe Starck in the ritzy 16e.

MUSÉE DAPPER Map p172

☎ 01 44 00 91 75; www.dapper.com.fr; 35 rue Paul Valéry, 16e; adult/senior/under 26yr €6/4/free, last Wed of month free; ⏰ 11am-7pm Wed-Mon; Ⓜ Victor Hugo

This fantastic museum of sub-Saharan African and Caribbean art collected and exhibited by the nonprofit Dapper Foundation (in a 16th-century *hôtel particulier* with wonderful 21st-century add-ons) stages a couple of major exhibitions each year. The collection consists mostly of carved wooden figurines and masks, which famously influenced the work of Picasso, Braque and Man Ray.

FONDATION PIERRE BERGÉ-YVES SAINT LAURENT Map p172

☎ 01 44 31 64 31; www.fondation-pb-ysl.net; 3 rue Léonce Reynaud, 16e; adult/10-25yr & senior €5/3; ⏰ 11am-6pm Tue-Sun; Ⓜ Alma Marceau

This foundation dedicated to preserving the work of the *haute couture* legend or-ganises two to three temporary exhibits (not necessarily related to YSL) per year, with an emphasis on fashion and art.

MUSÉE DU VIN Map p172

☎ 01 45 25 63 26; www.museeduvinparis.com; rue des Eaux, 5 square Charles Dickens, 16e; adult/senior & student €11.90/9.90; ⏰ 10am-6pm Tue-Sun; Ⓜ Passy

The not-so-comprehensive Wine Museum, headquarters of the prestigious International Federation of Wine Brotherhoods, introduces visitors to the fine art of viticulture with various mock-ups and displays of tools. Admission includes a glass of wine at the end of the visit.

FLAMME DE LA LIBERTÉ Map p172

Ⓜ Alma-Marceau

This bronze Flame of Liberty sculpture – a replica of the one topping New York's Statue of Liberty – was placed here in 1987 on the centenary of the launch of the *International Herald Tribune* newspaper, as a symbol of friendship between

Clock inside the Musée d'Orsay

IZZET KERIBAR

France and the USA. On 31 August 1997 in the place d'Alma underpass below, Diana, Princess of Wales, was killed in a devastating car accident along with her companion, Dodi Fayed, and their chauffeur, Henri Paul, and the Flame of Liberty became something of a memorial to her, decorated with flowers, photographs, graffiti and personal notes. It was renovated and cleaned in 2002 and, this being the age of short (or no) memories, apart from a bit of sentimental graffiti on a wall nearby there are no longer any reminders of the tragedy.

CHAPELLE NOTRE DAME DE LA MEDAILLE MIRACULEUSE Map p164

☎ 01 49 54 78 88; www.chapellenotredamede lamedaillemiraculeuse.com, in French; 140 rue du Bac, 6e; ☺ 7.45am-1pm & 2.30-7pm Mon & Wed-Sun, 7.45am-7pm Tue; Ⓜ Rue du Bac or Vaneau

Across the street from Le Bon Marché department store, hidden at the end of a courtyard, is this extraordinary chapel where, in 1830, the Virgin Mary spoke to a 24-year-old novice called Catherine Labouré. In a series of three miraculous apparitions that took place in the chapel the young nun was told to have a medal made that would protect and grace those who wore it. The first Miraculous Medals were made in 1832 – the same year a cholera epidemic plagued Paris – and its popularity spread like wild fire as wearers of the medal found themselves miraculously cured or protected from the deadly disease. Devout Roman Catholics around the world still wear the medal today.

MUSÉE D'ORSAY Map p164

☎ 01 40 49 48 14; www.musee-orsay.fr; 62 rue de Lille, 7e; adult/18-25yr €8/5.50, plus temporary exhibitions €9.50/7, permanent exhibitions free for EU residents under 26yr, 1st Sun of month free; ☺ 9.30am-6pm Tue, Wed & Fri-Sun, to 9.45pm Thu; Ⓜ Musée d'Orsay or Solférino

In a former train station (1900) facing the Seine, this museum displays France's national collection of paintings, sculptures, objets d'art and other works produced between the 1840s and 1914, including the fruits of the impressionist, postimpressionist and art nouveau movements.

Many visitors head straight to the upper skylight-lit level to see the impressionist paintings by Monet, Renoir, Pissarro, Sisley, Degas and Manet and the postimpressionist works by Van Gogh, Cézanne, Seurat and Matisse. But there's a great deal to see on the ground floor, too, including early works by Manet, Monet, Renoir and Pissarro. The middle level has some magnificent art nouveau rooms.

English-language **guided tours** (☎ information 01 40 49 48 48; €6 plus admission fee), last 1½ hours and include 'Masterpieces of the Musée d'Orsay'. There are also tours and workshops designed with kids and families in mind. Details and hours for all are listed on its website.

To cut the length of time spent queuing to get into the museum, buy tickets in advance online or at **Kiosque du Musée d'Orsay** (☺ 9am-5pm Tue-Fri school holidays, Tue only rest of year), in front of the museum. With an advance ticket purchase you get in via the less-busy entrance C. Those who prefer their own pace can DIY with a 1½-hour **audioguide tour** (€5) covering 80 major works.

Museum tickets are valid all day, meaning you can leave and re-enter the museum as you please. The reduced entrance fee of €5.50 (€7 including temporary exhibition) applies to everyone after 4.15pm (6pm on Thursday). Those visiting the Musée Rodin (p178) on the same day save €2 with a combined ticket (€12).

INVALIDES & EIFFEL TOWER

SIGHTS

MUSÉE RODIN Map p172

☎ 01 44 18 61 10; www.musee-rodin.fr; 79 rue de Varenne, 7e; adult/18-25yr permanent or temporary exhibition €7/5, both exhibitions plus garden €10/7, free for EU residents under 26yr, 1st Sun of month free, garden only €1; ⏱ 10am-5.45pm Tue-Sun; Ⓜ Varenne

The Rodin Museum is one of the most relaxing spots in the city, with its garden bespeckled with sculptures and trees in which to contemplate *The Thinker*. Rooms on two floors of the 18th-century Hôtel Biron display vital bronze and marble sculptures by Auguste Rodin, including casts of some of his most celebrated works: *The Hand of God, The Burghers of Calais, Cathedral,* that perennial crowd-pleaser *The Thinker* and the sublime, the incomparable, that romance-hewn-in-marble called *The Kiss*. There are also some 15 works by Camille Claudel (1864–1943), sister to the writer Paul and Rodin's mistress. The garden closes its gates later than the museum: at 6.45pm April to September and at 5pm October to March. Buy tickets online to save queuing.

HÔTEL DES INVALIDES Map p172

Ⓜ Invalides, Varenne or La Tour Maubourg

A 500m-long expanse of lawn known as the **Esplanade des Invalides** separates Faubourg St-Germain from the Eiffel Tower area. At the southern end, laid out between 1704 and 1720, is the final resting place of Napoleon, who many French people consider to be the nation's greatest hero.

Hôtel des Invalides was built in the 1670s by Louis XIV to provide housing for 4000 *invalides* (disabled war veterans). On 14 July 1789, a mob fought its way into the building and seized 32,000 rifles before heading on to the prison at Bastille and the start of the French Revolution.

MUSÉE DES ÉGOUTS DE PARIS Map p172

☎ 01 53 68 27 81; www.egouts.tenebres.eu, in French; place de la Résistance, 7e; adult/student & 6-16yr €4.20/3.40; ⏱ 11am-5pm Sat-Wed May-Sep, to 4pm Sat-Wed Oct-Dec & Feb-Apr; Ⓜ Pont de l'Alma

The Paris Sewers Museum is a working museum whose entrance, a rectangular

BRUCE BI

Musée Rodin

Amusement park ride at Jardin d'Acclimatation

JEAN-BERNARD CARILLET

INVALIDES & EIFFEL TOWER

SIGHTS

⬎ IF YOU LIKE...

If you like **Parc du Champ de Mars** (p172), we think you'll like the far larger green space of the 845-hectare **Bois De Boulogne** (Boulogne Woods; Map p164). The vast park owes its informal layout to Baron Haussmann who, inspired by London's Hyde Park, planted 400,000 trees here. Along with various gardens and other sights, the wood has 15km of cycle paths and 28km of bridle paths through 125 hectares of forest. The Bois de Boulogne is served by metro lines 1 (Porte Maillot, Les Sablons), 2 (Porte Dauphine), 9 (Michel-Ange Auteuil) and 10 (Michel-Ange Auteuil, Porte d'Auteuil), and the RER C (Av Foch, Av Henri Martin).

- **Jardin d'Acclimatation** (☎ 01 40 67 90 82; www.jardindacclimatation.fr; av du Mahatma Gandhi; admission €2.90, under 3yr free; ☽ 10am-7pm Apr-Sep, to 6pm Oct-Mar; Ⓜ Les Sablons) Families will be most interested in this great amusement park for kids, which includes puppet shows, boat rides, a small water park and art exhibits.
- **Parc de Bagatelle** (☎ 01 40 67 97 00; adult/7-25yr €5/2.50 June-Oct, free Nov-May; ☽ 9.30am-8pm June-Oct, 9.30am-5pm Nov-May) This enclosed park is renowned for its beautiful gardens.
- **Pré Catalan** (☽ 9.30am-5-8pm seasonal) The Catalan Meadow includes the Jardin Shakespeare, in which plants, flowers and trees mentioned in Shakespeare's plays are cultivated.
- **Rowing boats** (☎ 01 42 88 04 69; Lac Inférieur; per hr €15; ☽ 10am-6pm mid-Mar–mid-Oct, occasionally open weekends in winter; Ⓜ Av Henri Martin) Boats can be hired at the largest of the wood's lakes and ponds, Lac Inférieur.
- **Paris Cycles** (☎ 01 47 47 76 50; per hr €5; ☽ 10am-7pm mid-Apr–mid-Oct) Bicycles can be hired at two locations in the Bois de Boulogne: on av du Mahatma Gandhi (Ⓜ Les Sablons), across from the Porte Sablons entrance to the Jardin d'Acclimatation, and near the Pavillon Royal (Ⓜ Av Foch) at the northern end of Lac Inférieur.

Musee d'Art Moderne de la Ville de Paris (p175)

maintenance hole topped with a kiosk, is across the street from 93 quai d'Orsay, 7e. Raw sewage flows beneath your feet as you walk through 480m of odoriferous tunnels, passing artefacts illustrating the development of Paris' waste-water disposal system. The sewers keep regular hours except – God forbid – when rain threatens to flood the tunnels, and in January, when it is closed. Not recommended for anyone afraid of rats.

SLEEPING

Not surprisingly, these two very chic neighbourhoods are somewhat short on budget and midrange accommodation options.

HÔTEL SEZZ Map p172   Boutique Hotel €€€
☎ 01 56 75 26 26; www.hotelsezz.com; 6 av Frémiet, 16e; s €285-340, d & tw €335-470, ste €450-1800; Ⓜ Passy; 🍴 💻 🛜 🐾 ♿
Punning on the number of the posh arrondissement – 16 (*seize* in French) – in which it finds itself, this boutique bonanza

is heavy on design (think Christophe Pillet), technology and *l'esprit zen* (Zen spirit). The 27 rooms, more than half of which are suites, are spacious and done up in reds and blacks, and lots of glass. There's a hammam, Jacuzzi and massage room, and the bar specialises in Champagne. Each guest has their own personal assistant during their stay.

HÔTEL MUGUET Map p172   Hotel €€
☎ 01 47 05 05 93; www.hotelmuguet.com; 11 rue Chevert, 7e; s/d/tr €110/145/195; Ⓜ La Tour Maubourg; 🍴 💻 🛜
This hotel, strategically placed between Invalides and the Eiffel Tower, is a great family choice, with functional decor and generous-sized triples with armchair-bed to convert separate lounge area into kid's bedroom. From the 4th floor on, the Eiffel Tower sneaks into view, climaxing with room 62's fabulous full-frontal panorama. Several rooms stare at the equally arresting Hôtel des Invalides' Église du Dôme. Back down on ground level, a trio of rooms opens onto a courtyard garden.

CADRAN HÔTEL

Map p172   Boutique Hotel €€

☎ 01 40 62 67 00; www.paris-hotel-cadran.com; 10 rue du Champ de Mars, 7e; d €144-225, ste €163-228; Ⓜ École Militaire; ✖ ▯ 🛜

An address for gourmets, this concept hotel seduces guests with a designer ticktock clock theme and a bold open-plan reception spilling into a rather irresistible Bar à Chocolat (Chocolate Bar). Admire, taste and buy Christophe Roussel's colourful seasonal-flavoured *macarons* and chocolates (www.roussel-chocolatier. com), then retire to one of 41 futuristic rooms with all the mod cons.

HÔTEL DE VARENNE Map p172 Hotel €€

☎ 01 45 51 45 55; www.hoteldevarenne.com; 44 rue de Bourgogne, 7e; d €129-280; Ⓜ Varenne; ✖ ▯

Very refined, very classic and very quiet, this hotel tucked at the end of a courtyard garden has something of a country feel to it. Most of the two dozen rooms, which are spread over four floors, look into the courtyard and a very sizable choice is room 22. The Musée Rodin is within spitting distance.

HÔTEL LINDBERGH Map p164   Hotel €€

☎ 01 45 48 35 53; www.hotellindbergh.com; 5 rue Chomel, 7e; d €126-160, tr €180, q €190; Ⓜ Sèvres Babylone; ▯ 🛜

We still haven't figured out why this *hôtel de charme* is totally kitted out in Charles Lindbergh photos and memorabilia or named after him, but somehow it all works. The 26 guestrooms are done up in shades of chocolate and red, with silk fabric on the walls and rush matting on the floors. We like the room-number plates on the doors with little Paris landmarks, the ample-sized bathrooms and the very friendly staff.

HÔTEL DU CHAMP-DE-MARS

Map p172   Hotel €

☎ 01 45 51 52 30; www.hotelduchampde mars.com; 7 rue du Champ de Mars, 7e; s/d/tr €91/98/128; Ⓜ École Militaire; ▯ 🛜

This charming 25-room hotel is on everyone's wish list so book a good month or

Golden dome of Hôtel des Invalides (p178) with the Panthéon (p223) in the background

BRUCE BI

INVALIDES & EIFFEL TOWER

EATING

BRUCE BI

Musée des Égouts de Paris (p178)

two in advance if you want to wake up in the shadow of the Eiffel Tower. The attractive shop-front entrance leads into a colourful lobby. Rooms on the lower floors can be downright cupboardlike, though; go up higher (in floors and price) and you might earn a glimpse of Mademoiselle Eiffel herself.

EATING

Around the Eiffel Tower you can grab picnic supplies at **rue Cler** (p185) or choose from the restaurants on rue de Montessuy. And, for a truly memorable experience, you can even dine in the icon itself.

For afternoon tea, weekend brunch (€35) or a light lunch with the girls, no address is sweeter than legendary **Ladurée** (p258).

CAFÉ DE L'ESPLANADE
Map p172   Fusion €€€
☎ 01 47 05 38 80; 52 rue Fabert, 7e; starters €15-20, mains €25-45; ☻ lunch & dinner to 12.30am; Ⓜ La Tour Maubourg

An address to impress (so dress to impress), Café de l'Esplanade is one of those chic society places to be seen in between business deals – it *is* of the same Costes brothers ilk as **Café Marly** (p74) et al, much loved by politicians and journalists. Take one look at the astonishing view and you'll understand why. It's the only café-restaurant on the magnificent Esplanade des Invalides. No menus – just *à la carte* until half-past midnight.

58 TOUR EIFFEL Map p172   French €€
☎ 01 45 55 20 04; www.restaurants-toureiffel. com; 1st level, Champ de Mars, 7e; lunch mains €14-16, lunch menus €17.50/22.50, dinner mains €20-33, dinner menu €65; ☻ 11.30am-5.30pm & 6.30-11pm; Ⓜ Champ de Mars-Tour Eiffel or Bir Hakeim

If you're intrigued by the idea of a meal in the Tower, the 58 Tour Eiffel is a pretty good choice. It may not be the caviar and black truffles of Jules Verne (on the 2nd level), but Alain Ducasse did sign off on the menu, ensuring that this is much more than just another tourist cafeteria. That said, it's really the views from the 1st-floor bay windows that make it something special. For lunch, go first to the restaurant's outside kiosk (near the north pillar); for dinner, reserve online or by telephone.

BRASSERIE THOUMIEUX
Map p172   French, Brasserie €€
☎ 01 47 05 49 75; www.thoumieux.com, in French; 79 rue St-Dominique, 7e; starters/mains €10/25, menus €15 (lunch only) & €35; Ⓥ lunch & dinner to 11.30pm; Ⓜ La Tour Maubourg
Chef Christian Beguet has been here since 1979 – and that's just the tip of the iceberg. Founded in 1923, Thoumieux is an old-school institution just south of the Seine, loved by politicians and tourists alike. Duck thighs, veal, snails…the menu is typical brasserie and the service silky smooth. It has 10 rooms up top if you need to crash.

FIRMIN LE BARBIER Map p172 French €€
☎ 01 45 51 21 55; www.firminlebarbier.fr; 20 rue de Monttessuy, 7e; starters €9, mains €22, plat du jour €14 (lunch only); Ⓥ lunch Wed-Fri & Sun, dinner Tue-Sun; Ⓜ Pont de l'Alma
This discreet brick-walled bistro was opened by a retired surgeon turned gourmet, and his passion for a good meal is apparent in everything from the personable service to the wine list. The menu is traditional French (faux filet with polenta, decadent boeuf bourguignon), while the modern interior is bright and cheery and even benefits from an open kitchen – a rarity in smaller Parisian restaurants. The good news: it's a five-minute walk from the Eiffel Tower. The bad: it doesn't seat much more than 20 people – make sure to reserve.

LA CANTINE RUSSE
Map p172   Russian €€
☎ 01 47 20 56 12; www.lacantinerusse.com; 26 av de New York, 16e; starters €9-22, mains €15-24, menus €17 (lunch only) & €32; Ⓥ lunch & dinner to midnight Mon-Sat; Ⓜ Alma Marceau
Established for the overwhelmingly Russian students at the prestigious Conservatoire Rachmaninov in 1923, this 'canteen' is still going strong more than eight decades later. At communal tables you can savour herrings served

Pastry shop, rue Cler markets (p185)

OLIVER STREWE

INVALIDES & EIFFEL TOWER

EATING

INVALIDES & EIFFEL TOWER

EATING

Le Bon Marché department store (p186)

with blinis, aubergine 'caviar', chicken Kiev, beef Stroganov, *chachliks* (marinated lamb kebabs) and, to complete the tableau, *vatrouchka* (cream cheese cake).

BELLOTA BELLOTA
Map p172   Spanish, Tapas €€
☎ 01 53 59 96 96; www.bellota-bellota.com; 18 rue Jean Nicot, 7e; mains €19, 2-/3-course menu €24/29; ⊙ lunch & dinner to 11pm Tue-Sat; Ⓜ La Tour Maubourg

This Spanish-style tapas bar with a clutch of great big Iberian hams strung in the window is perfect for lunch before or after the **Musée d'Orsay** (p177), or an aperitif at the end of the day. As much drinking as dining venue, this atmospheric little place lures punters in with a fabulous tiled floor, grey painted chairs and more black-footed piggy legs than you'll ever be able to eat dangling from the ceiling.

CAFÉ CONSTANT
Map p172   French, Contemporary €€
☎ 01 47 53 73 34; www.cafeconstant.com; in French; 139 rue Ste-Dominique, 7e; starters/

mains/desserts €11/16/7; ⊙ lunch & dinner to 10.30pm Tue-Sun; Ⓜ École Militaire or Port de l'Alma

Take a former Michelin-starred, deadsimple corner café and what do you get? This jam-packed address with original mosaic floor, simple wooden tables and a huge queue out the door every meal time. The pride and joy of Christian and Catherine Constant, the café doesn't take reservations but you can enjoy a drink at the bar (or on the pavement outside) while you wait. Cuisine is creative bistro, mixing old-fashioned grandma staples like *purée de mon enfance* (mashed potato from my childhood) with Sunday treats like foie gras–stuffed quail and herbroasted chicken.

LA GRANDE ÉPICERIE
Map p164   Wok & Sandwich Bar €
☎ 01 46 39 81 00; www.lagrandeepicerie.fr; 26 rue de Sèvres, 7e; lunch €10-15; ⊙ 8.30am-9pm Mon-Sat; Ⓜ Sèvres-Babylone

Join the hordes of workers from the offices in this area for a quick, tasty lunch at the Espace Pic Nic, in the ground-floor food hall of stylish **Le Bon Marché department store** (p186). Hover around the bar over a wok-cooked hot dish, a design-your-own sandwich (pick the bread type and fillings yourself; a self-designed salad or an 11-piece sushi plate. Pay marginally less to take the same away, or build your own gourmet picnic from the food hall.

AMORINO Map p172   Ice Cream €

☎ 01 43 26 57 46; 4 rue de Buci, 6e; ⏰ noon-midnight; Ⓜ St-Germain des Prés

Though not such dedicated *lécheurs* (lickers) as some, we're told that **Berthillon** (p94) has serious competition and Amorino's homemade ice cream (yogurt, caramel, kiwi, strawberry etc) is, in fact, better. It has no less than 10 other branches in Paris, including **Amorino Luxembourg** (Map p196; ☎ 01 42 22 66 86; 4 rue Vavin, 6e; Ⓜ Vavin); **Amorino Île St-Louis** (Map p82; ☎ 01 44 07 48 08; 47 rue St-Louis en l'Île, 4e; Ⓜ Pont Marie); and **Amorino Cler** (Map p172; 42 rue Cler, 6e; Ⓜ École Militaire).

SELF-CATERING

Food shops cluster on rue de Seine and rue de Buci. The open-air food markets on **rue Cler** (Map p172; rue Cler, 7e; ⏰ 7am or 8am-7pm or 7.30pm Tue-Sat, 8am-noon Sun; Ⓜ École Militaire) have huge arrays of fine fresh produce.

Baguettes might be a common-as-muck staple but watching them being made is a rare treat that can be enjoyed at *boulangerie* **Besnier** (Map p172; ☎ 01 45 51 24 29; 40 rue de Bourgogne, 7e; ⏰ 7am-8pm Mon-Fri Sep-Jul).

DRINKING

An undisputable day rather than night venue, with government ministries and embassies outweighing drinking venues hands-down, the 7e arrondissement does

have a redeeming feature for socialites, in the shape of some lovely cafés.

CAFÉ LE BASILE Map p164   Café

☎ 01 42 22 59 46; 34 rue de Grenelle, 7e; ⏰ 7am-9pm Mon-Sat; Ⓜ Rue du Bac

Don't bother looking for a name above this hip student café, framed by expensive designer fashion shops – there isn't one. Well-worn Formica tables, petrol-blue banquettes and a fine collection of 1950s lights and lampshades keep the sleek crowd out, the retro crowd in. A fabulous find for a hot chocolate or beer, light lunch or flop between lectures.

ENTERTAINMENT & ACTIVITIES

FAT TIRE BIKE TOURS

Map p172   Bicycle Hire

☎ 01 56 58 10 54; www.fattirebiketoursparis. com; 24 rue Edgar Faure, 15e; 1hr/day/week €4/25/100; ⏰ 9am-7pm, after 11.30am only May-Aug; Ⓜ La Motte-Picquet Grenelle

Fat Tire is a friendly Anglophone outfit that rents three-speed cruisers, kids' bikes, trailers, tandems and so on. Show a driver's licence or passport and leave €250 deposit on your credit card. It organises fantastic bike tours too; see p273.

LA PAGODE Map p164   Film

☎ 01 45 55 48 48; 57bis rue de Babylone, 7e; adult/student €7/5; Ⓜ Vaneau

A classified historical monument, this Chinese-style pagoda was shipped to France, piece by piece, in 1895 by Monsieur Morin (the then proprietor of Le Bon Marché), who had it rebuilt in his garden on rue de Babylone as a love present for his wife. The wife clearly wasn't that impressed – she left him a year later. But Parisian *cinéphiles* who flock here to revel in its eclectic programme are. La Pagode has been a fantastic, atmospheric cinema since 1931 – don't miss a moment or two in its bamboo-enshrined garden.

SHOPPING

By the Seine, square on quai Voltaire and a trio of parallel streets south, 120 art and antiques galleries gather under the exclusive **Carré Rive Gauche** (Map p164; www.carrerivegauche.com; Ⓜ Rue du Bac or Solférino) umbrella. While the western half of bd St-Germain and rue du Bac boast a striking collection of contemporary furniture, kitchen and design shops, including **Kartell** (Map p164), **Conran Shop** (Map p164) and Paris' biggest shop window in the shape of **Knoll** (Map p164).

LE BON MARCHÉ
Map p164   Department Store
☎ 01 44 39 80 00; www.bonmarche.fr, in French; 24 rue de Sèvres, 7e; Ⓨ 10am-8pm Mon-Wed & Fri, 10am-9pm Thu & Sat; Ⓜ Sèvres-Babylone
Built by Gustave Eiffel as Paris' first department store in 1852, Le Bon Marché (which translates as 'good market' but also means 'bargain') is less frenetic than its rivals across the river, but no less chic. It has excellent men's and women's fashion collections, and a designer *'snack chic'* café on the 1st floor. But the icing on the cake is its glorious food hall, **La Grande Épicerie de Paris** (26 rue de Sèvres; Ⓨ 8.30am-9pm Mon-Sat, Ⓜ Sèvres-Babylone), which sells, among other edibles, vodka-flavoured lollipops with detoxified ants inside and fist-sized Himalayan salt crystals to grate over food.

ST-GERMAIN DES PRÉS & MONTPARNASSE

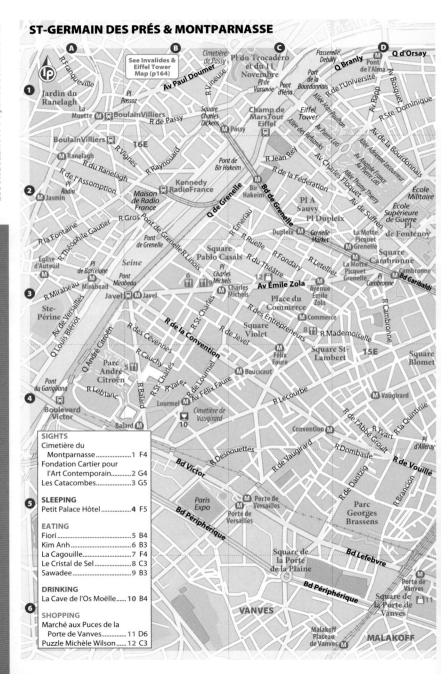

SIGHTS	
Cimetière du Montparnasse	1 F4
Fondation Cartier pour l'Art Contemporain	2 G4
Les Catacombes	3 G5

SLEEPING	
Petit Palace Hôtel	4 F5

EATING	
Fiori	5 B4
Kim Anh	6 B3
La Cagouille	7 F4
Le Cristal de Sel	8 C3
Sawadee	9 B3

DRINKING	
La Cave de l'Os Moëlle	10 B4

SHOPPING	
Marché aux Puces de la Porte de Vanves	11 D6
Puzzle Michèle Wilson	12 C3

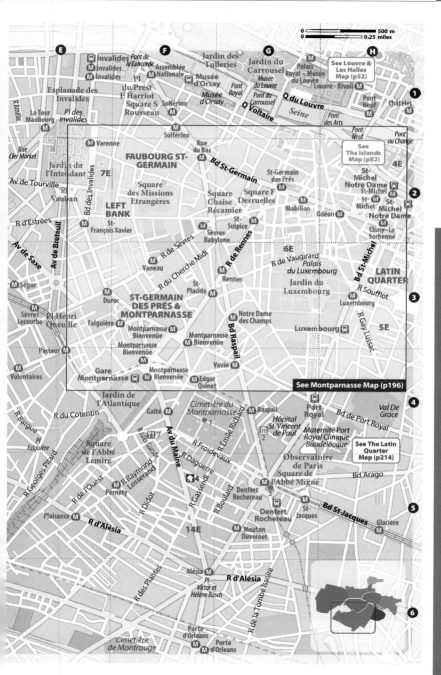

ST-GERMAIN DES PRÉS & MONTPARNASSE

HIGHLIGHTS

HIGHLIGHTS

1 JARDIN DU LUXEMBOURG

The picturesque Jardin du Luxembourg has always been a favourite of lovers and artists, adults and children, first-time visitors and locals. Everyone flocks to enjoy the formal terraces and chestnut groves, to manoeuvre sailboats on a pond and wander among apple orchards. In the summer, it's one of the most sublime spots in the city to take a picnic and sunbathe. Year-round, do as Parisians do: pick up a newspaper, find an empty bench or chair and press pause in this urban oasis.

↘ OUR DON'T MISS LIST

❶ PALAIS DU LUXEMBOURG
The park is a backdrop to the Palais du Luxembourg, built in the 1620s for Marie de Médici, Henri IV's consort, to assuage her longing for the Pitti Palace in Florence, where she had spent her childhood. Since 1958 the palace has housed the **Sénat** (Senate, upper house of French parliament; ☎ reservations 01 44 54 19 49; www.senat.fr; rue de Vaugirard, 6e; adult/18-25yr €8/6), which can be visited by guided tour at 10.30am one Saturday per month.

❷ ORANGERY
The palace's 57m-long orangery (1834) shelters lemon and orange trees, palms, grenadiers and oleanders from the cold. And at its southern side you'll find the park's top spot for catching rays, which always has loads of chairs available.

❸ HÔTEL DU PETIT LUXEMBOURG
The heavily guarded Hôtel du Petit Luxembourg (at rue de Vaugirard,

Clockwise from top: Toy sailboats on the Grand Bassin in front of Palais du Luxembourg; Flower bed; Toy sailboat; Jardin du Luxembourg in summertime

6e) was the modest 16th-century pad where Marie de Médici lived while Palace du Luxembourg was being built. The president of the Senate has called it home since 1825.

❹ SAILBOATS
Rent 1920s toy sailboats (€2/3.20 per 30/60 minutes) to sail on the water at the octagonal **Grand Bassin**. Nothing beats seeing your little boat topple its way out onto this charming pond. It's as much fun for kids as it is for adults, but even if you don't rent a boat, the accompanying laughter is as endearing as the sight of the tiny vessels bumping into one another.

❺ PUPPET SHOWS
Another multi-age pleaser, get a guaranteed giggle at the marionette shows that take place at the pint-sized **Théâtre des Marionnettes du Jardin du Luxembourg** (☎ 01 43 26 46 47; ticket €4; 🕒 3.30pm Wed, 11am & 3.30pm Sat & Sun, daily during school hols). It doesn't matter whether you understand French or not – the characters' costumes and movements speak for themselves.

⌐ THINGS YOU NEED TO KNOW
Best photo op Southern side of the sailboat pond. **Best place to pick up picnic supplies** Food hall at nearby **Le Bon Marché** (p186) **Total area** 24 hectares. **See p198 for further information.**

HIGHLIGHTS

2

⬆ PEOPLE-WATCHING

Lap up the subtle buzz of chic St-Germain des Prés at traffic- and people-busy crossing **Carrefour de l'Odéon**, before grabbing a culinary pew at **Le Comptoir du Relais** (p204) or **Les Éditeurs** (p206), where you can enjoy watching the stylish Parisians stream by as you sip a warming cup of coffee. The action in this area is so intoxicating it even has its own label: *Germanopratine* (St-Germain life).

3

⬆ ÉGLISE ST-SULPICE

You may recognise Paris' second-largest **church** (p198), from Dan Brown's *The Da Vinci Code*. Italianate outside, neoclassical in, it also boasts spectacular frescoes by Eugéne Delacroix; don't miss those in the Chapelle des Sts-Anges (Chapel of the Holy Angels). You can hear the 20m-tall organ in full glory during Sunday's 10.30am Mass or the occasional Sunday-afternoon concert.

4

⬎ SKULLS & BONES

Venture into the subterranean **Les Catacombes** (p195) to ogle the freakishly large number of bones and skulls surrounding you. Millions of Parisians are neatly packed along each and every wall of the 1.7km of underground corridors. During WWII these tunnels were used as a headquarters for the Resistance.

5

⬎ UP ON THE SKYSCRAPER

Zip up on a 38-second ride (it's Europe's fastest lift) to the 59th-floor observation terrace of **Tour Montparnasse** (p196). The building may be an unsightly eyesore of a skyscraper, but the views from the top take in a spread of the major sights – the Eiffel Tower, Jardin du Luxembourg and a striking panorama of the cityscape.

6

⬎ ÉGLISE ST-GERMAIN DES PRÉS

The bell tower above the western entrance of **Paris' oldest church** (p197) has barely changed since AD 990. The Chapelle de St-Symphorien, part of the original 6th-century abbey that was the foundation of this chic neighbourhood, is believed to be the resting place of St Germanus (AD 496–576), the first bishop of Paris.

2 WILL SALTER; 3 KRZYSZTOF DYDYNSKI; 4 JULIET COOMBE; 5 WILL SALTER; 6 KRZYSZTOF DYDYNSKI

2 Les Éditeurs (p206); 3 Eugène Delacroix painting, Église St-Sulpice (p198); 4 Skulls and bones in Les Catacombes (p195); 5 Tour Montparnasse (p196); 6 Église St-Germain des Prés (p197)

ST-GERMAIN DES PRÉS & MONTPARNASSE

BEST...

BEST...

⬎ CLASSIC FRENCH CUISINE

- **Brasserie Lipp** (p206) All the favourites in a traditional brasserie.
- **Le Petit Zinc** (p205) Enjoy lavish seafood platters and an original art nouveau interior at this restaurant masquerading as a brasserie.
- **Bouillon Racine** (p206) Built as a soup kitchen early in the 20th century, this restaurant boasts breathtaking art nouveau splendour.

⬎ HISTORIC CAFÉS

- **Café La Palette** (p209) Paul Cézanne's former haunt, resplendent with *fin-de-siècle* decor.
- **Les Deux Magots** (p209) Another literary stalwart, whose former regulars included Hemingway. Their hot chocolate is a must.
- **Café de Flore** (p209) Sartre, Simone de Beauvoir, Hemingway and André Breton hung out at Paris' most-famous literary café.

⬎ MUSEUMS

- **Musée National Eugène Delacroix** (p200) Embrace the romantic air and contemplate the array of oils, watercolours, pastels and drawings in the former artist's home.
- **Musée Bourdelle** (p196) Epic bronzes in sculptor Antoine Bourdelle's (a Rodin pupil) house and workshop.
- **Musée du Montparnasse** (p197) Temporary exhibits about Montparnasse's role in history.

⬎ SHOPPING

- **Marché aux Puces de la Porte de Vanves** (p212) One of Paris' friendliest flea markets.
- **Tea & Tattered Pages** (p211) Used books and a cosy tearoom in which to flip through them.
- **Pâtisserie Sadaharu Aoki** (p212) Paris' top pastry chef producing specialities with an Asian twist.

WILL SALTER

Les Deux Magots (p209)

DISCOVER ST-GERMAIN DES PRÉS & MONTPARNASSE

From the packed pavement terraces of literary café greats where Sartre, de Beauvoir and other postwar Left Bank intellectuals drank, to the pocket-sized studios of lesser-known romantic and Russian cubist artists, St-Germain des Prés oozes panache. Yet weave your way through the shopaholic crowds on bd St-Germain, past flagship *prêt-à-porter* stores and vast white spaces showcasing interior design, and there's little hint of its legendary bohemia. The arrival of the fashion industry changed all that jazz years ago.

Stroll past the portfolio of designer boutiques on rue du Cherche Midi, past heaps of fresh produce at the Rue Raspail market and watch it leap out at you: *La vie germanopratine* (St-Germain life) is *belle*.

Meanwhile, the unpretentious Montparnasse strikes a better balance than some perhaps: buzzing cafés, brasseries where Picasso and his mates put 1930s Paris to rights, a cemetery with plenty of personality and urban grit in the shape of a mainline train station and ugly tower with panoramic views to challenge Mme Eiffel.

SIGHTS

LES CATACOMBES Map p188
☎ 01 43 22 47 63; www.catacombes.paris.fr, in French; 1 av Colonel Henri Roi-Tanguy, 14e; adult/14-26yr €8/4; ☒ 10am-5pm Tue-Sun; Ⓜ Denfert Rochereau

Paris' most gruesome and macabre sight: in 1785 it was decided to solve the hygiene and aesthetic problems posed by Paris' overflowing cemeteries by exhuming the bones and storing them in the tunnels of three disused quarries. The Catacombes is one such ossuary, created in 1810. After descending 20m (130 steps) from street level, visitors follow 1.7km of underground corridors in which a mind-boggling amount of bones and skulls of millions of Parisians are neatly packed along each and every wall. During WWII these tunnels were used as a headquarters by the Resistance; so-called *cataphiles* looking for cheap thrills are often caught roaming the tunnels at night (there's a fine of €60).

The route through the Catacombes begins at a small, dark-green belle époque–style building in the centre of a grassy area of av Colonel Henri Roi-Tanguy. The exit is at the end of 83 steps on rue Remy Dumoncel (Ⓜ Mouton Duvernet), 700m southwest of av Colonel Henri Roi-Tanguy.

CIMETIÈRE DU MONTPARNASSE Map p188
☎ 01 44 10 86 50; 3 bd Edgar Quinet, 14e; ☒ 8am-6pm Mon-Fri, 8.30am-6pm Sat, 9am-6pm Sun mid-Mar–Oct, 8am-5.30pm Mon-Fri, 8.30am-6pm Sat, 9am-6pm Sun Nov–mid-Mar; Ⓜ Edgar Quinet or Raspail

Montparnasse Cemetery received its first 'lodger' in 1824. It contains the tombs of illustrious personages such as poet Charles Baudelaire, writer Guy de Maupassant, playwright Samuel Beckett, sculptor Constantin Brancusi, painter Chaim Soutine, photographer Man Ray, industrialist André Citroën, Captain Alfred Dreyfus of the infamous affair, actress

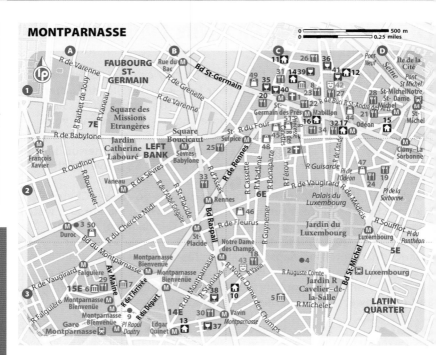

Jean Seberg, philosopher Jean-Paul Sartre and his lover, writer Simone de Beauvoir, and the crooner Serge Gainsbourg, whose grave is in division No 1 just off av Transversale.

TOUR MONTPARNASSE Map p196

☎ 01 45 38 52 56; www.tourmontparnasse56. com; rue de l'Arrivée, 15e; adult/student & 16-20yr/7-15yr €11/8/4.70; ⏱ 9.30am-11.30pm daily Apr-Sep, to 10.30pm Sun-Thu, to 11pm Fri & Sat Oct-Mar; Ⓜ Montparnasse Bienvenüe
The 210m-high Montparnasse Tower, a startlingly ugly, oversized lipstick tube built in 1973 with steel and smoked glass and housing offices for 5000 workers, affords spectacular views over the city. A lift whisks visitors up in 38 seconds to the indoor observatory on the 56th floor, with exhibition centre, video clips, multimedia terminals and Paris' highest café. Finish

with a hike up the stairs to the open-air terrace on the 59th floor.

FONDATION CARTIER POUR L'ART CONTEMPORAIN Map p196

☎ 01 42 18 56 50; www.fondation.cartier.fr; 261 bd Raspail, 14e; adult/11-26yr €7.50/5; ⏱ 11am-10pm Tue, to 8pm Mon & Wed-Sun; Ⓜ Raspail
This stunning contemporary building, designed by Jean Nouvel, is a work of art. It hosts temporary exhibits on contemporary art (from the 1980s to today) in a wide variety of media – from painting and photography to video and fashion.

MUSÉE BOURDELLE Map p196

☎ 01 49 54 73 73; www.bourdelle.paris. fr, in French; 18 rue Antoine Bourdelle, 15e; adult/14-26yr €7/3.50; ⏱ 10am-6pm Tue-Sun; Ⓜ Falguière

MONTPARNASSE

The Bourdelle Museum contains monumental bronzes in the house and workshop where sculptor Antoine Bourdelle (1861–1929), a pupil of Rodin, lived and worked. The three sculpture gardens are particularly lovely and impart a flavour of belle époque and post-WWI Montparnasse. The museum usually has a temporary exhibition going on alongside its permanent collection (free on the rare occasion there's no exhibition).

MUSÉE DU MONTPARNASSE
Map p196

☎ 01 42 22 91 96; www.museedumontparnasse.net, in French; 21 av du Maine, 15e; adult/12-18yr €5/4; ⏱ 12.30-7pm Tue-Sun;
Ⓜ Montparnasse Bienvenüe

Housed in the studio of Russian cubist artist Marie Vassilieff (1884–1957) down a surprisingly leafy alleyway off av du Maine,

Montparnasse Museum doesn't have a permanent collection; rather it recalls the great role Montparnasse played during various artistic periods of the 20th century, offered through temporary exhibitions.

ÉGLISE ST-GERMAIN DES PRÉS
Map p196

☎ 01 55 42 81 33; 3 place St-Germain des Prés, 6e; ⏱ 8am-7pm Mon-Sat, 9am-8pm Sun;
Ⓜ St-Germain des Prés

Paris' oldest standing church, the Romanesque St Germanus of the Fields, was built in the 11th century on the site of a 6th-century abbey and was the dominant place of worship in Paris until the arrival of Notre Dame. The **bell tower** over the western entrance has changed little since 990, although the spire dates only from the 19th century. The vaulted ceiling is a starry sky that seems to float forever upward.

ÉGLISE ST-SULPICE Map p196
☎ 01 46 33 21 78; place St-Sulpice, 6e;
🕙 7.30am-7.30pm; Ⓜ St-Sulpice

In 1646 work started on the twin-towered Church of St Sulpicius, which is lined inside with 21 side chapels and took six architects 150 years to finish. What draws most people is not its lovely Italianate facade with two rows of superimposed columns, nor its neoclassical decor influenced by the Counter-Reformation; rather, this church was the setting for a crucial discovery in Dan Brown's *The Da Vinci Code*.

The frescoes in the **Chapelle des Sts-Anges** (Chapel of the Holy Angels), first to the right as you enter, depict Jacob wrestling with the angel (to the left) and Michael the Archangel doing battle with Satan (to the right) and were painted by Eugène Delacroix between 1855 and 1861. The monumental, 20m-tall **organ loft** dates from 1781. Listen to it in its full glory during 10.30am Mass on Sunday or the occasional Sunday-afternoon organ concert.

JARDIN DU LUXEMBOURG Map p196
Ⓜ **Luxembourg**

Keen to know what the city does during its time off? Then stroll around the formal terraces, chestnut groves and green lawns of this 23-hectare park, where Parisians of all ages flock in all weather. Be it jogging, practising t'ai chi, gossiping with girlfriends on one of the garden's signature sage-green chairs, reading or romancing, the Jardin du Luxembourg is *the* voyeur's spot to peek on Parisians. Opening hours vary seasonally, opening sometime between 7.30am and 8.15am and closing sometime between 5pm and 10pm.

Urban **orchards** hang heavy with dozens of apple varieties in the southern part of the *jardin* (garden). Bees have produced honey in the nearby **Rucher du Luxembourg** since the 19th century; don't miss the annual Fête du Miel (Honey Festival), comprising two days of tasting and buying the aviary's sweet harvest in late September in the **Pavillon Davioud (55bis rue**

AMBROISE TÉZENAS

Fondation Cartier pour l'Art Contemporain (p196), building designed by Jean Nouvel

Tombeau de Napoléon 1er, Église du Dôme

RICHARD I'ANSON

⤷ IF YOU LIKE...

If you've already explored **Église St-Germain des Prés** (p197) venture to these lesser-known holy structures:

- **Église Notre Dame de l'Espérance** (Map p98; ☎ 01 40 21 49 39; 47 rue de la Roquette, 11e; 🕙 9am-5pm; Ⓜ Bastille) Head to the wonderful Church of Our Lady of Hope, designed by Bruno Legrand in 1997. Startling for both its modern design and its size (it stands 20m tall and is 11m wide), the interior is filled with all sorts of interesting elements and features, including Nicolas Alquin's *La Croix d'Espérance* (Cross of Hope) – made of an 18th-century oak beam and three gold squares representing the Trinity. Calligrapher Franck Lalou has etched fragments of the Scriptures onto the glass of the facade facing rue de la Roquette.

- **Église du Dôme** (Map p172; Hôtel des Invalides; 🕙 10am-7pm Jul & Aug, to 6pm Sep & Apr-Jun, to 5pm Oct-Mar) With its sparkling golden dome, this is one of the finest religious edifices erected under Louis XIV – it received the remains of Napoleon in 1840. The very extravagant **Tombeau de Napoléon 1er** (Napoleon's Tomb; 🕙 10am-6pm Apr-Sep, to 5pm Oct-Mar, closed 1st Mon of the month), in the centre of the church, comprises six coffins fitting into one another like a Russian *matryoshka* doll.

- **Chapelle Expiatoire** (Map p150; ☎ 01 44 32 18 00; www.monuments-nationaux.fr; square Louis XVI, 8e; adult/18-25yr €5/3.50, under 18yr free; 🕙 1-5pm Thu-Sat; ⓂSt-Augustin) The austere, neoclassical Atonement Chapel, opposite 36 rue Pasquier, sits atop the section of a cemetery where Louis XVI, Marie-Antoinette and many other victims of the Reign of Terror were buried after their executions in 1793. It was erected by Louis' brother, the restored Bourbon king Louis XVIII, in 1815.

ST-GERMAIN DES PRÉS & MONTPARNASSE

SIGHTS

OLIVIER CIRENDINI

Musée National Eugène Delacroix

⬋ MUSÉE NATIONAL EUGÈNE DELACROIX

The Eugène Delacroix Museum, in a courtyard off a leafy 'square', was the romantic artist's home and studio when he died in 1863, and contains many of his oils, watercolours, pastels and drawings. If you want to see his major works, such as *Liberty Leading the People,* visit the Musée du Louvre (p61) or the Musée d'Orsay (p177); here you'll find many of his more intimate works (eg *An Unmade Bed,* 1828) and his paintings of Morocco.

Things you need to know: Map p196; ☎ 01 44 41 86 50; www.musee-delacroix.fr; 6 rue de Furstemberg, 6e; adult/under 18yr €5/free, free for EU residents under 26yr, 1st Sun of month free; ☷ 9.30am-5pm Wed-Mon, to 5.30pm Sat & Sun Jun-Aug; Ⓜ Mabillon or St-Germain des Prés

d'Assas). This ornate pavilion is also the spot where green-fingered Parisians partake in gardening courses with the École d'Horticulture (64 bd St-Michel, 6e).

Luxembourg Garden offers all the delights of a Parisian childhood a century ago. At the octagonal Grand Bassin, 1920s toy sailboats can be rented (per 30/60 minutes €2/3.20) to sail on the water, and nearby ponies take tots for rides (€2.50). Complete the day with a romp around the kids' playground (adult/child/under 15 months €2.60/1.60/free; ☷ 10am–park close) – the green half is for kids aged seven to 12 years, the blue half for under-sevens – or a summertime waltz

on the old-fashioned carousel (merry-go-round).

FONDATION DUBUFFET Map p196
☎ 01 47 34 12 63; www.dubuffetfondation.com, in French; 137 rue de Sèvres, 6e; adult/under 10yr €6/free; ☷ 2-6pm Mon-Fri; Ⓜ Duroc
Situated in a lovely 19th-century *hôtel particulier* (private mansion) at the end of a courtyard, the foundation houses the collection of Jean Dubuffet (1901–85), chief of the Art Brut school (a term he himself coined to describe all works of artistic expression not officially recognised). Much of his work is incredibly modern and expressive.

MUSÉE ATELIER ZADKINE Map p196

☎ 01 55 42 77 20; www.zadkine.paris.fr, in French; 100bis rue d'Assas, 6e; admission free; ☽ 10am-6pm Tue-Sun

This museum covers the life and work of Russian cubist sculptor Ossip Zadkine (1890–1967), who arrived in Paris in 1908, and lived and worked in this cottage for almost 40 years. Zadkine produced an enormous catalogue of clay, stone, bronze and wood sculptures: one room displays figures he sculpted in contrasting walnut, pear, ebony, acacia, elm and oak.

SLEEPING

Excellent midrange hotels reign supreme in St-Germain: a particularly stylish crop of strikingly creative, designer boutique hotels is perfectly placed around the Vavin metro station between the Jardin du Luxembourg and Montparnasse. Predictably for such a well-heeled part of Paris, budget accommodation is seriously short-changed.

Montparnasse is an easy – and afford-able – area to plump for. East of Gare Montparnasse in the 14e, two- and three-star places stud rue Vandamme and rue de la Gaîté, though the latter is rife with sex shops and peep shows. The designer collection of boutique hotels around the Vavin metro station in the neighbouring 7e is as handy for Montparnasse as St-Germain.

HÔTEL RELAIS ST-GERMAIN

Map p196   Hotel €€€

☎ 01 43 29 12 05; www.hotel-paris-relais-saint -germain.com; 9 Carrefour de l'Odéon, 7e; s/d €220/285, ste €395; Ⓜ Odéon; 🛇 💻 📶

What rave reports this elegant four-star hotel with flowerboxes and baby-pink awning gets, and for good reason. Ceilings are beamed, furniture is antique and fabrics are floral (and very fine indeed) inside this 17th-century townhouse. Mix this with a chic contemporary air, ample artwork to admire and one of Paris' most talked-about bistros **Le Comptoir** (p204)

BRUCE BI

Musée Bourdelle (p196)

as next-door neighbour. Absolutely delicious, darling!

HÔTEL D'ANGLETERRE
Map p196   Hotel €€€

☎ 01 42 60 34 72; www.hotel-dangleterre.com; 44 rue Jacob, 6e; s €140, d €200-240, ste €320; Ⓜ St-Germain des Prés; 💻 📶
The loyal guests take breakfast in the courtyard of this former British Embassy, where the Treaty of Paris ending the American Revolution was signed, and where Hemingway once lodged (in room No 14 on 20 December 1921). Breakfast is included.

HÔTEL DES MARRONNIERS
Map p196   Hotel €€

☎ 01 43 25 30 60; www.hotel-marronniers.com; 21 rue Jacob, 6e; s €135, d €175-190, tr €220, q €260; Ⓜ St-Germain des Prés; 🎯 💻 📶
At the end of a small courtyard 30m from the main street, this 37-room hotel has a delightful conservatory leading on to a magical garden – a true oasis in the heart of St-Germain. From the 3rd floor up,

rooms ending in 1, 2 or 3 look on to the garden; the rooms on the two uppermost floors – the 5th and the 6th – have pretty views over the courtyard and the roofs of central Paris.

HÔTEL DELAMBRE Map p196   Hotel €€

☎ 01 43 20 66 31; www.delambre-paris-hotel.com; 35 rue Delambre, 14e; s €90, d €140-160; Ⓜ Montparnasse Bienvenüe; 🎯 💻 📶 ♿
This very attractive 30-room hotel just east of Gare Montparnasse takes wrought iron as a theme and uses it both in functional pieces (bed frames, lamps, shelving) and decorative items throughout. Room 7 has its own little terrace while rooms 1 and 2 look onto a small private courtyard. The writer André Breton (1896–1966) lived here in the 1920s. Wi-fi costs €4.50 per hour and parking is €11 per day.

HÔTEL LE CLÉMENT Map p196   Hotel €€

☎ 01 43 26 53 60; www.clement-moliere-paris-hotel.com; 6 rue Clément, 6e; d €126-148, tr €165; Ⓜ St-Germain des Prés; 🎯 💻

Jardin du Luxembourg (p198)

JONATHAN SMITH

Excellent value for the style and tranquillity it offers, the Clément has 28 stylish rooms, some of which overlook the Marché St-Germain (eg room 100). Note though that the rooms on the very top floor have sloping ceilings. The people who run the hotel clearly know what they're doing; it's been in the same family for over a century.

HÔTEL DANEMARK
Map p196   Boutique Hotel €€

☎ 01 43 26 93 78; www.hoteldanemark.com; 21 rue Vavin, 6e; d €110-178; Ⓜ Vavin; 🔀 ▣
This scrumptious boutique hotel southwest of the Jardin du Luxembourg has 15 tastefully furnished rooms and eclectic contemporary decor contrasting with ancient stone walls. Public areas and its corner rooms are full of vibrantly coloured furniture and objects that match and contrast. The bedrooms are well soundproofed and of a generous size (minimum 20 sq metres) for a boutique hotel in central Paris, and all have bathtubs. Book online to get the best rates.

HÔTEL DU LYS Map p196   Hotel €€
☎ 01 43 26 97 57; www.hoteldulys.com; 23 rue Serpente, 6e; s €100, d €105-120, tr €140; Ⓜ Odéon
Located in a 17th-century *hôtel particulier*, this 22-room midrange hotel has been in the same family for six decades. We love the beamed ceiling and the *chinoiserie* wallpaper in the lobby; rooms to go for include the blue-toned room 13 with its striped ceiling and two windows, or the darker (but more atmospheric) room 14 in terracotta and with rustic old furniture. Unusually rates include breakfast.

HÔTEL DE NESLE Map p196   Hotel €
☎ 01 43 54 62 41; www.hoteldenesleparis.com; 7 rue de Nesle, 6e; s €55-65, d €75-100; Ⓜ Odéon or Mabillon

The Nesle, a relaxed, colourfully decorated hotel in a quiet street west of place St-Michel, is such a fun place to stay. Most of its 20 rooms are painted with brightly coloured naive murals inspired by French literature. But its greatest asset is the huge (by Parisian standards) garden – a back yard really – accessible from the 1st floor, with pathways, trellis and even a small fountain. For a garden-facing room choose room 12.

PETIT PALACE HÔTEL Map p188   Hotel €
☎ 01 43 22 05 25; www.paris-hotel-petit -palace.com; 131 av du Maine, 14e; d €60-85, tr €99; Ⓜ Gaîté; ▣
A palace in the conventional sense it is not; an excellent-value two-star hotel run by the same family since the 1950s it is. On a main boulevard beaded with locally loved cafés and bistros, this hotel has 41 smallish but spotless rooms, several of which sleep three or four comfortably, making it a solid family choice. Look for an austere marble-clad facade cheered up with geraniums in the window. Wi-fi costs €4.50 per hour and parking is €11 per day.

EATING

Rue St-André des Arts and its continuation, rue du Buci, are lined with places to dine as lightly or lavishly as your heart desires, as is the stretch between Église St-Sulpice and Église St-Germain des Prés (especially rue des Canettes, rue Princesse and rue Guisarde). Quintessential Parisian bistros abound here.

Since the 1920s, the area around bd du Montparnasse has been one of the city's premier avenues for enjoying Parisian café life, though younger Parisians deem the place somewhat *démodé* and touristy these days. Glam it's not. But it does boast a handful of legendary brasseries and cafés which warrant a culinary visit.

Le Petit Zinc

SGA/IMAGEBROKER

LA COUPOLE

Map p196   French, Brasserie €€€

☎ 01 43 20 14 20; www.lacoupoleparis.com, in
French; 102 bd du Montparnasse, 14e; starters
€6.50-20, mains €12.50-35; ☷ 8.30am-1am Sun-
Thu, to 1.30am Fri & Sat; Ⓜ Vavin

The famous mural-covered columns
(painted by such artists as Brancusi and
Chagall), dark wood panelling and soft
lighting have hardly changed an iota since
the days of Sartre, Soutine, Man Ray, the
dancer Josephine Baker and other regulars. The reason for visiting this enormous,
450-seat brasserie, designed by the Solvet
brothers and opened in 1927, is more history than gastronomy. You can book for
lunch, but you'll have to queue for dinner;
though there's always breakfast. The more
expensive *menus* are available until 6pm
and after 10.30pm.

LE COMPTOIR DU RELAIS

Map p196   French, Bistro €€€

☎ 01 44 27 07 97; 9 Carrefour de l'Odéon, 6e;
starters/mains €15/20, menu €50; ☷ lunch &
dinner to 12.30am; Ⓜ Odéon

Simply known as Le Comptoir (The
Counter) among the in crowd, this gourmet bistro has provoked a real stir ever
since it opened. The culinary handiwork
of top chef Yves Camdeborde, it cooks
up seasonal bistro dishes with a seriously
creative and gourmet twist – fancy asparagus and foie gras salad? Bagging a table at
lunchtime is just about doable providing
you're here at 12.30pm sharp, but forget
evening dining – more gastronomic than
at *midi* – unless you have a table reservation (weeks in advance for weekends).

LA CAGOUILLE

Map p188   French, Seafood €€

☎ 01 43 22 09 01; www.la-cagouille.fr; 10 place
Constantin Brancusi, 14e; starters €10-15, mains
€16-45, 2-/3-course menu €23/38; ☷ lunch &
dinner to 10.30pm; Ⓜ Gaîté

Chef Gérard Allemandou, one of the best
seafood cooks (and cookery book writers)
in Paris, gets rave reviews for his fish and
shellfish dishes at this café-restaurant opposite 23 rue de l'Ouest. The *menus* here
are exceptionally good value.

KGB Map p196   Fusion €€

☎ 01 46 33 00 85; http://zekitchen-galerie.fr, in French; 25 rue des Grands Augustins, 6e; pasta/mains €21/28, lunch menus €27 & €34; ☺ lunch & dinner to 11pm Tue-Sat; Ⓜ St-Michel

KGB (as in 'Kitchen Galerie Bis') is the latest creation of William Ledeuil of Ze Kitchen Galerie fame. Overtly art gallery in feel, this small dining space plays to a hip crowd with its casual platters of Asian-influenced *hors d'œvres* (€16/19/22 for 4/5/6), creative pastas (*orecchiette* studded with octopus, squid and crab the day we were here) and marmite-cooked meats. Roast pigeon with ginger and cranberry condiment anyone?

CRÈMERIE RESTAURANT POLIDOR
Map p196   French €€

☎ 01 43 26 95 34; http://restaurantpolidor.info, in French; 41 rue Monsieur le Prince, 6e; starters €4.50-17, mains €11-22, menus €22 & €32; ☺ lunch & dinner to 12.30am Mon-Sat, to 11pm Sun; Ⓜ Odéon

A meal at this quintessentially Parisian *crèmerie-restaurant* is like a trip to Victor Hugo's Paris: the restaurant and its decor date from 1845 and everyone knows about it (read: touristy). Still, *menus* of tasty, family-style French cuisine ensure a never-ending stream of punters eager to sample *bœuf bourguignon*, *blanquette de veau à l'ancienne* (veal in white sauce) and the most famous *tarte Tatin* in Paris! Expect to wait. No credit cards.

LE PETIT ZINC
Map p196   French, Brasserie €€

☎ 01 42 86 61 00; www.petit-zinc.com, in French; 11 rue St-Benoît, 6e; starters/mains €15/30, 2-course lunch €20.30; ☺ noon-2am; Ⓜ St-Germain des Prés

Not a 'little bar' but a wonderful, large brasserie serving mountains of fresh seafood, traditional French cuisine and regional specialities from the southwest in true art nouveau splendour. The term brasserie is used loosely here; you'll feel more like you're in a starred restaurant, so book ahead and dress accordingly.

CHEZ ALLARD Map p196   French, Bistro €€

☎ 01 43 26 48 23; 41 rue St-André des Arts, 6e; starters €8-20, mains €25, menu €34; ☺ lunch & dinner to 11.30pm Mon-Sat; Ⓜ St-Michel

A definite Left Bank favourite is this charming bistro where the staff couldn't be kinder or more professional – even during its enormously busy lunchtime. And the food is superb. Try a dozen snails, some *cuisses de grenouilles* (frogs' legs) or *un poulet de Bresse* (France's most legendary chicken, from Burgundy) for two. Enter from 1 rue de l'Éperon.

SAWADEE Map p188   Thai €€

☎ 01 45 77 68 90; 53 av Émile Zola, 15e; menus €15 (lunch) & €21-33; ☺ lunch & dinner to 10.30pm Mon-Sat; Ⓜ Charles Michels

For 20 years this well-known restaurant has been bidding *sawadee* (welcome) to Thai-food lovers – and is in most guidebooks to prove it. The decor is rather impersonal, but the sophisticated cuisine more than makes up for it. Twist your tongue around prawn or chicken soup flavoured with lemon grass, spicy beef salad (a real treat), satay sticks (chicken, beef, lamb and pork) with peanut sauce and other classic dishes of Siam.

LE CRISTAL DE SEL Map p188   French €€

☎ 01 42 50 35 29; www.lecristaldesel.fr, in French; 13 rue Mademoiselle, 15e; starters €10-15, mains €20-28, 2-/3-course lunch menu €15/18; ☺ lunch & dinner to 10pm Tue-Sat; Ⓜ Commerce

The raved-about stage of young rising chef Karl Lopez, this modern bistro has a distinct kitchen feel with its small brightly lit white walls, white-painted beams and gaggle of busy chefs behind the bar. The only decorative feature is a candle-lit crystal of rose-tinted salt on each table – a sure sign that food is what The Salt Crystal is all about. Lopez's *tarte à la bergamote fraîche meringuée* (lemon meringue pie) – divine – has to be the zestiest in Paris. Reservations essential.

LES ÉDITEURS Map p196   French, Café €€
☎ 01 43 26 67 76; 4 Carrefour de l'Odéon, 6e; starters €10-18, mains €18-25; ⏲ 8am-2am; Ⓜ Odéon

This place goes to great lengths to describe itself as café, restaurant, library, bar and *salon de thé,* but for us it's a place to eat and/or people-watch. It is intended for writers – there are more than 5000 books on hand and it's done up to feel like a slightly faded and dingy library – but it has floor-to-ceiling windows through which you can watch the Germanopratin (yes, there is an adjective for St-Germain des Prés) goings-on. Breakfasts and Sunday brunch are big here.

BOUILLON RACINE
Map p196   French, Classical €€
☎ 01 44 32 15 60; 3 rue Racine, 6e; starters €6.50-14.50, mains €15.50-28, menus €14.90 (lunch) & €29.50; ⏲ lunch & dinner to 11pm; Ⓜ Cluny La Sorbonne

We've never seen anything quite like this 'soup kitchen', built in 1906 to feed market workers. A gorgeous art nouveau palace with mirrored walls, floral motifs and ceramic tiling, the interior is a positive delight. Oh, and the food? Wholly classic inspired by age-old recipes such as roast snails, *caille confite* (preserved quail) and lamb shank with liquorice. Finish off your foray in gastronomic history with an old-fashioned sherbet.

CHEZ HANAFOUSA
Map p196   Japanese €€
☎ 01 43 26 50 29; 4 passage de la Petite Boucherie, 6e; menus €13.50 (lunch) & €29-72; ⏲ lunch & dinner to 11.30pm; Ⓜ St-Germain des Prés

Dining at this understated Japanese restaurant is a spectacular choice guaranteed to impress. Sit around a steely-topped U-shaped 'hot table' and watch fish, meat, spices, vegetables and herbs chopped, sliced, ground and flamed before your very eyes – all the set menus (bar the quick, good-value miso-and-sushi lunchtime choice) feature *teppanjaki* (hot-plate cooking). End the show with a flaming vanilla ice-cream fritter or less flamboyant green-tea cheesecake with wasabi ice-cream.

BRASSERIE LIPP
Map p196   French, Brasserie €€
☎ 01 45 48 53 91; www.brasserie-lipp.fr; 151 bd St-Germain, 6e; starters €10-15, mains €15-25; ⏲ 9am-1am; Ⓜ St- Germain des Prés

Politicians rub shoulders with intellectuals, while waiters in black waistcoats, bow ties and long white aprons serve brasserie favourites like *choucroute garnie* and *jarret de porc aux lentilles* (pork knuckle with lentils) at this celebrated wood-panelled café, opened by Léonard Lipp in 1880.

KIM ANH Map p188   Vietnamese €€
☎ 01 45 79 40 96; 49 av Émile Zola, 15e; starters €13-15, mains €20, menu €34; ⏲ dinner to 10.30pm Tue-Sun; Ⓜ Charles Michels

A travel guide hotspot situated across the road from Sawadee, this place is the antithesis of the typically Parisian canteen-style Vietnamese restaurant. Kim Anh greets its customers with tapestries, white tablecloths, fresh flowers and extraordinarily fresh and flavoursome food, all elaborately presented. The *émincé de*

WILL SALTER

Bouillon Racine

bœuf à la citronnelle (beef with lemon grass) is a skilful combination of flavours, but the true sensation is the caramelised langoustine.

FISH LA BOISSONNERIE

Map p196   Seafood €€

☎ 01 43 54 34 69; 69 rue de Seine, 6e; starters/mains €8/15; ⏲ lunch & dinner to 10.45pm Tue-Sun; Ⓜ Mabillon

A hybrid of a Mediterranean place run by a New Zealander (of Cosi fame; p208) and an American, with its rustic communal seating and bonhomie, Fish has surely taken its cue from London, where such places have been a mainstay for several years. The wine selection is excellent – it's almost as much a wine bar as a restaurant – and the wonderful old mosaic on the front facade is a delight.

DA ROSA

Map p196   Mediterranean, Delicatessen €

☎ 01 45 21 41 30; www.restaurant-da-rosa.com; 62 rue de Seine, 6e; cheese, meat & fish platters €10-30; ⏲ 10am-11pm; Ⓜ Mabillon

Gourmets can spend a little or a lot at this modern *épicerie* (delicatessen) and *cantine* (hip, casual eating place), a real foodie address with its vast array of savoury hams, salamis, pâtés, caviars, cheeses and other unique savoury products from France, Spain, Portugal and Italy. Be it foie gras, smoked salmon, Iberian ham or marble-cooled *lardo di colonnata* from Carrara, 'only the best' is very much the philosophy at Da Rosa. Everything on the menu can be bought to take home.

FIORI Map p188   Italian, Pizza €

☎ 01 45 54 90 90; 52-56 rue Balard, 15e; pizza €9-12, pasta €10-16; ⏲ lunch & dinner; Ⓜ Balard

Breadsticks, spiced olive oil…you'll find all the trademarks of a good Italian at this down-to-earth address, smart on the edge of Parc André-Citroën. Come lunchtime it gets packed with hungry suits from nearby offices and families out for a romp in the park. Grab a seat on its sunny pavement terrace and dig into a Real McCoy pizza.

LA CABANE À HUÎTRES

Map p196   French, Oysters €

☎ 01 45 49 47 27; 4 rue Antoine Bourdelle, 14e; starters €10-17, dozen oysters €13-17, menu €18; ☻ lunch & dinner Wed-Sat; Ⓜ Montparnasse-Bienvenüe

One of Paris' best oyster addresses; this earthy wooden-styled *cabane* (cabin) with just nine sought-after tables is the pride and joy of fifth-generation oyster farmer Fançis Dubourg, who splits his week between the capital and his oyster farm in Arcachon on the Atlantic Coast. Geared totally towards dedicated gourmets, the fixed menu features a dozen oysters, foie gras de Landes (from Gascony in southwest France) or *magret de canard fumé* (smoked duck breast) followed by Pyreneen *brebis* cheese or sweet *canelé* (a rum, vanilla and cinnamon-spiced cake).

CUISINE DE BAR Map p196   Sandwiches €

☎ 01 45 48 45 69; 8 rue du Cherche Midi, 6e; breakfast €7.60-12, lunch €12; ☻ 8.30am-7pm Tue-Sat; Ⓜ Sèvres-Babylone; ⓦ

As next-door-neighbour to one of Paris' most famous bakers, this is not any old sandwich bar. Rather, it is a chic spot to lunch between designer boutiques on open sandwiches cut from that celebrated Poilâne bread and fabulously filled with gourmet goodies such as foie gras, smoked duck, gooey St-Marcellin cheese and Bayonne ham. Its breakfasts and afternoon teas are equally lush.

COSI Map p196   Sandwich Bar €

☎ 01 46 33 35 36; 54 rue de Seine, 6e; sandwich menus €10-15; ☻ noon-11pm; Ⓜ Odéon

An institution in the 6th for a quick cheap eat in or out, Cosi could easily run for Paris' most imaginative sandwich maker: with sandwich names like Stonker, Tom Dooley and Naked Willi, how could you expect otherwise? Classical music playing in the background and homemade Italian bread, still warm from the oven, only adds to Cosi's natural sex appeal which, incidentally, is of New Zealand origin.

SELF-CATERING

Food shops cluster on rue de Seine and rue de Buci. The covered **Marché St-Germain** (Map p196; 4-8 rue Lobineau, 6e; ☻ 8.30am-1pm & 4-7.30pm Tue-Sat, 8.30am-1pm Sun; Ⓜ Mabillon) and organic **Marché Raspail** (Map p196) have huge arrays of fine fresh produce.

DRINKING

LE ZÉRO DE CONDUITE Map p196   Bar

☎ 01 46 34 26 35; www.zerodeconduite.fr, in French; 14 rue Jacob, 6e; ☻ 8.30pm-1.30am Mon-Thu, 6pm-2am Fri & Sat, 9pm-1am Sun; Ⓜ Odéon

Originality, if nothing else, ensures that this *bijou* drinking hole, in the house where Richard Wagner lived briefly in the 1840s, gets a mention. Serving cocktails in *biberons* (baby bottles) and throwing *concours de grimaces* (face-pulling competitions), it goes all out to rekindle your infancy. Bizarre, yes, but obviously some enjoy sucking cocktails through a teat. Board games, dice, cards and Trivial Pursuit complete the playful scene. Advance table reservations are highly recommended.

PRESCRIPTION COCKTAIL CLUB

Map p196   Cocktail Bar

☎ 01 46 34 67 73; 23 rue Mazarine, 6e; ☻ 7pm-2am Mon-Thu, 7pm-4am Fri & Sat; Ⓜ Odéon

With bowler and flat-top hats as lampshades and a 1930s-speakeasy–New York air, this cocktail club really is an address to safeguard. It's all very Parisian-cool and getting past the doorman can be tough, but once in it's friendliness and old-fashioned cocktails all round.

CAFÉ DE FLORE Map p196   Café

☎ 01 45 48 55 26; 172 bd St-Germain, 6e;
⏰ 7.30am-1.30am; Ⓜ St-Germain des Prés

The red upholstered benches, mirrors and marble walls at this art deco landmark café haven't changed much since the days when the likes of Jean-Paul Sartre, Simone de Beauvoir, Albert Camus and Pablo Picasso wagged their chins here. Its busy terrace draws in lunching ladies, posh business-folk and foreigners in search of the past.

LES DEUX MAGOTS Map p196   Café

☎ 01 45 48 55 25; 170 bd St-Germain, 6e;
⏰ 7am-1am; Ⓜ St-Germain des Prés

This erstwhile literary haunt dates from 1914 and is known as the favoured hang-out of Sartre, Hemingway and André Breton. It's touristy, but just once you can give in to the nostalgia and sit on this inimitable terrace where passing celebrities, retiring philosophers and remnants of noblesse sip its famous shop-made hot chocolate.

CAFÉ LA PALETTE Map p196   Café, Bar

☎ 01 43 26 68 15; 43 rue de Seine, 6e; ⏰ 8am-2am Mon-Sat; Ⓜ Mabillon

In the heart of gallery land, this *fin-de-siècle* café and erstwhile stomping ground of Paul Cézanne and Georges Braque attracts a grown-up set of fashion people and local art dealers. Its summer terrace is beautiful.

LE SELECT Map p196   Café

☎ 01 42 22 65 27; 99 bd du Montparnasse, 6e;
⏰ 7.30am-2.30am; Ⓜ Vavin

This café is a Montparnasse institution that has changed little since 1923. Students congregate in the early evening; regulars take over as the night wears on. *Tartines* made with Poilâne bread are a speciality.

LE ROSEBUD Map p196   Cocktail Bar

☎ 01 43 35 38 54; 11bis rue Delambre, 14e;
⏰ 7pm-2am; Ⓜ Edgar Quinet or Vavin

Enjoy an expertly mixed Champagne cocktail or whisky sour amid the quiet

OLIVER STREWE

Café de Flore

Café La Palette (p209)

elegance of polished wood and aged leather.

LA CAVE DE L'OS À MOËLLE

Map p188   Wine Bar

☎ 01 45 57 28 28; rue Vasco de Gama, 15e; ⓨ noon-3pm & 7.30-10.30pm Tue-Sat, noon-4pm & 7.30-10.30pm Sun; Ⓜ Lourmel

Warming the cockles with a *vin chaud* (mulled wine) and chunk of *pain d'épice* (honey spiced bread) around a wine-barrel-turned-table on the pavement outside this cosy wine bar is a real winter delight. Should hunger pains strike, its lunchtime *formule à buffet* (€22.50) is excellent value.

ENTERTAINMENT & ACTIVITIES

LE WAGG Map p196   Clubbing

☎ 01 55 42 22 00; www.wagg.fr, in French; 62 rue Mazarine, 6e; admission incl 1 drink Fri & Sat €12, Sun €12, before/after midnight Thu free/€10; ⓨ 11pm-6am Thu-Sat, 3pm-midnight Sun; Ⓜ Odéon

The Wagg is a UK-style Conran club (associated with the popular Fabric in London), beautifully dressed in slick fixtures and contemporary design, but with a somewhat stifled vibe. Last time we looked it had been taken over by the salsa craze – indeed, it opens early on Sunday to host a two-hour salsa class followed by *une soirée 100% cubaine*.

LUCINAIRE Map p196   Classical Music

☎ 01 42 22 26 50, reservations 01 45 44 57 34; www.lucinaire.fr, in French; 53 rue Notre Dame des Champs, 6e; admission Sun-Thu €12, Fri & Sat €14, under 25yr €10; ⓨ box office 11.30am-12.30pm & 1.30pm-10.30pm, restaurant & bar 10am-11pm; Ⓜ Notre Dame des Champs

Sunday-evening concerts are a permanent fixture on the impressive repertoire of this dynamic Centre National d'Art et d'Essai (National Arts Centre) sandwiched between the Jardin du Luxembourg and Montparnasse. Be it classical guitar, baroque, French *chansons* or oriental music, these weekly concerts starting at 6.30pm are a real treat.

SHOPPING

The northern wedge of the 6e between Église St-Germain des Prés and the Seine is a dream to mooch with its bijou art galleries, antique shops, stylish vintage clothes and midrange fashion boutiques (Ventilo, Cacherel, Penny Black, Vanessa Bruno, Joseph etc). Don't miss **Cour du Commerce St-André** (Map p196), an enchanting glass-covered passageway built in 1735 to link a pair of Jeu de Paume (old-style tennis) courts.

IVOIRE Map p196   Art & Antiques
☎ 01 43 54 71 09; 57 rue Bonaparte, 6e;
☽ 9am-noon & 2-6pm Tue-Fri; Ⓜ St-Germain des Prés
This family-run business dating from 1913 is a two-man team comprising father Pierre Heckmann (in his mid-80s) and son Jean-Pierre (apprenticed at age 14 and not far off from retirement himself). Sculpting and restoring ivory, bone and nacre is their trade, and their art is extraordinary. The workshop interior, last refitted in 1937, is original.

TEA & TATTERED PAGES
Map p196   Books & Comics
☎ 01 40 65 94 35; 24 rue Mayet, 6e; ☽ 11am-7pm Mon-Sat, noon-6pm Sun; Ⓜ Duroc
More than 15,000 volumes are squeezed onto two floors at this secondhand English-language bookshop with tearoom.

VILLAGE VOICE Map p196 Books & Comics
☎ 01 46 33 36 47; www.villagevoicebookshop.com; 6 rue Princesse, 6e; ☽ 2-7.30pm Mon, 10am-7.30pm Tue-Sat, noon-6pm Sun; Ⓜ Mabillon

With an excellent selection of contemporary North American fiction and European literature, lots of readings and helpful staff, the Village Voice is a favourite.

SHU UEMURA Map p196   Cosmetics
☎ 01 45 48 02 55; 176 bd St-Germain, 6e;
☽ 11am-8pm Sun-Wed, to midnight Thu & Fri;
Ⓜ St-Germain des Prés
Curly fake eyelashes, lime-marmalade lip gloss (yep, it's green), 71 shades of lipstick and badger-hair make-up brushes: this Japanese cosmetics boutique founded by the Hollywood make-up guru who painted Shirley MacLaine's face in the film *My Geisha* (1962) is extraordinary. Treat yourself to a 1½-hour lesson (€150) at its make-up school.

SGA/IMAGEBROKER
Jardin du Luxembourg (p198)

MARCHÉ AUX PUCES DE LA PORTE DE VANVES

Map p188   Flea Market

av Georges Lafenestre & av Marc Sangnier, 14e; 🕑 7am-6pm or later Sat & Sun; Ⓜ Porte de Vanves

The Porte de Vanves flea market is the smallest and, some say, friendliest of the lot. Av Georges Lafenestre has lots of 'curios' that don't quite qualify as antiques. Av Marc Sangnier is lined with stalls of new clothes, shoes, handbags and household items for sale.

PÂTISSERIE SADAHARU AOKI

Map p196   Food & Drink

☎ 01 45 44 48 90; www.sadaharuaoki.com; 35 rue de Vaugirard, 6e; 🕑 11am-7pm Tue-Sat, 10am-6pm Sun; Ⓜ Rennes or St-Sulpice

'Exquisite' fails to describe the creations of one of Paris' top pastry chefs, Tokyo-born Sadaharu Aoki. Too beautiful to eat, his gourmet works include 'eye-shadow' palettes, boxes of 72 different flavoured macaroons and green-tea chocolate. He also has a boutique in the **Latin Quarter** (Map p196; ☎ 01 45 35 36 80; 56 bd de Port Royal, 5e; 🕑 10am-7pm Tue-Sat, to 6pm Sun; Ⓜ Port Royal) and inside **Galeries Lafayette** (p161).

PIERRE HERMÉ Map p196   Food & Drink

☎ 01 43 54 47 77; www.pierreherme.com; 72 rue Bonaparte, 6e; 🕑 10am-7pm Sun-Fri, to 7.30pm Sat; Ⓜ Odéon or Luxembourg

It's the size of chocolate box but once in, your tastebuds will go wild. Pierre Hermé is one of Paris' top chocolatiers and his two boutiques are a veritable feast of perfectly presented petits fours, cakes, chocolate, nougats, macaroons and jam. His second **branch** (☎ 01 47 83 89 96; 185 rue Vaugirard, 15e; 🕑 10am-7pm Mon-Wed, to 7.30pm Thu-Sat, to 6pm Sun; Ⓜ Pasteur) is in the 15e arrondissement.

THE LATIN QUARTER

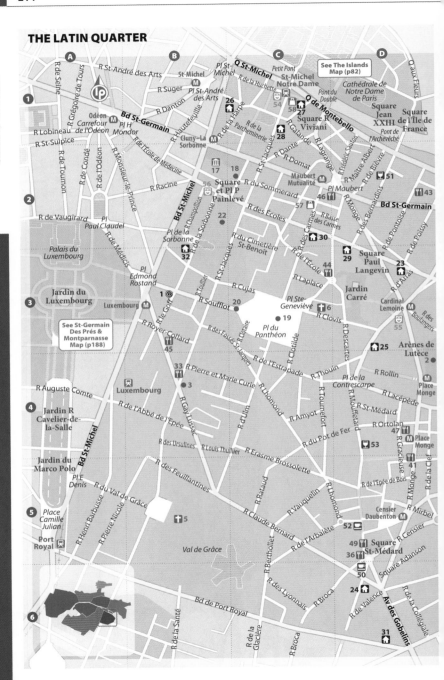

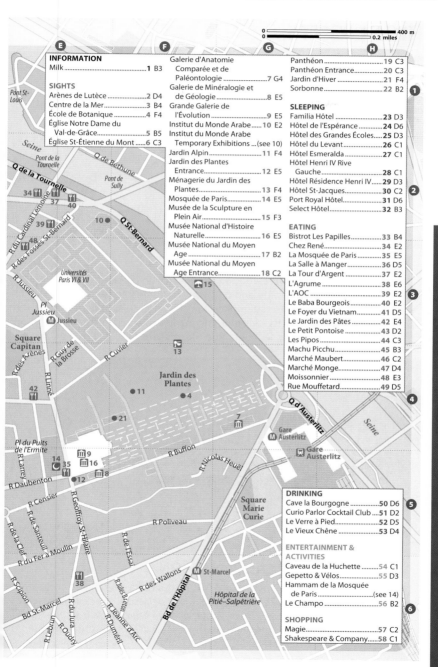

INFORMATION
Milk **1** B3

SIGHTS
Arènes de Lutèce **2** D4
Centre de la Mer **3** B4
École de Botanique **4** F4
Église Notre Dame du
  Val-de-Grâce **5** B5
Église St-Étienne du Mont **6** C3
Galerie d'Anatomie
  Comparée et de
  Paléontologie **7** G4
Galerie de Minéralogie et
  de Géologie **8** E5
Grande Galerie de
  l'Évolution **9** E5
Institut du Monde Arabe **10** E2
Institut du Monde Arabe
  Temporary Exhibitions ...(see 10)
Jardin Alpin **11** F4
Jardin des Plantes
  Entrance **12** E5
Ménagerie du Jardin des
  Plantes **13** F4
Mosquée de Paris **14** E5
Musée de la Sculpture en
  Plein Air **15** F3
Musée National d'Histoire
  Naturelle **16** E5
Musée National du Moyen
  Age **17** B2
Musée National du Moyen
  Age Entrance **18** C2
Panthéon **19** C3
Panthéon Entrance **20** C3
Jardin d'Hiver **21** F4
Sorbonne **22** B2

SLEEPING
Familia Hôtel **23** D3
Hôtel de l'Espérance **24** D6
Hôtel des Grandes Écoles **25** D3
Hôtel du Levant **26** C1
Hôtel Esmeralda **27** C1
Hôtel Henri IV Rive
  Gauche **28** C1
Hôtel Résidence Henri IV.......**29** D3
Hôtel St-Jacques **30** C2
Port Royal Hôtel **31** D6
Select Hôtel **32** B3

EATING
Bistrot Les Papilles **33** B4
Chez René **34** E2
La Mosquée de Paris **35** E5
La Salle à Manger **36** D5
La Tour d'Argent **37** E2
L'Agrume **38** E6
L'AOC **39** E2
Le Baba Bourgeois **40** E2
Le Foyer du Vietnam **41** D5
Le Jardin des Pâtes **42** E4
Le Petit Pontoise **43** D2
Les Pipos **44** C3
Machu Picchu **45** B3
Marché Maubert **46** C2
Marché Monge **47** D4
Moissonnier **48** E3
Rue Mouffetard **49** D5

DRINKING
Cave la Bourgogne **50** D6
Curio Parlor Cocktail Club **51** D2
Le Verre à Pied **52** D5
Le Vieux Chêne **53** D4

**ENTERTAINMENT &
ACTIVITIES**
Caveau de la Huchette **54** C1
Gepetto & Vélos **55** D3
Hammam de la Mosquée
  de Paris ....(see 14)
Le Champo **56** B2

SHOPPING
Magie **57** C2
Shakespeare & Company **58** C1

HIGHLIGHTS

↘ FOODIE HEAVEN

Ogle the fishmongers' shiny seafood slapped on ice and greengrocers' delicately displayed fruit and veggies, try and find your favourite cheese (we dare you to purchase just one wedge), contemplate the butchers' selection and inhale the scent of fresh flowers; with its early morning market and medley of stall-clad shop fronts with fresh produce piled high, **Rue Mouffetard** (p231) begs a meander.

↘ THE NEOCLASSICAL PANTHÉON

Let your soul soar inside the **Panthéon** (p223). Built as a church and completed the year the Revolution broke out, this sublime neoclassical structure now serves as a mausoleum for *'les grands hommes de l'époque de la liberté francaise'* (great men of the era of French liberty), though women like Marie Curie are buried here, too.

THE LATIN QUARTER

HIGHLIGHTS

↘ INSTITUTE OF THE ARAB WORLD

Savour the exterior as much as the interior of the **Institut du Monde Arabe** (p221), a stunning example of 1980s architecture. A motorised fusion of Arab and Western architectural styles, no Parisian facade is more extraordinary or clever. Inside, temporary exhibits represent the exterior's cultures.

↘ REPLENISH IN THE HAMMAM

Get a taste of multicultural Paris at the city's 1920s **Mosquée de Paris** (central mosque; p221). Indulge in a steam bath in its *hammam*, pamper yourself with a massage or sip fresh mint tea and feast on couscous in the fabulous North African restaurant – all within the mosque's ornate Moorish walls.

↘ RELAX AT THE SORBONNE

Chapelle de la Sorbonne, the **university's** (p223) gold-domed church where the mortal remains of Cardinal Richelieu lie buried, is the standout feature of this pretty 'village'. After exploring, take a breather on the campus' tranquil square, **Place de la Sorbonne**, and watch the *crème de la crème* of academia pass by.

1 Variety of cheeses at rue Mouffetard market (p231); 2 Late afternoon light on the Panthéon (p223); 3 Institut du Monde Arabe (p221); 4 Mosquée de Paris (p221); 5 Sorbonne (p223) university at night

LATIN QUARTER LITERARY LOOP WALK

Paris' reputation for liberal thought and relaxed morals lured writers and artists in the 1920s. This walking tour starts at Metro Cardinal Lemoine and ends at Boulevard St-Michel. It covers roughly 3km and takes about one to 1½ hours.

❶ JAMES JOYCE'S FLAT

Start at Cardinal Lemoine metro station. Walk southwest along rue du Cardinal Lemoine, peering down the passageway at No 71. Irish writer James Joyce (1882–1941) lived (and finished editing *Ulysses)* in the courtyard flat at the back (marked 'E') when he arrived in Paris in 1921.

❷ ERNEST HEMINGWAY'S APARTMENT

Further south at 74 rue du Cardinal Lemoine is the apartment where Ernest Hemingway (1899–1961) lived with his first wife, Hadley, from January 1922 until August 1923. Just below was Bal au Printemps, a popular *bal musette* (dancing club) that served as the model for the one where Jake Barnes meets Brett Ashley in Hemingway's *The Sun Also Rises.*

❸ PAUL VERLAINE'S GARRET

Hemingway lived on rue du Cardinal Lemoine, but wrote in a top-floor garret of a hotel round the corner at 39 rue Descartes, the very hotel where the poet Paul Verlaine (1844–96) died. Ignore the incorrect plaque.

❹ PLACE DE LA CONTRESCARPE

Rue Descartes runs south into place de la Contrescarpe, now a well-scrubbed square with four Judas trees and a fountain, but once a 'cesspool' (said Hemingway), especially Café des Amateurs at No 2-4, now Café Delmas.

❺ GEORGE ORWELL'S BOARDING HOUSE

Rue Mouffetard (from *mofette,* meaning 'skunk') runs south of place de la Contrescarpe. Turn right onto rue du Pot de Fer where in 1928 George Orwell (1903–50) stayed in a cheap boarding house above No 6 while working as a dishwasher. Read about it and the street, which he called 'rue du Coq d'Or' (Street of the Golden Rooster), in *Down and Out in Paris and London* (1933).

❻ PLACE DU PANTHÉON

Turn north onto rue Tournefort (the street where much of Balzac's novel *Père Goriot* takes place) and go left into rue de l'Estrapade. From

THE LATIN QUARTER LITERARY LOOP WALK

0 ——————— 400 m
0 ——————— 0.2 miles

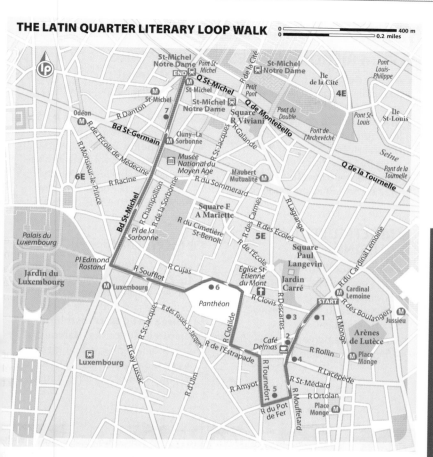

here follow Hemingway's own directions provided in *A Moveable Feast* as he made his way to a favourite café on place St-Michel. Turn north onto rue Clotilde and walk along the eastern side of vast place du Panthéon to the corner of rue Clovis. Just around the corner on rue Clovis is **Église St-Étienne du Mont** (p224).

❼ BOULEVARD ST-MICHEL

Continue around the northern edge of place du Panthéon and walk west along rue Soufflot. Turn right onto bd St-Michel, past the **Musée National du Moyen Age** (p224). The cafés on place St-Michel were taken over by tourists decades ago, but **Shakespeare & Company** (p233) is around the corner at 37 rue de la Bûcherie.

BEST...

⬐ KID-FRIENDLY VENUES

- **Arènes de Lutèce** (p224) Watch *boules* and *pétanque* in an ancient amphitheatre.
- **Grande Galerie de l'Évolution** (opposite) Play safari in Paris: this Natural History Museum gallery is a big must for kids.
- **Ménagerie du Jardin des Plantes** (p222) The zoo at the Jardin de Plantes.

⬐ MULTICULTURAL CUISINE

- **Le Foyer Du Vietnam** (p231) A warm bowl of *pho* in simple surrounds.
- **Machu Picchu** (p231) Peruvian fare at bargain prices.
- **La Mosquée de Paris** (p229) North African *tajine* inside a mosque.

⬐ SHOPPING

- **Rue Mouffetard** (p231) One of the most engaging market streets in Paris.
- **Magie** (p234) Legend has it this is the world's oldest magic shop.
- **Shakespeare & Company** (p233) A legend in its own time; browse the packed shelves of the city's most famous English-language bookshop just across the river from Notre Dame.

⬐ MUSEUMS

- **Musée National du Moyen Age** (p224) Time travel back to the Middle Ages – the gardens at this museum are particularly enchanting.
- **Musée National d'Histoire Naturelle** (opposite) Natural history from elephants to minerals.
- **Centre de la Mer** (p225) Oceanography exhibits and aquariums.

Souvenir shop, rue Mouffetard (p231)

DISCOVER THE LATIN QUARTER

There is no better strip to see, smell and taste the Quartier Latin (Latin Quarter), 5e, than rue Mouffetard, a thriving market street that is something of a local mecca with its titillating line-up of patisseries, *fromageries* (cheese shops) and fishmongers, interspersed by the odd *droguerie-quincaillerie* (hardware store) – easily spotted by the jumble of laundry baskets, buckets etc piled on the pavement in front.

The centre of Parisian higher education since the Middle Ages, the Latin Quarter is so-called because conversation between students and professors was in Latin until the Revolution. Academia remains a focal point of life – the Sorbonne is here – though its near monopoly on Parisian academic life is not what it was. But bury your nose in one of the quarter's late-opening bookshops, linger in a café, eat cheap in its abundance of budget restaurants or clink drinks during a dozen different happy hours and there will almost certainly be a student or academic affiliated with the Sorbonne sitting next to you.

SIGHTS

MUSÉE NATIONAL D'HISTOIRE NATURELLE

☎ 01 40 79 30 00; www.mnhn.fr; 57 rue Cuvier, 5e; Ⓜ Censier Daubenton or Gare d'Austerlitz

Housed in three buildings on the southern edge of the Jardin des Plantes, the National Museum of Natural History was created in 1793 and became a site of significant scientific research in the 19th century.

A highlight for kids: life-sized elephants, tigers and rhinos play safari in the **Grande Galerie de l'Évolution** (Great Gallery of Evolution; 36 rue Geoffroy St-Hilaire, 5e; adult/4-13yr €7/5, permanent collection free for EU residents under 26yr; ☺ 10am-6pm Wed-Mon), where imaginative exhibits on evolution and humanity's effect on the global ecosystem, including global warming, fill 6000 sq metres.

Giant natural crystals dance with sunlight in the **Galerie de Minéralogie et de Géologie** (Mineralogy & Geology Gallery; 36 rue Geoffroy St-Hilaire; adult/4-13yr €8/6; ☺ 10am-6pm Wed-Mon).

Displays on comparative anatomy and palaeontology (the study of fossils) fill the **Galerie d'Anatomie Comparée et de Paléontologie** (2 rue Buffon; adult/4-13yr €7/5, free for EU residents under 26yr; ☺ 10am-5pm Mon & Wed-Fri, 10am-6pm Sat & Sun).

MOSQUÉE DE PARIS

☎ 01 45 35 97 33; www.mosquee-de-paris.org, in French; 2bis place du Puits de l'Ermite, 5e; adult/7-25yr €3/2; ☺ 9am-noon & 2-6pm Sat-Thu; Ⓜ Censier Daubenton or Place Monge

Paris' central mosque, with its striking 26m-high minaret, was built in 1926 in the ornate Moorish style popular at the time. Visitors must be modestly dressed and remove their shoes at the entrance to the prayer hall. The complex includes a North African–style **restaurant** (p229) and **hammam** (p233).

INSTITUT DU MONDE ARABE

☎ 01 40 51 38 38; www.imarabe.org; 1 place Mohammed V, 5e; Ⓜ Cardinal Lemoine or Jussieu

The Institute of the Arab World, set up by France and 20 Arab countries to promote

THE LATIN QUARTER

SIGHTS

Jardin des Plantes with Grande Galerie de l'Évolution in the background

↘ JARDIN DES PLANTES

Paris' 24-hectare botanical garden, founded in 1626 as a medicinal herb garden for Louis XIII, is idyllic to stroll or jog around. You'll find a **rosery, iris garden**, the Eden-like **Jardin d'Hiver** (Winter Garden) or **Serres** (Greenhouses), the **Jardin Alpin**, with 2000 mountainous plants; and the gardens of the **École de Botanique**, where students of the School of Botany 'practice' and green-fingered Parisians savvy up on horticultural techniques.

During the Prussian siege of Paris in 1870, most of the animals in the **Ménagerie du Jardin des Plantes** were eaten by starving Parisians. Though a recreational animal park, the medium-sized zoo dating to 1794 in the northern section of the garden does much research into the reproduction of rare and endangered species.

A two-day combined ticket covering all of the Jardin des Plantes' sights, including the park's mightily impressive **Grande Galerie de l'Évolution** (p221), costs adult/child €20/15.

Things you need to know: main garden (☎ 01 40 79 56 01, 01 40 79 54 79; rue Cuvier, 5e; 🕐 7.30am-7pm; Ⓜ Gare d'Austerlitz, Censier Daubenton or Jussieu); **Jardin Alpin** (Alpine Garden; admission Mon-Fri free, Sat & Sun adult/4-15yr/under 4yr €1/0.50/free; 🕐 8-4.40pm Mon-Fri, 1.30-6pm Sat, 1.30-6.30pm Sun Apr-Oct); **Ménagerie du Jardin des Plantes** (adult/4-15yr/under 4yr €8/6/free; 🕐 9am-6pm Mon-Sat, 9am-6.30pm Sun)

cultural contacts between the Arab world and the West, is housed in a highly praised building (1987) that successfully mixes modern and traditional Arab and Western elements. Thousands of *mushrabiyah* (or *mouche-arabies,* photo-electrically sensi-

tive apertures built into the glass walls), inspired by the traditional latticed-wood windows that let you see out without being seen, are opened and closed by electric motors in order to regulate the amount of light and heat that reach the interior of the building.

The institute hosts some fascinating **temporary exhibitions (enter at 1 rue des Fossés Bernard; adult/13-25yr/under 12yr €7/4/ free, parent accompanying child €5;** ☷ **10am-6pm Tue-Sun)**. Its permanent museum, closed for renovation since April 2010, will focus on painting a global vision of the Arab world through 9th- to 19th-century art and artisanship, instruments from astronomy and other fields of scientific endeavour in which Arab technology once led the world, contemporary Arab art and so forth.

PANTHÉON

☎ **01 44 32 18 00; www.monum.fr; place du Panthéon, 5e; adult/18-25yr €8/5, free for EU residents under 26yr, 1st Sun of month Oct-Mar free;** ☷ **10am-6.30pm Apr-Sep, to 6pm Oct-Mar;** Ⓜ **Luxembourg**

The domed landmark was commissioned by Louis XV around 1750 as an abbey church dedicated to Ste Geneviève in thanksgiving for his recovery from an illness, but due to financial and structural problems it wasn't completed until 1789 – not a good year for church openings in Paris. Two years later the Constituent Assembly turned it into a secular mausoleum and bricked up most of the windows.

The Panthéon is a superb example of 18th-century neoclassicism. It reverted to its religious duties two more times after the Revolution but has played a secular role ever since 1885, when God was evicted in favour of Victor Hugo. Among the crypt's 80 or so permanent residents are Voltaire, Jean-Jacques Rousseau, Louis Braille, Émile Zola and Jean Moulin. The first woman to be interred in the Panthéon was the two-time Nobel Prize-winner Marie Curie (1867–1934), reburied here (along with her husband, Pierre) in 1995.

SORBONNE

12 rue de la Sorbonne, 5e; Ⓜ **Luxembourg or Cluny-La Sorbonne**

The *crème de la crème* of academia flock to this distinguished university, one of the world's most famous. Founded in 1253 by Robert de Sorbon, confessor to Louis IX,

Grande Galerie de l'Évolution (p221)

KRZYSZTOF DYDYNSKI

THE LATIN QUARTER

SIGHTS

Église St-Étienne du Mont at sunset

↘ IF YOU LIKE...

If you are impressed by the famed **Panthéon** (p223), head to the lesser-known **Église St-Étienne du Mont** (Church of Mount St Stephen; ☎ 01 43 54 11 79; 1 place Ste-Geneviève, 5e; ☾ 8am-noon & 2-7pm Tue-Sat, 9am-noon & 2.30-7pm Sun; Ⓜ Cardinal Lemoine). Built between 1492 and 1655, this church contains Paris' only surviving **rood screen** (1535), separating the chancel from the nave; the others were removed during the late Renaissance because they prevented the faithful assembled in the nave from seeing the priest celebrate Mass. In the nave's southeastern corner, a chapel contains the **tomb of Ste Geneviève**. A highly decorated **reliquary** nearby contains all that is left of her earthly remains – a finger bone. Ste Geneviève, patroness of Paris, was born at Nanterre in AD 422 and turned away Attila the Hun from Paris in AD 451.

as a college for 16 impoverished theology students, the Sorbonne soon grew into a powerful body with its own government and laws. Today, it embraces most of the 13 autonomous universities – 35,500-odd students in all – created when the University of Paris was reorganised after the student protests of 1968.

MUSÉE NATIONAL DU MOYEN AGE

☎ 01 53 73 78 00; www.musee-moyenage.fr; 6 place Paul Painlevé, 5e; adult/18-25yr €8.50/6.50, free for EU residents under 26yr,

1st Sun of the month free; ☾ 9.15am-5.45pm Wed-Mon; Ⓜ Cluny-La Sorbonne or St-Michel The National Museum of the Middle Ages occupies both a *frigidarium* (cooling room), which holds remains of Gallo-Roman *thermes* (baths) dating from around AD 200, and the 15th-century **Hôtel des Abbés de Cluny**, Paris' finest example of medieval civil architecture.

ARÈNES DE LUTÈCE

49 rue Monge, 5e; admission free; ☾ 9am-9.30pm Apr-Oct, 8am-5.30pm Nov-Mar; Ⓜ Place Monge

The 2nd-century Roman amphitheatre, Lutetia Arena, once sat around 10,000 people for gladiatorial combats and other events. Found by accident in 1869 when rue Monge was under construction, it's now used by neighbourhood youths for playing football, and by old men for *boules* and *pétanque* (a variant on the game of bowls).

CENTRE DE LA MER

☎ 01 44 32 10 90; www.oceano.org, in French; Institut Océanographique, 195 rue St-Jacques, 5e; adult/3-12yr €5/2.50; ⏰ 10.30am-12.30pm & 1.30-5.30pm Mon-Fri; Ⓜ Luxembourg

France has a long history of success in the field of oceanography (think Jacques Cousteau and, well, Jules Verne), and the Sea Centre cruises through that science, as well as marine biology, via temporary exhibitions, aquariums, scale models and audiovisuals. Kids will love the aquariums and the audiovisuals.

SLEEPING

There are dozens of attractive two- and three-star hotels in the Seine-side Latin Quarter (5e arrondissement), particularly popular with students since the Middle Ages and visiting academics. This makes rooms hardest to find during conferences and seminars March to June and in October.

HÔTEL RÉSIDENCE HENRI IV   Hotel €€€

☎ 01 44 41 31 81; www.residencehenri4.com; 50 rue des Bernardins, 5e; d €230-340; Ⓜ Maubert Mutualité; 🍴 🖥 ♿

This exquisite late-19th-century hotel at the end of a quiet cul-de-sac near the Sorbonne has eight rooms and five two-room apartments – all with kitchenette (microwave, fridge, stove, crockery and cutlery). They are of a generous size – a minimum 17 sq metres for the rooms and 25 sq metres for the apartments – and all look out onto the street and leafy square, while the bathrooms all face a courtyard. Room 1 on the ground floor is wheelchair accessible. Rates vary widely; check the internet.

HÔTEL HENRI IV RIVE GAUCHE   Hotel €€

☎ 01 46 33 20 20; www.henri-paris-hotel.com; 9-11 rue St-Jacques, 5e; s/d/tr €159/185/210; Ⓜ St-Michel Notre Dame or Cluny-La Sorbonne; 🍴 🖥 📶 ♿

This three-star hotel with 23 rooms awash with antiques, old prints and fresh flowers is an oasis in the Latin Quarter just steps from Notre Dame and the Seine. Exuding a real air of 'country chic', the lobby with its 18th-century fireplace, terracotta tiles and portraits could almost be in a manor house in Normandy. Front rooms have stunning views of the Église St-Séverin and its buttresses. Rates are cheapest online.

SELECT HÔTEL   Boutique Hotel €€

☎ 01 46 34 14 80; www.selecthotel.fr; 1 place de la Sorbonne, 5e; d €164-205, tr €228-295; Ⓜ Cluny-La Sorbonne; 🍴 🖥 📶

Smack dab in the heart of the studenty Sorbonne area, the Select is a very Parisian art deco mini-palace, with an atrium and cactus-strewn winter garden, an 18th- century vaulted breakfast room and 67 stylish bedrooms. The rooms are not always as large as you'd hope for, but the design solutions are ingenious, making great use of a minimum of space. The 1920s-style cocktail bar with an attached 'library' just off the lobby is a delight.

THE LATIN QUARTER

SLEEPING

Musée National du Moyen Age (p224)

GLENN BEANLAND

HÔTEL ST-JACQUES   Hotel €€
☎ 01 44 07 45 45; www.hotel-saintjacques.com;
35 rue des Écoles, 5e; s €110, d €125-215, tr
€200; Ⓜ Maubert Mutualité; 🍴 💻 🤶 ⬚ ♿
This very stylish 36-room hotel has rooms
with balconies overlooking the Panthéon.
Audrey Hepburn and Cary Grant, who
filmed some scenes of *Charade* here in
the 1960s, would commend the mod cons
that complement the original 19th-century
details (trompe l'oeil ceilings that look like
cloud-filled skies, an iron staircase and so
on). The cabaret-themed breakfast room
and bowl of jelly beans in the lobby is a
welcome touch.

HÔTEL DES GRANDES
ÉCOLES   Hotel €€
☎ 01 43 26 79 23; www.hotel-grandes-ecoles.
com; 75 rue du Cardinal Lemoine, 5e; d €115-
140; Ⓜ Cardinal Lemoine or Place Monge;
💻 🤶 ♿
This wonderful, very welcoming 51-
room hotel just north of place de la
Contrescarpe has one of the loveliest situ-
ations in the Latin Quarter, tucked away
in a courtyard off a medieval street with
its own private garden. Choose a room in
one of three buildings but our favourites
are those in the garden annexe, especially
the five that are on the ground floor and
have direct access to the garden (rooms
29 to 33).

HÔTEL DU LEVANT   Hotel €€
☎ 01 46 34 11 00; www.hoteldulevant.com;
18 rue de la Harpe, 5e; s €76, d €103-170, tr
€180-230, q €250-270; Ⓜ Cluny-La Sorbonne or
St-Michel; 🍴 💻 🤶
It's hard to imagine anything more central
than this 47-room hotel in the heart of
the Latin Quarter; you'll never lack for a
kebab day or night. The lobby, done up in
yellows and reds, is warm and welcoming;
the breakfast room is nicely decorated
with a large *faux naïf* mural and lots of
19th-century fashion engravings. Rooms
are of a decent size, with furnishings two
steps beyond pure functional, and feature
modern bathrooms.

FAMILIA HÔTEL   Hotel €€

☎ 01 43 54 55 27; www.familiahotel.com;
11 rue des Écoles, 5e; s €86, d €97-127, tr/q
€149/176; Ⓜ Cardinal Lemoine; ⊠ ▯ ⊚
This very welcoming and well-situated
family-run hotel has sepia murals of
Parisian landmarks in most rooms and is
one of the most attractive 'almost budget'
options on this side of the Seine. Eight
rooms have little balconies, from which
you can catch a glimpse of Notre Dame.
We love the flower-bedecked window, the
lovely parquet floors and the complimen-
tary breakfast.

HÔTEL ESMERALDA   Hotel €€

☎ 01 43 54 19 20; www.hotel-esmeralda.fr;
4 rue St-Julien le Pauvre, 5e; s €75, d €90-110,
tr/q €130/150; Ⓜ St-Michel
Tucked away in a quiet street with million-
dollar views of Notre Dame (choose room
12!), this no-frills place is about as central
to the Latin Quarter as you're ever likely
to get. Its charm is no secret though, so
book at least two months in advance. At
these prices and location, the 19 rooms –

the three cheapest singles have washbasin only – are no great shakes, so expect
little beyond the picture-postcard view
through the window.

HÔTEL DE L'ESPÉRANCE   Hotel €

☎ 01 47 07 10 99; www.hoteldelesperance.fr;
15 rue Pascal, 5e; s/d €75/80; Ⓜ Censier Daubenton; ⊠ ▯ ⊚ ♿
An eclectic mix of B&W photos, paintings
and a rather intrusive flat-screen TV strew
the salon walls of this immaculately kept
38-room hotel, a couple of minutes' walk
south of lively rue Mouffetard. Furnishings
are *faux* antique: think floral canopy beds
with drapes to match. The couple who run
it are an absolute charm and very service orientated; grab ice for drinks in your
room from the downstairs ice-machine.

PORT ROYAL HÔTEL   Hotel €

☎ 01 43 31 70 06; www.hotelportroyal.fr; 8 bd
de Port Royal, 5e; s €41-89, d €52.50-89; Ⓜ Les
Gobelins; ♿
This 46-room hotel, owned and managed
by the same family since 1931, is one of

Hôtel des Grandes Écoles

MARTIN MOOS

those refreshingly unassuming one-star hotels that really doesn't yearn for any more stars. Its six floors are served by a lift, but the cheapest (washbasin-clad) rooms share a toilet and shower (buy a token for €2.50 at reception). Rooms are spotless and very quiet, especially those that peep down on a small glassed-in courtyard. Predictably, this value-for-money place is no secret, so book ahead. No credit cards.

EATING

From cheap-eat student haunts to chandelier-lit palaces loaded with history, the 5e arrondissement has something to suit every budget and culinary taste. Rue Mouffetard is famed for its food market and food shops, while its side streets, especially pedestrian rue du Pot au Fer, cook up some fine budget dining.

LA TOUR D'ARGENT

French, Classical €€€

☎ 01 43 54 23 31; www.latourdargent.com; 15 quai de la Tournelle, 5e; menus lunch/dinner €75/160; ⏱ lunch Wed-Sun, dinner to 9pm Tue-Sun; Ⓜ Cardinal Lemoine or Pont Marie

A much-vaunted riverside address, the Silver Tower is famous – for its *caneton* (duckling), Michelin stars that come and go, rooftop garden with Notre Dame view and fabulous history harking back to 1582. Its wine cellar is one of Paris' best, dining is dressy and exceedingly fine. Reserve eight to 10 days ahead for lunch, three weeks ahead for dinner. Buy fine food and accessories in its boutique opposite.

BISTROT LES PAPILLES

French, Bistro €€

☎ 01 43 25 20 79; www.lespapillesparis.com, in French; 30 rue Gay Lussac, 5e; 2-course menu Tue-Fri €22 & €24.50, 4-course menu €31; ⏱ lunch & dinner Tue-Sat; Ⓜ Luxembourg

This hybrid bistro, wine cellar and *épicerie* with sunflower-yellow facade is one of those fabulous dining experiences that packs out the place (reserve a few days in advance to guarantee a table). Dining is at simply dressed tables wedged beneath bottle-lined walls, and fare is market-driven: each weekday cooks up a different *marmite du marché* (€16). But what really sets it apart is its exceptional wine list. Taste over lunch then stock your own *cave* (wine cellar) at Les Papilles' *cave à vin*.

L'AGRUME

French, Bistro €€

☎ 01 43 31 86 48; 15 rue des Fossés St-Marcel, 5e; starters/mains €14/30, menus lunch €14 & €16, dinner €35; ⏱ lunch & dinner Tue-Sat; Ⓜ Censier-Daubenton

Lunching at this much vaunted, pocket-sized contemporary bistro on an unknown street on the Latin Quarter's southern fringe is magnificent value and a real gourmet experience. Snagging a table at L'Agrume – meaning 'Citrus Fruit' – is tough; reserve several days ahead.

L'AOC

French, Classical €€

☎ 01 43 54 22 52; www.restoaoc.com; 14 rue des Fossés St-Bernard, 5e; 2-/3-course lunch €21/29; ⏱ lunch & dinner to 11.30pm Tue-Sat; Ⓜ Cardinal Lemoine

'Bistrot carnivore' is the strapline of this tasty little number concocted around France's most respected culinary products. The concept here is AOC (*appellation d'origine contrôlée*), meaning everything has been reared or made according to strict guidelines designed to protect a product unique to a particular village, town or area. The result? Only the best! Rare is the chance to taste *porc noir de Bigorre*, a type of black piggie bred in the Pyrénées.

Le Petit Pontoise

JEAN-BERNARD CARILLET

LE PETIT PONTOISE French, Bistro €€

 01 43 29 25 20; 9 rue de Pontoise, 5e; starters €8-13.50, starters €10-15, mains €17.50-25; lunch & dinner to 10.30pm; M Maubert Mutualité

Plop yourself down at a wooden table, note the lace curtains hiding you from the world, and pig out on fantastic old-fashioned classics like *rognons de veau à l'ancienne* (calf kidneys), *boudin campagnard* (black pudding) and sweet apple purée or roast quail with dates at this great bistro. Dishes might seem simple, but you'll leave pledging to return.

CHEZ RENÉ French, Bistro €€

01 43 54 30 23; 14 bd St-Germain, 5e; starters €6-10, mains €15-29; lunch & dinner to 11pm Tue-Sat; M Cardinal Lemoine or Maubert Mutualité

Proud owner of one of bd St-Germain's busiest pavement terraces, Chez René has been an institution since the 1950s. Perfect for punters seeking no surprises, cuisine is quintessentially bistro: think *pot au feu* (beef stew), *coq au vin* (chicken cooked in wine), *rognons de veau* (calf kidneys) etc accompanied by your pick of *garnitures* (fries, boiled potatoes, fresh spinach or other veg of the season etc) and sauces.

LA MOSQUÉE DE PARIS

North African €€

01 43 31 38 20; www.la-mosquee.com; 39 rue Geoffroy St-Hilaire, 5e; starters €5.50-7, mains €15-20; lunch & dinner to 10.30pm; M Censier-Daubenton or Place Monge

Dig into one of 11 types of couscous (from €12 to €21), two hands' worth of *tajines* (from €13.50 to €17) or a meaty grill (€14.50) at this authentic restaurant tucked within the walls of the city's **central mosque** (p221). Feeling decadent? Plump for a peppermint tea and calorie-loaded *pâtisserie orientale* between trees and chirping birds in the North African–style **tearoom** (9am-11.30pm) or, better still, a *formule orientale* (€58) which includes a body scrub, 10-minute massage and lounge in the *hammam* (Turkish bath) as well as lunch, mint tea and sweet pastry.

Patio, Mosquée de Paris (p221)

BRUCE BI

MOISSONIER   French, Lyonnais €€
☎ 01 43 29 87 65; 28 rue des Fossés St-Bernard,
5e; starters/mains €10/20; ⏱ lunch & dinner to
9.30pm Tue-Sat; Ⓜ Cardinal Lemoine
It's Lyon, not Paris, that French gourmets
venerate as the French food capital (they
have a point). Indeed, take one bite of
a big fat *andouillette* (pig-intestine sausage), *tablier de sapeur* (breaded, fried
stomach), traditional *quenelles* (fish-
flavoured dumplings) or *boudin noir aux
pommes* (black pudding with apples) and
you'll realise why. A perfect reflection of
one of France's most unforgettable regional cuisines, Moissonier is worth the
wait. Look for the elegant oyster-grey
facade opposite the university.

LE BABA BOURGEOIS   French €€
☎ 01 44 07 46 75; http://lebababourgeois.com,
in French; 5 quai de la Tournelle, 5e; menus
lunch €16.90 & €19.90, dinner €25.90 & €29.90;
⏱ lunch & dinner to 10.30pm Tue-Sat, brunch
Sun; Ⓜ Cardinal Lemoine or Pont Marie
It's all very trendy, le BB. Bang-slap on
the Seine with a pavement terrace facing Notre Dame, this contemporary eating
and drinking space is a former architect's
studio. Its interior screams 1970s Italian
design and the menu – *tartes salées* (savoury tarts) and salads – makes for a simple stylish bite any time. Sunday ushers in
a splendid all-day buffet brunch, *à volonté*
(all you can eat for €27).

LES PIPOS   French, Wine Bar €€
☎ 01 43 54 11 40; www.les-pipos.com, in
French; 2 rue de l'École Polytechnique, 5e; plats
du jour €15.90-28.50; ⏱ 8am-2am Mon-Sat;
Ⓜ Maubert Mutualité
A feast for the eyes and the senses, this
bar à vins is constantly propped up by a
couple of regulars over 60. Bistro tables
wear red and white, and are so close you
risk disturbing the entire house should
you need the loo midway through your
meal. Its *charcuteries de terroir* (regional
cold meats and sausages) is mouth-watering, as is its cheese board, which includes
all the gourmet names (bleu d'Auvergne,
St-Félicien, St-Marcellin etc). Indeed, take
one glance at the titles on the bookshelf

(feel free to browse) and you'll realise Les Pipos' overtly casual, laidback scene is a guise for feasting on the finer things in a French foodie's life. No credit cards.

MACHU PICCHU   South American €

☎ 01 43 26 13 13; 9 rue Royer-Collard, 5e; starters €6.50-8.20, mains €8.50-14.90, lunch menu €10.50; ☽ lunch & dinner to 10.30pm Mon-Fri; Ⓜ Luxembourg

Students adore this place, named after the lost city of the Incas in Peru. But doesn't Peruvian food mean guinea-pig fricassee? No. This hidey-hole, going strong since the 1980s, serves excellent meat and seafood dishes as well as a bargain-basement lunch *menu* and *plats du jour* (€6). No credit cards.

LE JARDIN DES PÂTES   Organic, Pasta €

☎ 01 43 31 50 71; 4 rue Lacépède, 5e; pasta €9-14; ☽ lunch & dinner to 11pm; Ⓜ Place Monge

A crisp white-and-green facade handily placed next to a Vélib' station flags the Pasta Garden, a simple, smart 100% *bio* (organic) place where pasta comes in every guise imaginable – barley, buckwheat, rye, wheat, rice, chestnut and so on. Our favourite: *pâtes de chataignes* (chestnut pasta) with duck breast, nutmeg, crème fraîche and mushrooms.

LA SALLE À MANGER   French €

☎ 01 55 43 91 99; 138 rue Mouffetard, 5e; lunch €10-15; ☽ 8.30am-6.30pm Mon-Fri, to 7pm Sat & Sun; Ⓜ Censier-Daubenton

With a sunny pavement terrace beneath trees enviably placed at the foot of foodie street rue Mouffetard, the Dining Room is prime real estate. Its 360-degree outlook – market stalls, fountain, church and garden with playground for tots – could not be prettier and its salads, *tartines* (open

toasted sandwiches), tarts and pastries ensure packed tables at breakfast, lunch and weekend brunch.

LE FOYER DU VIETNAM   Vietnamese €

☎ 01 45 35 32 54; 80 rue Monge, 5e; starters €3-6, mains €6-10; ☽ lunch & dinner to 10pm Mon-Sat; Ⓜ Place Monge

The 'Vietnam Club', with its self-proclaimed *ambiance familiale* (family atmosphere), might be nothing more than a long room with peeling walls and tables covered in oilcloths and plastic flowers, but everyone flocks here to feast on its hearty house specialities, 'Saigon' or 'Hanoi' soup (noodles, soya beans and pork flavoured with lemon grass, coriander and chives) included. Dishes come in medium or large portions and the price/quality ratio is astonishing. Students can fill up for €7.

SELF-CATERING

Shop with Parisians at a trio of lively outdoor food markets, framed (as with every market), by some lovely food shops:

Marché Maubert (place Maubert, 5e; ☽ 7am-2.30pm Tue, Thu & Sat; Ⓜ Maubert Mutualité) This market, spread over a small triangle of intersecting streets, reigns over St-Germain des Prés, the poshest part of the bohemian 5e.

Marché Monge (place Monge, 5e; ☽ 7am-2pm Wed, Fri & Sun; Ⓜ Place Monge) This is one of the better open-air neighbourhood markets on the Left Bank.

Rue Mouffetard (rue Mouffetard around rue de l'Arbalète, 5e; ☽ 8am-7.30pm Tue-Sat, 8am-noon Sun; Ⓜ Censier Daubenton) Rue Mouffetard is the city's most photogenic commercial market street and it's the place where Parisians send tourists (travellers go to Marché Bastille or Rue Montorgueil).

DRINKING

Rive Gauche romantics, well-heeled café society types and students by the gallon drink in the 5e arrondissement, where classic recipes, nostalgic formulas and a flurry of early-evening happy hours ensure a quintessential Parisian soirée. It's all good fun here, though not ground-breaking.

CURIO PARLOR COCKTAIL CLUB   Bar, Club
☎ 01 44 07 12 47; 16 rue des Bernardins, 5e; ⏱ 7pm-2am Tue-Thu, 7pm-4am Fri & Sat; Ⓜ Maubert Mutualité

This hybrid bar-club looks to the inter-war *années folles* (crazy years) of 1920s Paris, London and New York for inspiration. Its racing-green facade with simple brass plaque on the door is the height of discretion: go to its Facebook page to find out which party is happening when.

LE VIEUX CHÊNE   Bar
☎ 01 43 37 71 51; 69 rue Mouffetard, 5e; ⏱ 4pm-2am Sun-Thu, to 5am Fri & Sat; Ⓜ Place Monge

This rue Mouffetard institution is reckoned to be Paris' oldest bar. Indeed, a revolutionary circle met here in 1848 and it was a popular *bal musette* (dancing club) in the late 19th and early 20th centuries. Today it's popular with students, and hosts jazz on weekends.

LE VERRE À PIED   Café
☎ 01 43 31 15 72; 118bis rue Mouffetard, 5e; ⏱ 8am-9pm Tue-Sat, to 4pm Sun; Ⓜ Censier Daubenton

This *café-tabac* is a pearl, where little has changed since 1870. Its nicotine-hued mirrored wall, moulded cornices and original bar make it part of a dying breed, and it oozes the charm, glamour and romance of an old Paris everyone loves. Stall holders from the rue Mouffetard market yo-yo in and out, contemporary photography and art adorns one wall. Lunch is a busy, lively affair, and live music quickens the pulse a couple of evenings a week.

CAVE LA BOURGOGNE   Café, Wine Bar
☎ 01 47 07 82 80; 144 rue Mouffetard, 5e; ⏱ 9am-10.30pm; Ⓜ Censier Daubenton

A prime spot for lapping up rue Mouffetard's contagious 'saunter-all-day' spirit, this neighbourhood hang-out sits on square St-Médard, one of the Latin Quarter's loveliest squares: think flower-bedecked fountain, centuries-old church and tastebud-titillating market stalls. Inside, old ladies and their pet dogs meet for coffee around dark wood tables alongside a local wine-sipping set. In summer everything spills outside.

ENTERTAINMENT & ACTIVITIES

CAVEAU DE LA HUCHETTE   Jazz & Blues
☎ 01 43 26 65 05; www.caveaudelahuchette.fr; 5 rue de la Huchette, 5e; admission Sun-Thu €12, Fri & Sat €14, under 25yr €10; ⏱ 9.30pm-2.30am Sun-Wed, to 4am Thu-Sat; Ⓜ St-Michel

Housed in a medieval *caveau* (cellar) used as a courtroom and torture chamber during the Revolution, this club has hosted virtually all the jazz greats since the end of WWII. It's touristy, but the atmosphere can be more electric than at the more serious jazz clubs. Sessions start at 10pm.

LE CHAMPO   Cinemas
☎ 01 43 54 51 60; www.lechampo.com, in French; 51 rue des Écoles, 5e; adult/student & under 20yr €7.50/6, 2pm matinée €5; Ⓜ St-Michel or Cluny-La Sorbonne

This is one of the most popular of the many Latin Quarter cinemas, featuring

WILL SALTER

Shakespeare & Company

classics and retrospectives looking at the films of actors and directors such as Alfred Hitchcock, Jacques Tati, Alain Resnais, Frank Capra and Woody Allen. One of the two *salles* (cinemas) has wheelchair access. A couple of times a month Le Champo screens films all night for night owls, kicking off at midnight (three films plus breakfast €15).

HAMMAM DE LA MOSQUÉE DE PARIS
Hammams & Spas

☎ 01 43 31 38 20; www.la-mosquee.com; 39 rue Geoffroy St-Hilaire, 5e; admission €15; ⏱ men 2-9pm Tue, 10am-9pm Sun, women 10am-9pm Mon, Wed, Thu & Sat, 2-9pm Fri; Ⓜ Censier Daubenton or Place Monge

Massages at this atmospheric hammam cost €1 a minute and come in 10-, 20- or 30-minute packages. Should you fancy an exfoliating body scrub and mint tea, get the 10-/30-minute massage *formule* (€38/58). There are lunch deals for rumbling tummies. Bring a swimsuit but hire a towel/dressing gown (€4/5). No kids under 12.

GEPETTO & VÉLOS
Bicycle Hire

☎ 01 43 54 19 95; www.gepetto-et-velos.com, in French; 59 rue du Cardinal Lemoine, 5e; half-/ full day/weekend/week €9/15/25/60; ⏱ 9am-1pm & 2-7.30pm Tue-Sat; Ⓜ Cardinal Lemoine

New and secondhand bicycles, plus repairs. To rent, show your passport and leave a €325 deposit.

SHOPPING

Bookworms in particular will love this part of the Left Bank, not particularly known for its shopping but home to some fine bookshops nonetheless, Paris' most famous English-language bookshop included.

SHAKESPEARE & COMPANY
Books & Comics

☎ 01 43 26 96 50; 37 rue de la Bûcherie, 5e; ⏱ 10am-11pm Mon-Fri, 11am-11pm Sat & Sun; Ⓜ St-Michel Notre Dame

Paris' most famous English-language bookshop sells new and used books and is a charm to browse (grab a read and sink into

THE LATIN QUARTER

SHOPPING

one of the two cinema chairs near the stairs out back); the staff's picks are worth noting and there's a dusty old library on the 1st floor. This isn't the original Shakespeare & Company owned by Sylvia Beach, who published James Joyce's *Ulysses;* that one was closed down by the Nazis.

MAGIE
Games & Hobbies
☎ 01 43 54 13 63; www.mayette.com, in French; 8 rue des Carmes, 5e; ⏲ 1-8pm Mon-Sat; Ⓜ Maubert Mutualité

One of a kind, this 19th-century (1808) magic shop is said to be the world's oldest, and since 1991 in the hands of world-famous magic pro Dominique Duvivier. Professional and hobbyist magicians flock here to discuss king sandwiches, reverse assemblies, false cuts and other card tricks with him and his daughter, Alexandra. Should you want to learn the tricks of the trade, Duvivier has magic courses up his sleeve.

↘ DAY TRIPS

DAY TRIPS

HIGHLIGHTS

1 CHÂTEAU DE VERSAILLES

BY SYLVAIN POSTOLLE, OFFICIAL GUIDE, CHÂTEAU DE VERSAILLES

Versailles, as the official residence of the kings of France, is magnificent – the only place where the daily life of the monarchy before the French Revolution can really be felt. My favourite moment is the evening, after the crowds have gone, when I quietly walk from room to room lecturing to just a small group…extraordinary.

HIGHLIGHTS

⩘ SYLVAIN POSTOLLE'S DON'T MISS LIST

❶ KING'S PRIVATE APARTMENT

This is the most fascinating part of the palace as it shows the king as a man and very much reflects his daily life in the 18th century. Of the 10 or so rooms, the most famous is his bedroom – where he not only slept, but also held ceremonies. He had lunch here each day at 1pm and also supper, which up to 150 courtiers and people invited from outside the court would watch! By the 1780s, the king's life had be-

come more private – he had an official supper just once a week, on Sunday.

❷ HERCULES SALON

I love one particular perspective inside the palace: from the Hercules Salon you can see all the rooms comprising the King's State Apartment, and to the right, through the gallery leading to the opera house. The salon served as a passageway for the king to go from his state apartment to the chapel to celebrate daily mass.

Clockwise from top: Bassin d'Apollon; Hallway, Château de Versailles; Ceiling paintings; Manicured gardens; Interior of the Royal Chapel

DAY TRIPS

HIGHLIGHTS

❸ THE ROYAL CHAPEL

This is an exquisite example of the work of a very important architect of the time, Jules Hardouin-Mansart (1646–1708). The paintings, very representative of art fashions at the end of the reign of Louis XIV, are also stunning: they evoke the idea that the French king was chosen by God and as such was his lieutenant on earth. This is the chapel where, in 1770, the future king Louis XVI wed Marie Antoinette in 1770 – the beginning of the French Revolution.

❹ ENCELADE GROVE

Versailles' gardens are extraordinary; my favourite spot has to be this grove, typical of the gardens created for Louis XIV by André Le Nôtre. A gallery of trellises surrounds a pool with a statue of Enceladus, chief of the Titans, who was punished for his pride by the gods from Mount Olympus. When the fountains are on, it's impressive.

↘ THINGS YOU NEED TO KNOW

Nightmare queues Avoid by arriving early or after 4pm **Day to avoid** Tuesday – many Paris museums are closed, so Versailles queues are even more horrific **Absolute must** Buy tickets in advance on www.chateauversailles.fr or from a Fnac branch or SNCF train station. **See our author's review, p238.**

DAY TRIPS

Paris is encircled by the romantically named, 12,000-sq-km Île de France (literally 'Island of France'). It is shaped by five rivers and Seine tributaries: the Epte in the northwest, the Aisne (northeast), the Eure (southwest), the Yonne (southeast) and the Marne (east). From this relatively small area the kingdom of France began to expand beginning around 1100.

Today the region's excellent rail and road links with the French capital and its exceptional sights – châteaux, cathedrals, towns that hosted and inspired Impressionist painters, theme parks – make it especially popular with day-trippers from Paris.

The official Paris Île de France website (www.nouveau-paris-ile-de-france.fr) is a treasure trove of information on the area.

VERSAILLES

Seven hundred rooms, 67 staircases, 352 chimneys, 2153 windows, 6300 paintings, 2100 sculptures and statues, 15,000 engravings, 5000 decorative art objects and furnishings, more than five million château visitors annually: no wonder visiting France's most famous, grandest palace can be overwhelming. Six days a week (the château is shut Monday) tourist

madness consumes the prosperous, leafy and bourgeois suburb of Versailles (population 84,225), political capital and seat of the royal court from 1682 until 1789, when Revolutionary mobs massacred the palace guard and dragged Louis XVI and Marie-Antoinette back to Paris to eventually lop off their heads.

It was during the reign of the Sun King Louis XIV (1643–1715) that **Château de Versailles** (☎ 01 30 83 78 00; www.châteauversailles.fr; palace ticket adult/EU citizen under 26 & everyone under 18yr €15/free, from 3pm €10/free, Passeport sold until 3pm adult/EU citizen under 26 & everyone under 18yr €20/free Wed-Fri & €25/free Tue, Sat & Sun Apr-Oct, €18/free Nov-Mar; ☷ 9am-6.30pm Tue-Sun Apr-Oct, 9am-5.30pm Tue-Sun Nov-Mar) was built. The basic palace ticket and more elaborate Passeport both include an English-language audioguide and allow visitors to freely visit the King's and Queen's State Apartments, chapel, the Dauphin's Apartments and various galleries.

Intended to house his court of 6000 people, the sheer scale and decor of Versailles reflected not only the absolute power of the French monarchy but also Louis XIV's taste for profligate luxury and

---

⬎ TO MAKE VERSAILLES VISITS LESS HELLISH

- It can't be stressed enough: buy your château ticket in advance of stepping foot in Versailles – online (www.chateauversailles.fr) or from a branch of Fnac.
- Should you arrive in Versailles ticketless, bulldoze straight to the tourist office to buy a Passeport. It will save you time.
- By noon queues spiral out of control: visit the palace first thing in the morning or after 4pm; avoid Tuesday and Sunday, its busiest days.

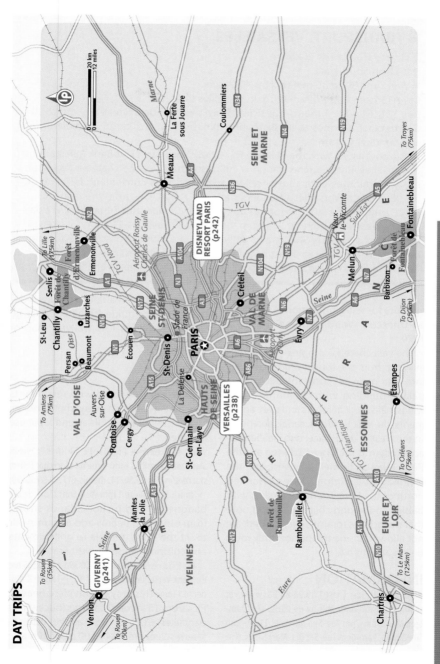

DAY TRIPS

20 km
12 miles

Marne

La Ferté
sous Jouarre

Coulommiers

N34

SEINE ET
MARNE

N4

N19

To Troyes
(75km)

Meaux

A4

N36

TGV

N2

**DISNEYLAND
RESORT PARIS
(p242)**

TGV
Sud-Est

Vaux-
le-Vicomte

Aéroport Roissy
Charles de Gaulle

A5

Fontainebleau

Forêt
de
Fontainebleau

To Lille
(175km)

Forêt
d'Ermenonville

TGV Nord

A1M

Ermenonville

A1

SEINE
ST-DENIS

N3

Créteil

N104

N19

Melun

N7

Barbizon

Senlis

Forêt de
Chantilly

Stade de
France

VAL DE
MARNE

N6

Seine

A6

To Dijon
(250km)

St-Leu

Chantilly

N16

Luzarches

N1

Écouen

A3

Aéroport
d'Orly

Évry

N7

Persan

Oise

Beaumont

St-Denis

PARIS

A6

Étampes

To Amiens
(75km)

VAL D'OISE

Auvers-
sur-Oise

A15

La Défense

HAUTS
DE-SEINE

A86

A20

ESSONNES

Pontoise

Cergy

**VERSAILLES
(p238)**

To Orléans
(75km)

N13

St-Germain
en-Laye

A13

N10

Atlantique

A10

N14

Mantes
la Jolie

Seine

D

E

TGV

EURE ET
LOIR

Forêt de
Rambouillet

A11

Vernon

**GIVERNY
(p241)**

YVELINES

N12

Rambouillet

To Le Mans
(125km)

N10

To Rouen
(35km)

To Rouen
(50km)

Eure

Chartres

⚓ TRANSPORT: VERSAILLES

Distance from Paris 28km

Direction Southwest

Travel time 30 to 35 minutes by RER/train

Car A13 from Porte d'Auteuil, exit 'Versailles Château'

Bus 171 (€1.60 or 1 metro/bus ticket) from the Pont de Sèvres (15e) metro station to place d'Armes every six to nine minutes 5am (5.30am/6.30am Saturday and Sunday) to 1am.

RER train Fastest way: the RER line C5 (€2.95) from Paris' Left Bank RER stations to Versailles–Rive Gauche station is 700m southeast of the château; trains run every 15 minutes until shortly before midnight. Less convenient: RER line C8 (€2.95) stops at Versailles-Chantiers station, a 1.3km walk from the château.

SNCF train From Paris' Gare St-Lazare (€3.70) SNCF operates 70-odd trains a day to Versailles–Rive Droite, 1.2km from the château. Versailles-Chantiers is likewise served by half-hourly SNCF trains daily from Gare Montparnasse (€2.95); trains on this line continue to Chartres (€11.50, 35 to 60 minutes).

Taxi Book a taxi in Versailles on ☎ 01 39 50 50 00 (www.taxis-abeille.com).

appetite for self-glorification. It has been on Unesco's World Heritage List since 1979.

The vast château complex – get a folding map from the tourist office – divides into four main sections: the 580m-long palace building with its innumerable wings, halls, bedchambers and state apartments; the vast **gardens**, canals and pools to the west of the palace; two smaller palaces known as the **Grand Trianon** and the **Petit Trianon** to the northwest; and the **Hameau de la Reine** (Queen's Hamlet) north of the Petit Trianon. Families with babies and young children should note that pushchairs (prams), even folded, are not allowed inside the palace; they must be left at Entrée A.

INFORMATION

Tourist Office (☎ 01 39 24 88 88; www.versailles-tourisme.com; 2bis av de Paris; ☺ 10am-6pm Mon, 9am-7pm Tue-Sun Apr-Sep, 11am-5pm Sun & Mon, 9am-6pm Tue-Sat Oct-Mar) Sells the Passeport to Château de Versailles, a detailed visitor's guide (small €8.50, large €15) and also an IGN walking map of the area (€10.20).

EATING

Rue de Satory is lined with restaurants serving cuisine from everywhere: Indian, Chinese, Lebanese, Tunisian and Japanese included.

À la Ferme (☎ 01 39 53 10 81; www.alaferme-versailles.com; 3 rue du Maréchal Joffre; starters/mains €6.50/14, menus €17.90 & €22.50; ☺ lunch & dinner to 11pm Wed-Sun) Cow-hide banquettes and rustic garlands strung from old wood beams add a country air to 'At the Farm', temple to grilled meats and cuisine from southwest France.

Le Phare St-Louis (☎ 01 39 53 40 12; 33 rue du Vieux Versailles; menus €11-18; ☺ lunch & dinner to 11pm) This cosy Breton place heaves. Pick from 15 savoury galettes (buckwheat pancakes; €3.60 to €9.80) and 40-odd different sweet crêpes (€3.60 to €7.10).

SELF-CATERING

Marché & Halles Notre Dame (place du Marché Notre Dame; ⊙ inside 7am-1pm & 3.30-7.30pm Tue-Sat, 7.30am-1pm Sun, outside 7.30am-2pm Tue, Fri & Sun) Indoor and outdoor food market.

GIVERNY

The prized drawcard of this tiny village (population 525), northwest of Paris en route to Rouen, is the **Maison de Claude Monet** (House of Claude Monet; ☎ 02 32 51 28 21; www.fondation-monet.com; 84 rue Claude Monet; adult/student/7-11yr/under 7yr €6/4.50/3.50/free; ⊙ 9.30am-6pm Apr-Oct), the home and flower-filled garden of one of the leading Impressionist painters and his family from 1883 to 1926. Here Monet painted some of his most famous series of works, including *Décorations des Nymphéas* (Water Lilies). Unfortunately, the hectare of land that Monet owned here has become two distinct areas, cut by the Chemin du Roy, a small railway line that has been converted into the D5 road.

The northern area of the property is **Clos Normand**, where Monet's famous pastel pink-and-green house and the **Atelier des Nymphéas** (Water Lilies Studio) stand.

From the Clos Normand's far corner a foot tunnel leads under the D5 to the **Jardin d'Eau** (Water Garden). Having bought this piece of land in 1895 after his reputation had been established (and his bank account had swelled), Monet dug a pool, planted water lilies and constructed the famous **Japanese bridge**, since rebuilt. Draped with purple wisteria, the bridge blends into the asymmetrical foreground and background, creating the intimate atmosphere for which the 'Painter of Light' was famous.

INFORMATION

Vernon Tourist Office (☎ 02 32 51 39 60; http://giverny.org; 36 rue Carnot; ⊙ 9am-noon & 2.30-6.30pm Mon-Sat, 10am-noon Sun May-Oct, 10am-noon & 2-5pm Tue-Sat Nov-Apr) The closest tourist office is in Vernon, 7km northwest of Giverny.

DAY TRIPS

GIVERNY

↘ TRANSPORT: GIVERNY

Distance from Paris 74km

Direction Northwest

Travel time 45 minutes by train to Vernon, then 20 minutes by bus or bicycle

Car Route A13 from Paris' Port de St-Cloud (direction Rouen), exit No 14 to route N15 (direction Vernon, Giverny and Bonnières)

SNCF train From Paris' Gare St-Lazare there are two early-morning SNCF trains to Vernon (€12.50, 1¼ hours), from where seasonal **shuttle buses** (€4 return; ⊙ Apr-Oct) continue from the station to Giverny, 7km to the southeast. Miles more fun is to hire a bike for €12 a day from the café facing the station, **Bar-Restaurant du Chemin de Fer** (☎ 02 32 21 16 01; 1 pl de la Gare; ⊙ 6.30am-11pm); take your passport as a deposit. **Cyclo News** (☎ 02 32 21 24 08; 7 cours du Marché aux Chevaux; ⊙ 8:30am-7.30pm Tue-Sat), about 800m from the Vernon train station, rents bikes for the same amount. Between 5pm and 9pm there's roughly one train an hour back to Paris.

EATING

Many Giverny restaurants are only open in season.

Auberge du Vieux Moulin (☎ 02 32 51 46 15; www.vieuxmoulingiverny.com; 21 rue de la Falaise; salads €12, lunch menus €15-18, dinner menus €24-35; ☯ lunch daily, dinner to 10pm Fri & Sat Apr-Oct, lunch Fri-Sun Nov-Mar) The lovely little 'Old Mill Inn', a couple of hundred metres east of the Maison de Claude Monet, is an excellent place for lunch and has a lovely terrace.

DISNEYLAND RESORT PARIS

Europe's first Disney theme park opened amid much fanfare and controversy in 1992. Rocky start now a million moons away, what started out as Euro-Disney sees visitors (mostly families) pour into the park to scare themselves silly in the blood-curdling Tower of Terror, dance in a High School Musical, dive with Nemo, hit 70km/h in a Space Mountain rocket, shake Winnie the Pooh's paw and share a fiesta of other magical moments with Mickey and his Disney mates. And the kids can't seem to get enough. As its marketing bumph boasts, at Disneyland 'the party never stops'.

Disneyland Resort Paris (☎ 01 60 30 60 53, www.disneylandparis.com) comprises three areas plus a golf course: **Disney Village**, with its hotels, shops, restaurants and clubs; **Disneyland Park** (☯ 10am-8pm Mon-Fri, 9am-8pm Sat & Sun early May–mid-Jun & Sep-Mar, 9am-11pm early Jul-Aug), with its five theme parks; and **Walt Disney Studios Park** (☯ 9am-7pm late Jun-early Sep, 10am-7pm Mon-Fri & 9am-7pm Sat & Sun early Sep-late Jun), which brings film, animation and TV production to life

One-day **admission fees** (adult/3-11yr €52/44) include unlimited access to all rides and activities in *either* Disneyland Park or Walt Disney Studios Park. Those who opt for the latter can enter Disneyland Park three hours before it closes. Multiple-day passes are also available: a one-day pass (adult/child €65/57) allows entry to both parks for a day and its multiday

BARBARA VAN ZANTEN

Painters at Main Alley, Monet's garden, Giverny (p241)

equivalents (two days €111/94, three days €138/117) allow you to enter and leave both parks as often as you like over non-consecutive days used within one year. Some shows and activities such as a meal with Disney characters (from €22/15 per adult/child) or the 1½-hour Buffalo Bill's Wild West Dinner Show (from €58/44) cost extra.

Buy your tickets at tourist offices or train stations in Paris beforehand to avoid at least one queue (for tickets); once in, reserve your time slot on the busiest rides using FastPass, the park's ride reservation system (limited to one reservation at a time).

EATING

No picnics are allowed at Disneyland Paris. But there are ample themed restaurants to pick from, be it **Buzz Lightyear's Pizza Planet** (Discoveryland), **Planet Hollywood** or the *Happy Days*–inspired **Annette's Diner** (Disney Village), the meaty **Silver Spur Steakhouse** or Mexican **Fuente del Oro** (Frontierland)

> ### ⬎ TRANSPORT: DISNEYLAND RESORT PARIS
>
> **Distance from Paris** 32km
> **Direction** East
> **Travel time** 35 to 40 minutes by RER train
> **Car** Route A4 from Porte de Bercy, direction Metz-Nancy, exit No 14
> **RER train** Line A4 to Marne-la-Vallée/Chessy, Disneyland's RER station, from central Paris (€6.55). Trains run every 15 minutes or so, with the last train back to Paris just after midnight.

and the sea-faring **Blue Lagoon** for future pirates or African-themed **Hakuna Matata** (Adventureland). Most have *menus* and meal coupons (adults/children €24/10) are available. Opening hours vary. To avoid another queue, pick your place online and reserve a **table** (☎ **01 60 30 40 50**) in advance .

DAY TRIPS

DISNEYLAND RESORT PARIS

ARCHITECTURE

JOHN ELK III

Centre Pompidou (p68)

Parisians have never been as intransigent as, say, Londoners about accepting changes to their cityscape, nor as un-shocked by the new as New Yorkers appear to be. Several key eras and people are woven into Paris' architectural fabric, from von Haussmann's boulevards to the Centre Pompidou, named after its creator. Modern and historic complement each other, even if it sometimes takes time for Parisians to come on board with new additions – the Eiffel Tower, for example, was hated and labelled the 'metal asparagus' when it was first built; now it's cherished by locals and visitors alike.

ROMANESQUE

A religious revival in the 11th century led to the construction of a large number of *roman* (Romanesque) churches, so-called because their architects adopted many architectural elements (eg vaulting) from Gallo-Roman buildings still standing at the time. Romanesque buildings typically have round arches, heavy walls, few (and small) windows that let in very little light, and a lack of ornamentation that borders on the austere. The Église St-Germain des Prés (p197), built in the 11th century on the site of the Merovingian ruler Childeric's 6th-century abbey, has been altered many times over the centuries, but the Romanesque bell tower over the west entrance has changed little since AD 1000.

GOTHIC – RADIANT TO FLAMBOYANT

In the 14th century, the Rayonnant – or Radiant – Gothic style, which was named after the radiating tracery of the rose windows, developed. Light was welcomed into interiors by broad windows and translucent stained glass. One of the most influential Rayonnant buildings was Ste-Chapelle (p92), whose stained glass forms a curtain of glazing on the 1st floor. The two transept facades of the Cathédrale de Notre Dame de Paris (p89) are another fine example.

By the 15th century, decorative extravagance led to what is now called Flamboyant Gothic, so named because the wavy stone carving made the towers appear to be blazing or flaming (*flamboyant*).

EARLY RENAISSANCE

The Early Renaissance style of the 15th and early 16th centuries, in which a variety of classical components and decorative motifs (columns, tunnel vaults, round arches, domes etc) were blended with the rich decoration of Flamboyant Gothic, is best exemplified in Paris by the Église St-Eustache (p70). The Marais remains the best area for spotting reminders of the Renaissance in Paris proper, with some fine *hôtels particuliers* (private mansions) from this era, such as Hôtel Carnavalet, housing part of the Musée Carnavalet (p106).

BAROQUE

During the baroque period – which lasted from the tail end of the 16th to the late 18th centuries – painting, sculpture and classical architecture were integrated to create structures and interiors of great subtlety, refinement and elegance. With the advent of the baroque, architecture became more pictorial, with the painted ceilings in churches illustrating the Passion of Christ to the faithful, and palaces invoking the power and order of the state.

Salomon de Brosse, who designed Paris' Palais du Luxembourg in the Jardin du Luxembourg (p198) in 1615, set the stage for prominent early baroque architect François Mansart, designer of the Église Notre Dame du Val-de-Grâce (Map p214).

NEOCLASSICISM

Neoclassical architecture (see p248), which emerged in about 1740 and remained popular in Paris until well into the 19th century, had its roots in the renewed interest in classical forms. Neoclassicism was more profoundly a search for order, reason and serenity through the adoption of the forms and conventions of Graeco-Roman antiquity: columns, simple geometric forms and traditional ornamentation. Neoclassicism really came into its own under Napoleon, who used it extensively for monumental architecture intended to embody the grandeur of imperial France and its capital.

❯THE BEST

BRUCE BI

Musée du Quai Branly (p172)

ARCHITECTURAL ICONS

- **Arc de Triomphe** (p149)
- **Opéra Bastille** (p110)
- **Musée du Quai Branly** (p172)
- **Centre Pompidou** (p68)

PARIS IN FOCUS

ARCHITECTURE

THE BEST

JEAN-BERNARD CARILLET

Panthéon (p223)

NEOCLASSICAL SIGHTS

- Église St-Sulpice (p198)
- Arc de Triomphe (p149)
- Panthéon (p223)
- Palais Garnier (p150)

VON HAUSSMAN

Baron von Haussman's late 19th-century renovation of the medieval city's disease-ridden streets demolished more than 20,000 homes, making way for wide boulevards lined by 40,000 new apartments in neoclassical creamy stone, grey-metal roofed buildings. And the turn-of-the-century art nouveau movement, which emerged in Europe and the USA in the second half of the 19th century under various names (Jugendstil, Sezessionstil, Stile Liberty) caught on quickly in Paris. It was characterised by sinuous curves and flowing, asymmetrical forms reminiscent of creeping vines, water lilies, the patterns on insect wings and the flowering boughs of trees. Influenced by the arrival of exotic *objets d'art* from Japan, its French name came from a Paris gallery that featured works in the 'new art' style. In Paris, it ushered in signature sights including the Musée d'Orsay (p177), Grand Palais (p151) and Paris' ornate brasseries and wrought-iron metro entrances (p72).

CONTEMPORARY

Additions to the cityscape in the 20th century centred on French presidents' *grand projets* (huge public edifices through which French leaders seek to immortalise themselves). President George Pompidou's Centre Pompidou (p68), unveiled in 1977, prompted a furore, as did President François Mitterand's Louvre's glass pyramid (p62) in 1989. However, both are now widely admired and considered iconic Paris landmarks. Mitterand oversaw a slew of other costly *projets*, including the Opéra Bastille (p110). In 1995 the presidential baton shifted to Jacques Chirac – his pet *projet*, the Musée du Quai Branly (p172), opened in a Jean Nouvel–designed structure. Sarkozy has turned his attentions to the *banlieues* (suburbs) in particular and the Parisian metropolis as a whole. In 2007, he set up a commission to select 10 architects to head up multi-disciplinary teams. The remit: plans for transforming Paris into a model 'post-Kyoto metropolis of the 21st century'.

ART

WILL SALTER

Musée d'Orsay (p177)

Paris is a bottomless well when it comes to the arts. Its museums are among the richest in the world, with artwork representing the best of every historical period and school from the Romans to postmodernism. Viewing art and sculpture is an integral part of Parisians' leisure activities and accounts for Parisians' keen sense of the aesthetic.

PAINTING

The philosopher Voltaire wrote that French painting began with Nicolas Poussin, the greatest representative of 17th-century classicism, who frequently set scenes from ancient Rome, classical mythology and the Bible in ordered landscapes bathed in golden light. It's not a bad starting point.

In the 18th century Jean-Baptiste Chardin brought the humbler domesticity of the Dutch masters to French art. In 1785 the public reacted with enthusiasm to two large paintings with clear republican messages: *The Oath of the Horatii* and *Brutus Condemning His Son* by Jacques-Louis David. David became one of the leaders of the French Revolution, and a virtual dictator in matters of art, where he advocated a precise, severe classicism.

Jean-Auguste-Dominique Ingres, David's most gifted pupil in Paris, continued in the neoclassical tradition. The historical pictures to which he devoted most of his life (eg *Oedipus and the Sphinx*, the 1808 version of which is in the Louvre; p61) are now generally regarded as inferior to his portraits.

As for romanticism, Eugène Delacroix rules. Delacroix's most famous – if not best – work is *Liberty Leading the People,* which commemorates the July Revolution of 1830 and can also be seen at the Louvre.

Édouard Manet (1832–1883) used realism to depict the life of the Parisian middle classes, yet he included in his pictures numerous references to the Old Masters. He was a pivotal figure in the transition from realism to impressionism.

Impressionism, initially used as a term of derision, was taken from the title of an 1874 experimental painting by Claude Monet, *Impression: Soleil Levant* (Impression: Sunrise). Monet was the leading figure of the school. The impressionists' main aim was to capture the effects of fleeting light, painting almost universally in the open air – and light came to dominate the content of their painting.

Edgar Degas was a fellow traveller of the impressionists, but he preferred painting café life *(Absinthe)* and in ballet studios *(The Dance Class)* than the great outdoors. Paul Cézanne is celebrated for his still lifes and landscapes depicting the south of France, though he spent many years in Paris after breaking with the impressionists.

Cubism was effectively launched in 1907 with *Les Demoiselles d'Avignon* by the Spanish prodigy Pablo Picasso. Cubism, as developed by Picasso, Georges Braque and Juan Gris, deconstructed the subject into a system of intersecting planes and presented various aspects simultaneously. Good examples are Braque's *Houses at l'Estaque* and *Woman Playing the Mandolin* by Picasso.

In the 1920s and '30s the so-called École de Paris (School of Paris) was formed by a group of expressionists, mostly foreign born, including Amedeo Modigliani from Italy, Foujita from Japan and Marc Chagall from Russia, whose works combined fantasy and folklore.

Dada, both a literary and artistic movement of revolt, started in Zürich in 1915. Among the most important proponents of this style in Paris were Chagall, and Piet Mondrian. The most influential, however, was the Spanish-born artist Salvador Dalí, who arrived in the French capital in 1929 and painted some of his most seminal works (eg *Sleep, Paranoia*) while residing here. To see his work, visit the Dalí Espace Montmartre (p134).

SCULPTURE

By the 14th century, sculpture was increasingly commissioned for the tombs of the nobility. In Renaissance Paris, Jean Goujon created the Fontaine des Innocents (p70). The baroque style is exemplified by Guillaume Coustou's *Horses of Marly* at the entrance to the av des Champs-Élysées.

In the mid-19th century, memorial statues in public places came to replace sculpted tombs. Sculptor Jean-Baptiste Carpeaux

❯THE BEST

BRUCE BI

Musée Rodin (p178)

ART & SCULPTURE MUSEUMS

PARIS IN FOCUS

ART

THE BEST

OLIVIER CIRENDINI

Musée Atelier Zadkine (p201)

MUSEUMS FOR 20TH & 21ST CENTURY ART

- Musée d'Art Moderne de la Ville de Paris (p175)
- Musée d'Orsay (p177)
- Musée Atelier Zadkine (p201)

began as a romantic, but his works – such as *The Dance* on the Palais Garnier and his fountain in the Jardin du Luxembourg – look back to the gaiety and flamboyance of the baroque era. At the end of the 19th century Auguste Rodin's work overcame the conflict between neoclassicism and romanticism. One of Rodin's most gifted pupils was his lover Camille Claudel, whose work can be seen along with that of Rodin in the Musée Rodin (p178).

One of the most influential sculptors to emerge in Paris before WWII was the Romanian-born Constantin Brancusi, whose work can be seen in the Atelier Brancusi, part of the Centre Pompidou (p68). Another sculptor who lived and worked in Paris and has a museum is Ossip Zadkine (p201).

In 1936 France put forward a bill providing for 'the creation of monumental decorations in public buildings' by allotting 1% of all building costs to public art. This did not really get off the ground for another half-century, until Daniel Buren's *Les Deux Plateaux* sculpture was commissioned at Palais Royal (p68). The whole concept mushroomed, and artwork started to appear everywhere in Paris, including in the Jardin des Tuileries (*The Welcoming Hands;* p66) and even in the metro (see the boxed text, p72).

DRINKING & NIGHTLIFE

WILL SALTER

Bofinger (p115)

A night out in Paris can mean anything from kicking back at a chilled wine bar serving bite-sized snacks, or a chic, design-driven lounge bar brimming with beautiful people to swilling champagne on the Champs-Elysées, or dancing till dawn on the tables of a mad-loud DJ bar. From jazz cellar to comic theatre, garage beat to go-go dancer, this is *the* capital of *savoir-vivre*, with spectacular nightlife and entertainment to suit every budget, every taste.

The French capital holds a firm place on the touring circuit of the world's finest performing artists and boasts dozens of historic and/or legendary concert venues: seeing a performance here is a treat. French and international opera, ballet and theatre companies (not to mention the cabaret's incorrigible cancan dancers) take to the stage in venues of mythical proportion – the Palais Garnier (p150), Comédie Française (p79) and the Moulin Rouge (p141) included. And away from the bright lights and media glare, a flurry of young, passionate, highly creative musicians, theatre aficionados and artists make up a fascinating fringe scene.

Most theatre productions, including those originally written in other languages, are performed in French in Paris, naturally enough. Very occasionally the odd itinerant English-speaking troupe plays at smaller venues around town. Consult *Pariscope* (http://spectacles.premiere.fr/pariscope/theatre, in French) or *L'Officiel des Spectacles* (www.offi.fr, in French) for details.

Drinking in Paris runs the gamut, too. You might find Parisians savouring wafer-thin slices of *saucisson* (sausage) over a glass of sauvignon on a pavement terrace at sundown; meeting after work for *une verre* (a glass) and *tartines* (open sandwiches) cut from

Poilâne bread; quaffing an early-evening apéritif in the same literary café as Sartre and Simone did; dancing on tables to bossa nova beats; or sipping martinis on a dark leather couch while listening to live jazz.

In a country where eating and drinking are inseparable, it's inevitable that the line between bars, cafés and bistros is blurred at best (no, you haven't drunk too much – indeed the French rarely go drunk-wild and really rather frown upon it). Practically every place serves food of some description, but those featured in our guide are favoured, first and foremost, as happening places to drink – be it alcohol, coffee or tea. Furthermore, the distinct lack of any hardcore clubbing circuit in the French capital means what might appear as a simple café at 5pm can morph quite comfortably into a DJ bar with pounding dance floor as the night rolls on.

THE BEST

Bottles of fine French wine

DRINKING SPOTS

- **Le Fumoir** (p78)
- **Le Bistrot du Peintre** (p121)
- **Prescription Cocktail Club** (p208)
- **Ice Kube** (p140)
- **Rue Oberkampf & rue Jean-Pierre Timbaud** (p120)
- **Rue Montmartre** (p125)

FAMILY TRAVEL

JOHN HAY

Jardin des Tuileries (p66)

Be it dining, celebrating or travelling, Parisians adore *les enfants* (children) and welcome them with open arms just about everywhere. They are great believers in doing things *en famille* (as a family) – making the capital a great place to kid around. As a large city, Paris does present its challenges, but the upside is a stack of unique activities for *les enfants* to indulge in.

SIGHTS & ACTIVITIES

Central Paris' residential make-up means you'll find playground equipment in parks all over the city. You can sail toy boats, laugh with the puppets and take a ride on the antique carousel at the Jardin du Luxembourg (p195) or head indoors to aquarium Cinéaqua (p175) – two words: shark tank. A trip to the Louvre (p61) can be a treat for older kids – they'll all be curious about one piece of art even little ones have heard about: the *Mona Lisa*. The Eiffel Tower (p171) and Musée National d'Histoire Naturelle (Museum of Natural History; p221) are solid kid-pleasers, while further afield, you might consider a day trip to the Disneyland Resort Paris (p242) theme park, a dream for kids and parents alike.

EATING OUT

Many restaurants accept little diners (confirm ahead), but they're expected to behave (bring crayons/books). Children's menus are common, but most restaurants don't have highchairs. Department-store cafeterias, such as **BHV** (Bazar de l'Hôtel de Ville; www.bhv.fr, in French), and chain restaurants, such as **Flunch** (www.flunch.fr), offer kid-friendly fare. In fine weather, good options include picking up sandwiches and crêpes from a street stall or packing a market-fresh picnic and heading to gardens such as the Jardin du Luxembourg (p198), where they can play to their hearts' content.

WAY TO GO

Paris' narrow streets and metro stairways are, in short, a trial if you have a pram or pushchair in tow. Car-rental firms have children's safety seats for hire at a nominal cost; book in advance. Children under four years of age travel free on public transport and generally receive free admission to sights. For older kids, discounts vary from place to place – anything from a euro off for over fours to free up to the age of 18.

The choice of baby food, infant formula, soy and cow's milk, nappies (diapers) and the like in French supermarkets is similar to that in any developed country, but remember that opening hours may be more limited. Pharmacies – of which a number are open 24/7, and others open for at least a few hours on a Sunday – also sell baby paraphernalia.

> ## ⬆ THE NITTY GRITTY
>
> - **Cots** Available upon request in many midrange and top-end hotels.
> - **Highchairs** Rare; bring your own screw-on seat.
> - **Kids' menu** A standard in most restaurants.
> - **Nappies (diapers)** Widely available in supermarkets and pharmacies.
> - **Changing facilities** Rare; bring a towel and improvise (no one minds).
> - **Strollers (pushchairs)** A strict no-no inside Château de Versailles; bring a baby sling.

BEDTIME

Weekly magazine *L'Officiel des Spectacles* advertises *gardes d'enfants* (babysitting) services. When booking accommodation, check availability and costs for a *lit bébé* (cot/crib).

FOOD & WINE

MARTIN MOOS

Cheese stall, Marché Maubert (p231)

No other cuisine can compare to French for freshness of ingredients and reliance on natural flavours – that's not a recent trend for things 'green' or 'organic' like elsewhere, but a predilection that dates back centuries. Add the use of refined, often very complex cooking methods and the typical Parisian's passion (some would say obsession) for anything concerned with the table and you will soon realise you are in a gourmet's paradise.

Do not think for a moment, though, that this passion for things culinary means that dining here (either out or in a private home) has to be a ceremonious or even formal occasion, full of pitfalls for the uninitiated. Just approach food and wine with half the enthusiasm that the Parisians themselves do, and you will be warmly received, tutored, encouraged and, of course, well fed.

WINE & CHEESE

Think France, think wine and cheese. The country counts upwards of 500 varieties of *fromage* (cheese) made from raw or pasteurised milk, or *petit-lait* (the whey left over after the milk fats and solids have been curdled with rennet). The selection at a *fromagerie* (cheese shop) or a Parisian market can be overwhelming – ask to sample before buying.

And wine and cheese is often a match made in heaven. In general, strong, pungent cheeses require a young, full-bodied red or a sweet wine, while soft cheeses with a refined flavour call for more quality and age in the wine. Some classic pairings include Alsatian Gewürztraminer and Munster, Côtes du Rhone red with Roquefort, Côte d'Or (Burgundy) red and Brie or Camembert, and mature Bordeaux with Emmental or

Cantal. Even Champagne can get into the act: drink it with Chaource, a mild cheese that smells of mushrooms.

A CRUST OF BREAD

Nothing is more French than *pain* (bread) – more than three-quarters of all French people eat it at every meal. All bakeries have *baguettes* (and the somewhat similar *flûtes*), which are long, thin and crusty loaves. What is simply called a *pain* is wider, softer on the inside and has a less crispy crust. Both types are at their best if eaten within four hours of baking; if you're not very hungry, ask for a *demi baguette* or a *demi pain*, which is half a loaf. A *ficelle* is a thinner, crustier version of a baguette.

CHARCUTERIE & WINE

Traditionally *charcuterie* is made only from pork, though a number of other meats –

PARIS IN FOCUS

THE BEST

WILL SALTER

Rue Montorgueil markets (p76)

FOOD MARKETS

- **Rue Montorgueil** (p76)
- **Rue Mouffetard** (p231)
- **Rue Cler** (p185)
- **Marché Bastille** (Map p108; bd Richard Lenoir, 11e; ☺ 7am-2.30pm Thu & Sun; Ⓜ Bastille or Richard Lenoir)

FOOD & WINE

from beef and veal to chicken and goose – are now used in making sausages, blood puddings, hams, and other cured- and salted-meat products.

Every region in France produces standard *charcuterie* favourites as well as its own specialities. Pâtés, terrines and *rillettes* – potted meat or even fish that is shredded, seasoned, mixed with fat and spread cold, like pâté, over bread or toast – are essentially

HOLGER LEUE

French bread and croissants

MACARON ME HAPPY

Like all French people, Parisians love *sucreries* (sweet things), and judging from the saliva-inducing window displays at pastry shops, they can't get enough. But one stands out: Ladurée (Map p144; ☎ 01 40 75 08 75; www.laduree.fr, in French; 75 av des Champs-Élysées, 8e; ⊙ 7.30am-11.30 Sun-Thu, 7.30-12.30am Fri, 8.30am-12.30am Sat; Ⓜ George V). Specialities at this most decadent of Parisian patisseries include its own inventions, *macarons* (especially the chocolate and pistachio variety) and *le baiser Ladurée* (layered almond cake). There's also a St-Germain branch (☎ 01 40 44 07 64 87; 21 rue Bonaparte, 7e; ⊙ 8.30am-7.30pm Mon-Fri, 8.30am-8.30pm Sat, 10am-7.30pm Sun; Ⓜ St-Germain des Prés).

charcuterie and are prepared in many different ways. They're all often nibbled on with wine, some of the most popular are *jambon* (ham, either smoked or salt-cured), *saucisse* (usually a small fresh sausage that is boiled or grilled before eating), *saucisson* (usually a large salami eaten cold) and *saucisson sec* (air-dried salami).

PARISIAN CUISINE

La cuisine parisienne (Parisian cuisine) and that of the Île de France surrounding the capital are basically indistinguishable from the cooking of France in general. Dishes specifically associated with these regions are few – *vol-au-vent,* a light pastry shell filled with chicken or fish in a creamy sauce; *potage Saint-Germain,* a thick green pea soup; *gâteau Paris-Brest,* a ring-shaped cake filled with *praline* (butter cream) and topped with flaked almonds and icing sugar; and the humble onion soup and pigs trotters described so intimately in Ernest Hemingway's *The Sun Also Rises. Frites* (deep-fried potatoes), and dishes such as *steak-frites,* have always been a Parisian speciality.

HISTORY

DAN HERRICK

Arc de Triomphe (p149)

As the capital, Paris is the administrative, business and cultural centre of France; virtually everything of importance in the republic starts, finishes or is currently taking place here. Throughout its illustrious history, political rebellion has remained a constant theme, and since before the French Revolution, it has been what urban planners call a 'hypertropic city' – the enlarged head of a nation-state's body.

The French have always said *'Quand Paris éternue, la France s'en rhume'* (When Paris sneezes, France catches cold), but there have been conscious efforts – going back at least four decades – by governments to decentralise Paris' role. During that time the population, and thus to a certain extent the city's authority, has actually shrunk. It dropped by 2% between 2004 and 2010.

THE BEGINNINGS TO THE RENAISSANCE

Paris was born in the 3rd century BC, when a tribe of Celtic Gauls known as the Parisii settled on what is now the Île de la Cité. Centuries of conflict between the Gauls and Romans ended in 52 BC, when Julius Caesar's legions crushed a Celtic revolt. Christianity

3rd Century BC	AD 845–86	1253
Celtic Gauls called Parisii arrive in the Paris area and set up huts on what is now the Île de la Cité, and engage in fishing and trading.	Paris is repeatedly raided by Vikings for more than four decades but ends in victory for the French.	La Sorbonne is founded by Robert de Sorbon as a theological college for impoverished students.

THE BEST

Musée d'Art et d'Histoire du Judaïsme (p108)

HISTORICAL SIGHTS

- **Archives Nationales** (p108)
- **Musée d'Art et d'Histoire du Judaïsme** (Museum of the Art and History of Judaism; p108)
- **Cimetière du Père Lachaise** (p107)
- **Les Catacombes** (p195)
- **Château de Versailles** (p238)

was introduced in the 2nd century AD, and Roman rule ended in the 5th century with the arrival of the Germanic Franks. In 508 Frankish king Clovis I united Gaul and made Paris his seat.

France's west coast was beset in the 9th century by Scandinavian Vikings (also known as Norsemen and, later, as Normans). Three centuries later, the Normans started pushing towards Paris, which had risen rapidly in importance: construction had begun on the cathedral of Notre Dame in the 12th century, the Louvre began life as a riverside fortress around 1200, the beautiful Ste-Chapelle was consecrated in 1248 and the Sorbonne opened in 1253.

The Vikings' incursions heralded the Hundred Years' War between Norman England and Paris' Capetian dynasty, bringing French defeat in 1415 and English control of the capital in 1420. In 1429 the 17-year-old Jeanne d'Arc (Joan of Arc) rallied the French troops to defeat the English at Orléans. With the exception of Calais, the English were eventually expelled from France in 1453.

The Renaissance helped Paris get back on its feet in the late 15th century. Less than a century later, however, turmoil ensued as clashes between Huguenot (Protestant) and Catholic groups culminated in the St Bartholomew's Day massacre in 1572, in which 3000 Huguenots died.

THE REVOLUTION TO A NEW REPUBLIC

A five-year-old Louis XIV ascended the throne in 1643 and ruled until 1715, virtually emptying the national coffers with his ambitious battling and building, including his extravagant palace at Versailles (p238). The excesses of the grandiose king and his heirs led to an uprising of Parisians on 14 July 1789, kick-starting the French Revolution. Within four years, the so-called Reign of Terror was in full swing.

The unstable postrevolutionary government was consolidated in 1799 under Napoleon Bonaparte, who declared himself first consul. In 1804 he had the Pope crown

1682	14 July 1789	1889
Louis XIV, the 'Sun King', moves his court from the Palais des Tuileries in Paris to Versailles.	The French Revolution begins when a mob storms the prison at Bastille.	The Eiffel Tower is completed in time for the opening of the Exposition Universelle (World Exhibition).

him emperor of the French, going on to conquer most of Europe before his defeat at Waterloo in present-day Belgium in 1815. He was exiled and died in 1821.

France struggled under a string of mostly inept rulers until a coup d'état in 1851 brought Emperor Napoleon III to power. At his behest, Baron Haussmann razed whole tracts of the city, replacing them with sculptured parks, a hygienic sewer system and – strategically – boulevards too broad for rebels to barricade. Napoleon III embroiled France in a costly war with Prussia in 1870, which ended within months with the French army's defeat and the capture of the emperor. When the masses in Paris heard the news, they took to the streets, demanding that a republic be declared.

20TH CENTURY HISTORY

Out of WWI's conflict came increased industrialisation, confirming Paris' place as a major commercial, as well as artistic, centre and establishing its reputation among freethinking intellectuals. This was halted by WWII and the Nazi occupation of 1940; Paris would remain under direct German rule until 25 August 1944. After the war, Paris regained its position as a creative nucleus and nurtured a revitalised liberalism that peaked with the student-led uprisings of May 1968 – the Sorbonne was occupied, the Latin Quarter blockaded and a general strike paralysed the country.

DENNIS JOHNSON

Bust in Louis XIV's bedchamber, Château de Versailles (p238)

1922	25 August 1944	1968
Sylvia Beach of the Shakespeare & Company bookshop (p233) publishes James Joyce's *Ulysses*.	Spearheaded by Free French units, Allied forces liberate Paris and the city escapes destruction.	Paris is rocked by student-led riots that bring the nation and the city to the brink of civil war.

PARIS IN FOCUS

HISTORY

THE BEST

CHRISTOPHER WOOD

Palais Garnier (p150)

HISTORIC NIGHTLIFE

- **Comédie Française** (p79)
- **Moulin Rouge** (p141)
- **Palais Garnier** (p150)
- **Au Lapin Agile** (p141)

Under centre-right President Jacques Chirac's watch, the late 1990s saw Paris seize the international spotlight with the rumour-plagued death of Princess Di in 1997, and France's first-ever World Cup victory in July 1998.

THE NEW MILLENIUM

In May 2001 Socialist Bertrand Delanoë was elected mayor, becoming widely popular for making Paris more liveable through improved infrastructure and green spaces. Chirac (himself a former Paris mayor) named Dominique de Villepin as prime minister in 2005. In October that year, the deaths of two teenagers who were electrocuted while allegedly hiding from police in an electricity substation sparked riots that quickly spread across Paris, and then across France. Consequently, the government promised to address the disenfranchisement felt by unemployed French youth, but one of Villepin's first efforts – the introduction of two-year work contracts for workers under 26 years old – was met by street protests and transport strikes by sympathetic unions around the country, sparking comparisons with May '68. Backed by a reputed 70% of the French public, Chirac overrode Villepin, scrapping the week-old law.

THE FRENCH RESISTANCE

Despite the infamy of 'la France Résistante' (the French Resistance), the underground movement never actually included more than 5% of the population. Resistance members engaged in railway sabotage, collected intelligence for the Allies, helped Allied airmen who had been shot down and published anti-German leaflets, among other activities. The impact of their pursuits might have been modest but the Resistance served as an enormous boost to French morale – not to mention fresh fodder for numerous literary and cinematic endeavours.

1977	1994	2001
The Centre Pompidou, the first of a string of *grands projets*, opens to great controversy.	Eurostar trains link Waterloo station in London with the Gare du Nord in Paris in just over three hours.	Socialist Bertrand Delanoë becomes the first openly gay mayor of Paris.

SARKOSIS

First there was Cécilia, his second wife – of 11 years – and mother of one of his three children. Within three months of the couple divorcing, Sarkozy had met, wooed and married Italian Carla Bruni, a singer and former supermodel. Dozens of biographies have been published on the couple, including one in which Bruni spills the beans on the intimacies of their relationship. In contrast to the fact that the French are normally unimpressed with celebrity, no one could get enough of the French president and his First Lady. In 2008 a psychiatrist in Paris identified people's unhealthy obsession with Sarkozy as 'Sarkosis'.

RECENT HISTORY

Chirac retired in 2007. With Dominique de Villepin's political career blighted, Chirac's centre-right successor, Nicolas 'Sarko' Sarkozy, beat Socialist Ségolène 'Ségo' Royal in the 2007 presidential elections, and appointed François Fillon prime minister. Sarkozy's win was widely attributed to his platform of economic reform, with many French claiming it was time for 'modernisation'. In his first year of office, Sarkozy complied, though not in the way people anticipated (see the boxed text, above). The French, who consider private lives to be emphatically that, were unimpressed at the *peopolisation* (media/celebrity hype) surrounding the presidency. The right subsequently suffered heavily at France's March 2008 municipal elections, including Paris mayor Delanoë's comfortable re-election.

Since then, Sarkozy's personal life has attracted less press than his political endeavours, particularly July 2008's constitutional reform, which squeaked through by two votes. These changes to President Charles de Gaulle's 1958 constitution include a two-term limit for presidents and, most controversially, give the president an annual parliamentary address – something barred for the French head of state since 1875 to separate executive and legislative powers. Opponents believe this to be a 'coronation' of the president (a contentious concept in France). The next presidential elections take place in 2012, with Socialist Delanoë tipped to be a contender.

2004–2005	2007	2010
The French electorate rejects the EU Constitution; Arab and African youths riot in Parisian suburbs.	Pro-American pragmatist Nicolas Sarkozy becomes France's new president.	Sarkozy's power base is weakened in nationwide local elections, receiving just 35% of the vote.

LIFESTYLE

PARIS IN FOCUS

LIFESTYLE

BRUCE B

Band playing on the banks of the Seine during Paris Plages (p48)

'Wow,' a fresh-off-the-plane traveller once exclaimed to us, 'Paris is so French!' Irony aside, he's right. It is. The capital of both the *region* – Île-de-France – and the country, Paris is defined by its walls (that is, the *Périphérique,* or ring road). This makes Paris in effect an 'island within an island' (or, as residents of other regions might say, a bubble).

Intra-muros (Latin for 'within the walls'), the city spans 105 sq metres and has a population of just under 2.2 million. This dense inner-city population defines life in Paris. Residential apartments are often miniscule and, as a result, communal spaces are the Parisians' backyards. Neighbourhood shops are the cornerstones of community life, and street markets, parks and other facets of day-to-day living evoke a village atmosphere. A lack of high-rises gives it all a human scale.

Parisians have a finely tuned sense of aesthetics, and take meticulous care in the presentation of everything from food to fashion – you'll never see a Parisian leave their apartment with just-out-of-the-shower wet hair. Smart casual is a fail-safe form of dress, but it's nearly impossible to overdress in this fashion-conscious city.

Etiquette – itself a French word – is extremely important in Paris. People who know each other well greet one another with *bises* (kisses), usually one glancing peck on each cheek (starting with the left). People always stand up when meeting one another for the first time (and usually shake hands). Conversations often revolve around philosophy, art and sports such as football and tennis; talking about money is generally taboo in public.

LITERARY PARIS

WILL SALTER

Shakespeare & Company (p233)

Flicking through a street directory reveals just how much Paris honours its literary history, with listings including Place Colette, avenues Marcel Proust and Emile Zola and rues Balzac and Ernest Hemingway. The city has nurtured countless French authors over the centuries who, together with expat writers who made their pilgrimage here, sealed Paris' literary reputation.

You can leaf through the capital's heritage in atmospheric bookshops – including the famed Shakespeare & Co (p233), which also features regular literary events and readings (often by emerging writers and in English), a prime way to embrace the written word in the present – and libraries; hang out in cafés and swish literary bars once frequented by the likes of Sartre, de Beauvoir and Hemingway – such as Café de Flore (p209) and Les Deux Magots (p209); and pay your respects to Oscar Wilde and other departed writers at Cemetière du Père Lachaise (p107). As Hemingway wrote in *A Moveable Feast*, 'There is never any ending to Paris'.

Lining both banks of the Seine through the centre of Paris, the open-air *bouqinistes* stalls selling secondhand (and often out-of-print) books, rare magazines, postcards and old advertising posters are a definitive Parisian experience – haggling over volumes is the norm here. The name comes from *bouquiner*, which means to read with pleasure. At night, their dark metal green stalls fold down and lock like suitcases. Many only open spring to autumn, but even in the depths of winter you'll find some to barter for antiquarian treasures.

For the best stroll through Paris' literary history, take our Latin Quarter Literary Loop (p218) walking tour.

PARKS & GARDENS

CRAIG PERSHOUSE

Jardin des Tuileries (p66)

Paris' elegantly laid out parks and gardens are idyllic for strolling around or simply laying back and soaking up the sunshine in – you'll find plenty of benches and cafés peppered about. Join Parisians soaking up a bit of greenery – few locals have private gardens or balconies – and press pause.

The most extraordinary of the traditional parks in central Paris is the Jardin du Luxembourg (p198), with its signature jade-green chairs to perch on and the formal, sculpture-filled Jardin des Tuileries (p66). The sprawling lawns of the Parc du Champ de Mars (p172), extending from the Eiffel Tower, and the Seine-hugging botanical garden, Jardin des Plantes (p222) are not to be missed. And one of Paris' charms is its small, secreted gardens tucked between its gracious old buildings. A comprehensive list by *arrondissement* is available at www.paris-walking-tours.com/parisgardens.html.

Paris Respire (Paris Breathes) kicks motorised traffic off certain streets at certain times to let pedestrians, cyclists and other non-motorised cruisers breathe. Specific tracks throughout the city are off-limits to cars on Sunday and public holidays: most notable are the central areas along both banks of the Seine (from 9am to 5pm); almost all of the central Marais (from 10am to 7.30pm summer, 10am to 6pm winter); the stretch in the Latin Quarter along rue Mouffetard extending north along rue Descartes (from 10am to 6pm); the Bastille's rue de la Roquette and surrounding streets (from 10am to 6pm); all the streets in Montmartre (from 11am to 6pm); and the immediate streets surrounding the Jardin du Luxembourg (from 10am to 6pm March to November). For updates on exact routes and detailed maps, see www.velo.paris.fr.

SHOPPING

Fashion on Ave des Champs-Élysées (p149)

KRZYSZTOF DYDYNSKI

Paris is famous for its luxury avenues with designer fashion and famous *grands magasins* (department stores), but the real charm of Parisian shopping resides in a stroll through the side streets, where tiny speciality shops and quirky boutiques sell everything from strawberry-scented Wellington boots to green-tea chocolates.

Shops are spread out across different neighbourhoods, inspiring very different styles of shopping. If what the French do best – fashion – is what you're after, then tread the *haute couture* (high fashion), luxury jewellery and designer perfume boardwalks near the Champs-Élysées. Just remember: the most exclusive designer boutiques require customers to buzz to get in – don't be shy about ringing the bell. For original fashion, both street and vintage, the addictive maze of boutique shopping in the Marais and St-Germain will keep you on your toes.

Fashion is but one wallet temptation. Parisian shopping is an exquisite Pandora's Box of fine, wine and tea; books, art and antiques. Check out the Marais neighbourhood or the large department stores for gifts and souvenirs –

❯ SPECIALITY STREETS

- **Rue du Pont Louis-Philippe, 4e** (Map p83; Ⓜ Pont Marie) Stationery and fine paper.
- **Rue Keller, 11e** (Map p99; Ⓜ Ledru Rollin) Comic books, mangas, DVDs.
- **Rue Victor Massé, 9e** (Map p126; Ⓜ Pigalle) Musical instruments.
- **Rue Drouot, 9e** (Map p145; Ⓜ Richelieu Drouot) Collectable postage stamps.

➤ TOP SHOPPING TIPS

- Start with an overview of Paris fashion at department stores like Le Bon Marché (p186), Galeries Lafayette (p161) and Le Printemps (p161).
- Clothes shopping in France is 'look but don't touch' style, meaning no disturbing perfectly folded piles of T-shirts or trying on shades without asking.
- Returning or exchanging a purchase without the *ticket de caisse* (receipt) is impossible. Keep the receipt safe and know you have one month to change the item.
- Buying a present for someone or simply fancy your purchase exquisitely gift-wrapped? Ask for *un paquet cadeau* (gift-wrapping). It costs nothing and is something practically every shop does – and very beautifully too.
- Don't want to DIY? Invest in a personalised shopping tour by foot or chauffeur: www.secretsofparis.com and www.chicshoppingparis.com are two of many.

be it a music box to enchant, a hammock to string between trees or a truffle to shave on pasta.

With its catwalk fashion and boutique fare Parisian shopping is not really for the dedicated bargain hunter. But there are bargains to be had – at the city's clutch of flea markets and twice a year during the annual soldes (sales) which see prices slashed by as much as 50%; sales usually last a month, starting in mid-January and again in mid-June.

Wherever you go, you'll be greeted with a '*Bonjour*' (Hello). Be sure to say '*Bonjour*', or *Bon Soir* (Good Evening; after 5pm or so) back – it's impolite not to.

↳ DIRECTORY & TRANSPORT

DIRECTORY
ACCOMMODATION
APARTMENTS & FLATS
If you are interested in renting a furnished flat for anything from a night to a month, consult one of the many agencies listed under 'Furnished Rentals' in the Hotels & Accommodation section of the **Paris Convention & Visitors Bureau** (www. parisinfo.com) website.

HOTELS
Paris may not be able to boast the number of budget hotels it did a decade or so ago, but the choice is still more than ample, especially in the Marais, around the Bastille and near the major train stations. Places with one star and those with the designations 'HT' (Hôtel de Tourisme) or 'NN' (Nouvelle Norme), which signifies that a hotel is awaiting its rating but remains of a certain standard of comfort, are much of a muchness. Be advised that some budget hotels in Paris do not accept credit cards.

Breakfast – usually a simple Continental affair of bread, croissants, butter, jam and coffee or tea – is served at most hotels with two or more stars and usually costs around €8.

BOOK YOUR STAY ONLINE

For more accommodation reviews and recommendations by Lonely Planet authors, check out the online booking service at www.lonely planet.com. You'll find the true, insider lowdown on the best places to stay. Reviews are thorough and independent. Best of all, you can book online.

PRICE GUIDE

Sleeping prices in this book are full price in high season and include bathroom. Exceptions are noted in specific listings.

Eating price ranges are based on a two-course meal.

		Sleeping	Eating
Budget	€	<€80	<€20
Midrange	€€	€80-180	€20-40
Top end	€€€	>€180	>€40

Some hotels in Paris have different rates according to the season and are noted as such throughout this guide. The high season is (roughly) from April to September while the low season is from October to March. There are usually bargains to be had during the late autumn (November) and winter months (January and February).

B&BS
Bed-and-breakfast (B&B) accommodation – known as *chambres d'hôte* in French – has never been anywhere near as popular in Paris as it has been in, say, London but that is changing. The city of Paris has inaugurated a scheme called **Paris Quality Hosts** (www.hqp.fr) to encourage Parisians to rent out their spare rooms. Expect to pay anything from €50 for a double. Most hosts will expect you to stay a minimum of three or four nights.

CLIMATE
The Paris basin lies midway between coastal Brittany and mountainous Alsace and is affected by both climates. The Île de France region, of which Paris is the centre, records among the lowest annual precipitation (about 640mm) in the nation, but rainfall is erratic; you're just as likely to be

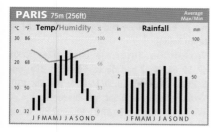

caught in a heavy spring shower or an autumn downpour as in a sudden summer cloudburst. Paris' average yearly temperature is just under 12°C (2°C in January, 19°C in July), but the mercury sometimes drops below zero in winter and can climb into the 30s in the middle of summer.

Check the Météo France website (www. meteofrance.com, in French) for a reliable three-day forecast. The national forecast can be heard on ☎ 0 899 701 234 in French or ☎ 0 899 701 111 in one of 11 different languages. Call charges for either number are €1.35 then €0.35 per minute.

COOKING COURSES

Cours de Cuisine Olivier Berté (Map p62; ☎ 01 40 26 14 00; www.coursdecuisineparis.com; 2nd fl, 7 rue Paul Lelong, 2e; Ⓜ Bourse), offers three-hour courses (adult/child €100/30) at 10.30am from Wednesday to Saturday with an additional class from 6pm to 9pm on Friday. Children's classes (ages seven and up) are on Wednesday at 3pm.

Much more expensive are the **Paris Cooking Classes with Patricia Wells** (www. patriciawells.com; US$5000) led by the incomparable American food critic and author. The class runs from Monday to Friday and includes market visits, tastings, local transport and daily lunch. A new private class is run by **Eye Prefer Paris** (www.eyeprefer paristours.com; €185; Ⓨ Wed-Sun). Courses last four and a half hours and focus on French cuisine with influences from Southeast Asia, the Middle East and Africa.

CUSTOMS REGULATIONS

Duty-free shopping within the EU was abolished in 1999. However, you can still enter an EU country with duty-free items from countries *outside* the EU, where the usual allowances apply: 200 cigarettes, 50 cigars or 250g of loose tobacco; 2L of still wine and 1L of spirits; 50g of perfume and 250cc of eau de toilette.

Do not confuse these with *duty-paid* items (including alcohol and tobacco) bought at normal shops in another EU country (eg Spain or Germany) and brought into France. Here allowances are: 800 cigarettes, 200 cigars, 400 small cigars or 1kg of loose tobacco; and 10L of spirits (more than 22% alcohol by volume), 20L of fortified wine or *aperitif*, 90L of wine or 110L of beer.

DISCOUNT CARDS

The **Paris Museum Pass** (www.parismuseum-pass.fr; 2/4/6 days €32/48/64) is valid for entry to some 38 venues in Paris – including the Louvre, Centre Pompidou, Musée d'Orsay and the Arc de Triomphe – but not the Eiffel Tower.

EMBASSIES & CONSULATES

Australia (Map p172; ☎ 01 40 59 33 00; www. france.embassy.gov.au; 4 rue Jean Rey, 15e; Ⓜ Bir Hakeim)

Canada (Map p144; ☎ 01 44 43 29 00; www. amb-canada.fr; 35 av Montaigne, 8e; Ⓜ Franklin D Roosevelt)

Ireland (Map p164; ☎ 01 44 17 67 00; www.embassyofireland.fr; 4 rue Rude, 16e; Ⓜ Argentine)

Japan (Map p144; ☎ 01 48 88 62 00; www. fr.emb-japan.go.jp; 7 av Hoche, 8e; Ⓜ Courcelles)

New Zealand (Map p172; ☎ 01 45 01 43 43; www.nzembassy.com/france; 7ter rue Léonard de Vinci, 16e; Ⓜ Victor Hugo)

South Africa (Map p172; ☎ 01 53 59 23 23; www.afriquesud.net; 59 quai d'Orsay, 7e; Ⓜ Invalides)

UK (Map p150; ☎ 01 44 51 31 00; http://ukin france.fco.gov.uk; 35 rue du Faubourg St-Honoré, 8e; Ⓜ Concorde)

USA (Map p150; ☎ 01 43 12 22 22; http://france. usembassy.gov; 2 av Gabriel, 8e; Ⓜ Concorde)

INSURANCE

A travel insurance policy to cover theft, loss and medical problems is a good idea. EU citizens on public-health insurance schemes should note that they're generally covered by reciprocal arrangements in France.

You may prefer a policy which pays doctors or hospitals directly rather than you having to pay on the spot and then claim it back later. If you have to claim later make sure you keep all documentation. Ensure that your policy covers ambulances or an emergency flight home.

Paying for your airline ticket with a credit card often provides limited travel accident insurance, and you may be able to reclaim the payment if the operator doesn't deliver. Ask your credit card company what it's prepared to cover.

INTERNET ACCESS

Wi-fi is widely available at midrange and top-end hotels in Paris as well as some 260 public hotspots (look for a network with 'gratuit' in the name). The public wi-fi scheme is limited, however (in some spots no more than 20 minutes); (the icon ☎ in this book indicates wi-fi is available).

Paris is awash with internet cafés:

Milk Latin Quarter (Map p214; ☎ 01 43 54 55 55; www.milklub.com; 17 rue Soufflot, 5e; per 15/30/60min €1.99/2.99/3.99; ☺ 24hr; Ⓜ Luxembourg); Les Halles branch (Map p62; ☎ 01 40 13 06 51; 31 bd de Sébastopol, 1er; ☺ 24hr; Ⓜ Les Halles)

Phon'net (Map p98; 74 rue de Charonne, 11e; per hr €2; ☺ 10am-midnight; Ⓜ Charonne or Ledru Rollin)

Taxiphone Internet (Map p126; ☎ 01 42 59 64 14; 2 rue de La Vieuville, 18e; per 5/10/20/30/60min €0.50/1/2/3/4, per 5hr €10; ☺ 9am-7.30pm Mon-Sat; Ⓜ Abbesses)

Web 46 (Map p108; ☎ 01 40 27 02 89; 46 rue du Roi de Sicile, 4e; per 15/30/60min €2.50/4/7, per 5hr €29; ☺ 9.30am-10.30pm Mon-Fri, 9.30am-9pm Sat, 11am-10.30pm Sun; Ⓜ St-Paul)

LEGAL MATTERS

The police can search anyone they want to at any time – whether or not there is probable cause.

France has two separate police forces. The Police Nationale, under the command of departmental prefects (and, in Paris, the Préfet de Police), includes the Police de l'Air et des Frontières (PAF; the border police). The Gendarmerie Nationale, a paramilitary force under the control of the Ministry of Defence, handles airports, borders and so on. During times of crisis (eg a wave of terrorist attacks), the army may be called in to patrol public places.

Be aware that the police can, without any particular reason, ask to examine your passport, visa, *carte de séjour* (residence permit) and so on. You are expected to have photo ID on you at all times.

French police are very strict about security. Do not leave baggage unattended; they are quite serious when they say that suspicious objects will be summarily blown up.

MEDICAL SERVICES

If you are not an EU citizen, it is imperative that you take out travel insurance before your departure. EU passport holders have access to the French social security system, which reimburses up to 70% of medical costs.

HOSPITALS

There are some 50 *assistance publique* (public health service) hospitals in Paris. If you need an ambulance while in the city, call ☎ 15; the EU-wide emergency number (with English speakers) is ☎ 112. For emergency treatment, call Urgences Médicales de Paris (☎ 01 53 94 94 94) or SOS Médecins (☎ 01 47 07 77 77 or 3624), both of which offer 24-hour house calls costing between €35 and €90 depending on the time of day and whether you have French social security.

PHARMACIES

Pharmacies with extended hours:
Pharmacie Bader (Map p82; ☎ 01 43 26 92 66; 12 bd St-Michel, 5e; ⊙ 9am-9pm; Ⓜ St-Michel)
Pharmacie des Champs (Map p144; ☎ 01 45 62 02 41; Galerie des Champs, 84 av des Champs-Élysées, 8e; ⊙ 24hr; Ⓜ George V)
Pharmacie des Halles (Map p62; ☎ 01 42 72 03 23; 10 bd de Sébastopol, 4e; ⊙ 9am-midnight Mon-Sat, 9am-10pm Sun; Ⓜ Châtelet)

ORGANISED TOURS
BICYCLE

Fat Tire Bike Tours (Map p172; ☎ 01 56 58 10 54; www.fattirebiketours.com; 24 rue Edgar Faure, 15e; ⊙ office 9am-6pm; Ⓜ La Motte-Picquet Grenelle) offers daytime bike tours of the city (adult/student €28/26; four hours), starting at 11am daily from mid-February to early January, with an additional departure at 3pm from April to October.

Bike About Tours (Map p108; ☎ 06 18 80 84 92; www.bikeabouttours.com; 4 Rue Lobau, 4e; ⊙ office 10am-7pm; Ⓜ Hôtel de Ville) is another expat-run tour group, offering 3.5-hour daytime tours (adult/student €30/28). Tours begin at 10pm and run from mid-February to November, with an extra 3pm tour from mid-May to September.

BOAT
CANAL CRUISES

Canauxrama (☎ 01 42 39 15 00; www.canauxrama.com; Bassin de la Villette, 13 quai de la Loire, 19e; adult/4-12yr/student & senior €15/8/11; ⊙ Mar-Nov, call in winter; Ⓜ Jaurès) has barges that run from the Bastille to Parc de la Villette along the Canal St-Martin and Canal de l'Ourcq. Departures are at 9.45am and 2.30/2.45pm from the Bastille and Parc de la Villette. Note that the boat goes at a very leisurely pace (2½ hours total) as it passes through four double locks. There is also an underground section (with an art installation).

Paris Canal Croisières (☎ 01 42 40 96 97; www.pariscanal.com; Bassin de la Villette, 19-21 quai de la Loire, 19e; adult/4-11yr/senior & 12-25yr €17/10/14; ⊙ late Mar–mid-Nov; Ⓜ Jaurès or Musée d'Orsay) has 2½-hour cruises from near the Musée d'Orsay (quai Anatole France) at 9.30am, departing from Parc de la Villette for the return trip at 2.30pm.

RIVER CRUISES

Bateaux-Mouches (Map p144; ☎ 01 42 25 96 10; www.bateauxmouches.com; Port de la Conférence, 8e; adult/senior & 4-12yr €10/5; ⊙ mid-Mar-mid-Nov; Ⓜ Alma Marceau) runs nine 1000-seat glassed-in tour boats. Cruises (70 minutes) run regularly from 10.15am to 11pm April to September and 13 times a day between 11am and 9pm the rest of the year.

Bateaux Parisiens (Map p144; ☎ 01 76 64 14 45; www.bateauxparisiens.com; Port de la Bourdonnais, 7e; adult/3-11yr €11/5; ⊙ every half hr 10am-10.30pm Apr-Sep, hourly 10am-10pm Oct-Mar; Ⓜ Pont de l'Alma) runs smaller boats that do one-hour river circuits with recorded commentary in 13 different languages.

BUS

L'Open Tour (Map p150; ☎ 01 42 66 56 56; www.pariscityrama.com; 13 rue Auber, 9e; 1 day adult/4-11yr €29/15, 2 consecutive days €32/15;

DIRECTORY

M Havre Caumartin or Opéra) runs open-deck buses along four circuits (central Paris; Montmartre–Grands Boulevards; Bastille–Bercy; and Montparnasse–St-Germain) daily year-round.

In season, the RATP's **Balabus** (☎ 3246; www.ratp.fr; €1.70 or 1 metro/bus ticket; ☾ departures 12.30-8pm from La Défense, 1.30pm from Gare de Lyon Sun Apr-Sep), designed for tourists, follows a 50-minute route to/from Gare de Lyon and La Défense, passing many of central Paris' most famous sights.

WALKING

The following organisations offer walking tours.

Ça Se Visite (☎ 01 43 57 59 50; www.ca-se-visite.fr, in French; €12) Meet local artists and craftspeople on resident-led 'urban discovery tours'. Reserve ahead for English tours.

Eye Prefer Paris (www.eyepreferparistours.com; €195 for 3 people) New Yorker turned Parisian leads offbeat tours of the city. Cooking classes also available.

Paris Go (☎ 01 53 30 74 40; www.parisgo.fr; €20) Two-hour thematic tours followed by drinks in a local café or bar. Reserve ahead for English tours.

Paris Greeter (www.parisiendunjour.fr; donation) See Paris through local eyes. Minimum two week's advance notice needed.

Paris Walks (☎ 01 48 09 21 40; www.paris-walks.com; adult/15-21/under 15 €12/10/8) Paris Walks offers thematic tours (fashion, chocolate, the French Revolution) in English.

TAXES & REFUNDS

France's value-added tax (VAT) is known as TVA *(taxe sur la valeur ajoutée)* and is 19.6% on most goods except medicine and books, for which it's 5.5%. Prices

that include TVA are often marked TTC *(toutes taxes comprises;* literally 'all taxes included').

If you're not an EU resident, you can get a TVA refund provided that: you're aged over 15; you'll be spending less than six months in France; you purchase goods worth at least €175 at a single shop on the same day (not more than 10 of the same item); the goods fit into your luggage; you are taking the goods out of France within three months after purchase; and the shop offers *vente en détaxe* (duty-free sales).

Present a passport at the time of purchase and ask for a *bordereau de vente à l'exportation* (export sales invoice) to be signed by the retailer and yourself. Most shops will refund less than the full amount (about 14%) to which you are entitled, in order to cover the time and expense involved in the refund procedure.

For more information contact the **customs information centre** (☎ 08 11 20 44 44; www.douane.minefi.gouv.fr; ☾ 8.30am-6pm Mon-Fri).

TELEPHONE

France's country code is ☎ 33. To call a number in Paris from outside France, dial your country's international access code (usually ☎ 00 but exceptions include ☎ 011 from the USA and ☎ 001 from Hong Kong), then ☎ 33 and then the local number, omitting the first '0'.

To call abroad from Paris, dial France's international access code (☎ 00), the country code, the area code (usually without the initial '0', if there is one) and the local number. International Direct Dial (IDD) calls to almost anywhere in the world can be placed from public telephones. The international reduced rate applies from 7pm to 8am weekdays and all day at the weekend.

For international directory enquiries, dial ☎ 3212. Note that the cost for this service is €3 per call.

MOBILE PHONES

You can use your smart phone or mobile phone (*portable*) in France provided that it is GSM (the standard in Europe which is becoming increasingly common elsewhere) and is tri-band or quad-band. It is a good idea to ensure it is 'unlocked', which means you can use another service provider while abroad. If you meet the requirements, you can check with your service provider about using it in France, but beware of calls being routed internationally, which can make a 'local' call very expensive indeed.

PHONECARDS

Public telephones in Paris usually require a *télécarte* (phonecard; €7.50/15 for 50/120 calling units), which can be purchased at post offices, *tabacs,* supermarkets, SNCF ticket windows, metro stations and anywhere you see a blue sticker reading '*télécarte en vente ici*' (phonecard for sale here).

You can buy prepaid phonecards in France such as Allomundo (www.allomundo.com, in French) that are up to 60% cheaper for calling abroad than the standard *télécarte*. They're available in denominations of up to €15 from *tabacs,* newsagents, phone shops and other sales points.

TOURIST INFORMATION

The main branch of the **Paris Convention & Visitors Bureau** (Office de Tourisme et de Congrès de Paris; Map p62; www.parisinfo.com; 25-27 rue des Pyramides, 1er; ☺ 9am-7pm Jun-Oct, 10am-7pm Mon-Sat & 11am-7pm Sun Nov-May;

Ⓜ **Pyramides**) is about 500m northwest of the Louvre.

TRAVELLERS WITH DISABILITIES

Paris is an ancient city and is thus not particularly well equipped for *les handicapés* (disabled people): kerb ramps are few and far between, older public facilities and bottom-end hotels usually lack lifts, and the metro, dating back more than a century, is mostly inaccessible for those in a wheelchair *(fauteuil roulant)*. But efforts are being made and early in the new millennium the tourist office launched its 'Tourisme & Handicap' initiative in which museums, cultural attractions, hotels and restaurants that provided access or special assistance or facilities for those with physical, mental, visual and/or hearing disabilities would display a special logo at their entrances. For a list of the places qualifying, visit the tourist office's website (www.parisinfo.com) and click on 'Practical Paris'.

VISAS

There are no entry requirements for nationals of EU countries. Citizens of Australia, the USA, Canada and New Zealand do not need visas to visit France for up to three months. Except for people from a handful of other European countries (including Switzerland), everyone, including citizens of South Africa, needs a so-called Schengen Visa, named after the Schengen Agreement that has abolished passport controls among 22 EU countries and has also been ratified by the non-EU governments of Iceland, Norway and Switzerland. A visa for any of these countries should be valid throughout the Schengen area, but it pays to double check with the embassy or consulate of each country you intend to visit.

TRANSPORT
AIR
Most international airlines fly through Paris; for flight, route and carrier info contact **Aéroports de Paris** (☎ 39 50, from abroad +33 1 70 36 39 50; www.aeroportsdeparis.fr).

AIRPORTS
The older, smaller of Paris' two major airports, **Aéroport d'Orly** (ORY; ☎ 39 50, from abroad +33 1 70 36 39 50; www.aeroportsdeparis. fr), is 19km south of the city.

Aéroport Roissy Charles de Gaulle (CDG; ☎ 39 50, from abroad +33 1 70 36 39 50; www.aeroportsdeparis.fr) is 28km northeast of central Paris in the suburb of Roissy

Charter companies and budget airlines land/take off at **Aéroport Paris-Beauvais** (BVA; ☎ 0 892 682 066; www.aeroportbeauvais. com), 75km north of central Paris.

GETTING INTO TOWN FROM THE AIRPORT
Children under four travel free and those between four and nine (inclusive) pay half-price on most of the services listed below; exceptions are noted.

Door-to-door alternatives include taxi (€35 to €50 between central Paris and Orly, €45 to €60 to/from Charles de Gaulle, €140 to €180 to/from Beauvais; see p279 for taxi telephone numbers); or a private minibus shuttle such as **Allô Shuttle** (☎ 01 41 10 98 11; www.alloshuttle.com), **Paris Airports Service** (☎ 01 55 98 10 80; www. parisairportservice.com) or **PariShuttle** (☎ 01 53 39 18 18; www.parishuttle.com). Count on from €20/30 per one/two person(s) (from €40 between 8pm and 6am) for Orly or Charles de Gaulle and from €140 for one to four people to/from Beauvais. Book in advance.

Aéroport d'Orly
Unless noted otherwise, these options to/ from Orly call at both terminals.

Air France bus 1 (☎ 0 892 350 820; http:// videocdn.airfrance.com/cars-airfrance; adult single/return €11.50/18.50; ☼ from Orly 6.15am-11.150pm, from Invalides 6am-11.30pm) This *navette* (shuttle bus) runs every 30 minutes to/from the eastern side of Gare Montparnasse (Map p196; 35 minutes) and Aérogare des Invalides (Map p172; 35 minutes) in the 7e. Children aged two to 11 pay half-price.

Noctilien bus 31 (☎ 32 46; www.noctilien. fr; adult €6.40 or 4 metro tickets; ☼ 12.30am-5.30pm) Part of the RATP's night service, Noctilien bus 31 links Gare de Lyon (Map p98), Gare d'Austerlitz (Map p215)

⮵ CLIMATE CHANGE & TRAVEL
Every form of transport that relies on carbon-based fuel generates CO_2, the main cause of human-induced climate change. Modern travel is dependent on aeroplanes, which might use less fuel per kilometer per person than most cars but travel much greater distances. The altitude at which aircraft emit gases (including CO_2) and particles also contributes to their climate change impact. Many websites offer 'carbon calculators' that allow people to estimate the carbon emissions generated by their journey and, for those who wish to do so, to offset the impact of the greenhouse gases emitted with contributions to portfolios of climate-friendly initiatives throughout the world. Lonely Planet offsets the carbon footprint of all staff and author travel.

and place d'Italie with Orly-Sud. It runs every hour and journey time is 45 minutes to an hour.

Orlybus (☎ 32 46; www.ratp.fr; adult €6.40; ⏱ from Orly 6am-11.20pm, from Paris 5.35am-11.05pm) This bus runs every 15 to 20 minutes between both terminals and metro Denfert-Rochereau (Map p189; 20 to 30 minutes) in the 14e, making several stops in the eastern 14e en route.

Orlyval (☎ 32 46; www.ratp.fr; adult €9.85; ⏱ 6am-11pm) From either terminal take the Orlyval automatic rail (€7.60) to the RER B station Antony, then RER B4 north (€2.25; 35 to 40 minutes to Châtelet, every four to 12 minutes). Orlyval tickets are valid for the subsequent RER and metro journey.

RER C & shuttle (☎ 32 46; www.ratp.fr; adult €6.20; ⏱ 5am-11.30pm) From the airport, hop aboard the airport shuttle bus (every 15 to 30 minutes) to the RER station Pont de Rungis-Aéroport d'Orly, then RER C2 train to Paris' Gare d'Austerlitz (50 minutes). Coming from Paris, be sure to get the shuttle at Pont de Rungis that goes to the correct terminal.

Aéroport Roissy Charles de Gaulle

Air France bus 2 (☎ 0 892 350 820; http://videocdn.airfrance.com/cars-airfrance; adult single/return €15/24; ⏱ 5.45am-11pm) Links the airport every 30 minutes with the Arc de Triomphe outside 1 av Carnot, 17e (Map p144; 45 minutes) and Porte Maillot metro station (17e) on line 1 (Map p164; 35 to 50 minutes). Children aged two to 11 pay half-price.

Air France bus 4 (☎ 0 892 350 820; http://videocdn.airfrance.com/cars-airfrance; adult single/return €16.50/27; ⏱ from CDG 7am-9pm, from Paris 6.30am-9.30pm) Links the airport every 30 minutes with Gare de Lyon (Map p98; 50 minutes) and Gare Montparnasse (Map p196; 55 minutes). Children aged two to 11 pay half-price.

Noctilien bus 140 & 143 (☎ 32 46; www.noctilien.fr; adult €4.80 or 3 metro tickets; ⏱ 12.30am-5.30pm) Part of the RATP night service, Noctilien bus 140 from Gare de l'Est and 143 from Gare de l'Est and Gare du Nord go to Roissy-Charles de Gaulle hourly.

RER B (☎ 32 46; www.ratp.fr; adult €8.5; ⏱ 5.20am-midnight) Though this line was under extensive renovation at the time of research, with replacement buses on duty, RER line B3 usually links CDG1 and CDG2 with the city (30 minutes; every 10 to 15 minutes).

Roissybus (☎ 32 46; www.ratp.fr; adult €9.10; ⏱ 5.30am-11pm) Direct public bus linking several points at both terminals with Opéra (cnr of rue Scribe and rue Auber) in the 9e (Map p52; 45 to 60 minutes, every 15 minutes).

Aéroport Paris-Beauvais

Navette Officielle (Official Shuttle Bus; ☎ 0 892 682 064, airport 0 892 682 066; one way €14) Leaves Parking Pershing (off Map p126), west of the Palais des Congrès de Paris, 3¼ hours before flight departures (board 15 minutes before) and leaves the airport 20 minutes after arrivals, dropping passengers south of the Palais des Congrès on place de la Porte Maillot (Map p164). Journey time is one to 1¼ hours.

BICYCLE

Vélib' (☎ 01 30 79 79 30; www.velib.paris.fr; day/week/year subscription €1/5/29, bike hire 1ˢᵗ/2ⁿᵈ/3ʳᵈ & each additional half-hr free/€2/4) has revolutionised how Parisians get around. Its almost 1500 *stations Vélib'* across the city – one every 300m – sport 20-odd bike stands a head.

To get a bike, you need a Vélib' account: one- and seven-day subscriptions can be done at the terminals found at docking stations with a major credit card provided

TRANSPORT

BOAT

it has a microchip (be warned North Americans). As deposit you'll need to pre-authorise a *caution* (deposit or guarantee) of €150, which is debited if your bike is not returned or is reported as stolen. If the station you want to return your bike to is full, swipe your card across the multilingual terminal to get 15 minutes for free to find another station. Bikes are geared to cyclists aged 14 and over, and are fitted with gears, antitheft lock with key, reflective strips and front/rear lights.

BOAT

For a flexible, hop-on-and-off approach, sail with **Batobus** (☎ 0 825 050 101; www. batobus.com; **adult 1-/2-/3-day pass €13/17/20, student €9/12/14, child 2-16yr €7/9/10;** ☽ **10am-9.30pm late May-Aug, 10am-7pm Sep-early Nov & mid-Mar–late May, 10.30am-4.30pm mid-Nov–early Jan & early Feb–mid-Mar, closed early Jan-early Feb).** Its fleet of glassed-in trimarans dock at eight small piers along the Seine and tickets are sold at each stop as well as tourist offices. Boats depart every 15 to 30 minutes from various stops.

BUS
LOCAL BUSES

Paris' bus system runs from 5.30am to 8.30pm Monday to Saturday; after that certain *service en soirée* (evening service) lines continue until between midnight and 12.30am. Services are drastically reduced on Sunday and public holidays, when buses run from 7am to 8.30pm.

NIGHT BUSES

Night buses pick up after the last metro (around 1.15am Sunday to Thursday, 2.15am Friday and Saturday). Buses depart hourly from 12.30am to 5.30pm. The RATP runs 47 night bus lines known as Noctilien (www.noctilien.fr), including direct or semidirect services out to the suburbs.

Noctilien services are included on your Mobilis or Paris Visite (see opposite) pass for the zones in which you are travelling. Otherwise you pay a certain number of standard €1.60 metro/bus tickets, depending on the length of your journey.

TICKETS & FARES

Normal bus rides embracing one or two bus zones cost one metro/bus ticket; longer rides require two or even three tickets. Transfers to other buses – but not the metro – are allowed on the same ticket as long as the change takes place 1½ hours between the first and last validation. This does not apply to Noctilien services.

METRO & RER NETWORKS
METRO

Metro lines have a terminus at each end; the name of the line depends on which direction you are travelling. To simplify matters further, on maps and plans each line has a different colour and number (from 1 to 14, plus 3b and 7b).

Each line has its own schedule, but trains usually start at around 5.30am, with the last train beginning its run between 12.35am and 1.15am (2.15am on Friday and Saturday).

RER

The **RER** (☎ 32 46; www.ratp.fr; ☽ **7am-9pm Mon-Fri, 9am-5pm Sat & Sun**) is faster than the metro but the stops are much farther apart. Some attractions, particularly those on the Left Bank (eg the Musée d'Orsay, Eiffel Tower and Panthéon), can be reached far more conveniently by the RER than by the metro.

TICKETS & FARES

The same RATP tickets are valid on the metro, the RER (for travel within the city limits), buses, trams and the Montmartre funicular. A ticket costs €1.60 (half-price for children aged four to nine years) and €11.60 for adults for a *carnet* (book) of 10 (NB: half-price carnets are not available for children).

TRAVEL PASSE

Navigo (www.navigo.fr, in French) provides you with a refillable weekly, monthly or yearly unlimited pass that you can recharge at machines in most metro stations. Pay €5 for a Nagivo Découverte (Navigo Discovery) card. Passes require a passport photo. A weekly ticket *(coupon hebdomadaire)* pass costs €17.20 for zones 1 and 2 and is valid from Monday to Sunday.

TOURIST PASSES

The Mobilis and Paris Visite passes are valid on the metro, RER, SNCF's suburban lines buses, night buses, trams and Montmartre funicular railway.

The Mobilis card coupon allows unlimited travel for one day in two/three/four/five/six zones and costs €5.90/7.90/9.80/13.20/16.70.

Paris Visite allows unlimited travel (including to/from airports) as well as discounted entry to certain museums and other discounts and bonuses. Passes are valid for either three or six zones. The zone

1 to 3 pass costs €8.80/14.40/19.60/28.30 for one/two/three/five days. Children aged four to 11 years pay half-price.

TAXI

To order a taxi, call Paris' **central taxi switchboard** (☎ 01 45 30 30 30, passengers with reduced mobility 01 47 39 00 91; ☽ 24hr).

TRAIN
SUBURBAN

The RER and the commuter lines of the **SNCF** (Sociéte' Nationale des Chemins de Fer; ☎ 0 891 362 020; www.transilien.com) serve suburban destinations outside the city limits (ie zones 2 to 6) in the Île de France. Purchase your ticket *before* you board the train or you won't be able to get out of the station when you arrive. You are not allowed to pay the additional fare when you get there.

MAINLINE & INTERNATIONAL

Information for **SNCF mainline services** (☎ 36 35, 0 892 353 535; www.voyages-sncf.com) is available by phone or internet.

Eurostar (☎ 0 892 353 539, in UK 0 8432 186 186; www.eurostar.com) links Gare du Nord with London's St-Pancras International train station in just over two hours, and **Thalys** (☎ 36 35, 0 892 353 536; www.thalys.com) trains go to Brussels, Amsterdam and Cologne.

⬇ GLOSSARY

(m) indicates masculine gender, (f) feminine gender, (pl) plural, (adj) adjective

arrondissement (m) – one of 20 administrative divisions in Paris; abbreviated on street signs as 1er (1st arrondissement), 2e or 2ème (2nd) etc

banlieues (f pl) – suburbs
billet (m) – ticket
billeterie (f) – ticket office or window
boulangerie (f) – bakery
boules (f pl) – a game played with heavy metal balls on a sandy pitch; also called *pétanque*
brasserie (f) – literally 'brewery'; a restaurant that usually serves food all day long

cacher (adj) – kosher
carnet (m) – a book of (usually) 10 bus, tram, metro or other tickets sold at a reduced rate
carte de séjour (f) – residence permit
cave (f) – (wine) cellar
chambre (f) – room
chanson française (f) – 'French song'; traditional musical genre where lyrics are paramount
charcuterie (f) – a variety of meat (usually pork) products that are cured, smoked or processed; shop selling these products
cimetière (m) – cemetery
cour (f) – courtyard

demi (m) – half; 330mL glass of beer
département (m) – administrative division of France

eau (f) – water
église (f) – church

entrée (f) – entrance; first course or starter
épicerie (f) – small grocery store
espace (f) – space; outlet
exposition universelle (f) – world exhibition

fête (f) – festival; holiday
ficelle (f) – string; a thinner, crustier 200g version of the baguette
fin de siècle (adj) – 'end of the century'; characteristic of the last years of the 19th century and generally used to indicate decadence
formule (f) – similar to a *menu* but allows choice of any two of three courses
fromagerie (f) – cheese shop

galerie (f) – gallery; covered shopping arcade (also called *passage couvert*)
galette (f) – a pancake or flat pastry, with a variety of (usually savoury) fillings
gare or **gare SNCF** (f) – railway station
gendarmerie (f) – police station; police force
grand projet (m) – huge, public edifice erected by a government or individual politician
Grands Boulevards (m pl) – 'Great Boulevards'; the eight contiguous thoroughfares stretching from place de la Madeleine eastwards to place de la République

halles (f pl) – covered food market
hammam (m) – steam room, Turkish bath
haute cuisine (f) – 'high cuisine'; classic French cooking style typified by elaborately prepared multicourse meals

hôtel de ville (m) – city or town hall
hôtel particulier (m) – private mansion (especially in the Marais district)

intra-muros – 'within the walls' (Latin); refers to central Paris defined by the 20 *arrondissements*

jardin (m) – garden

marché (m) – market
marché aux puces (m) – flea market
menu (m) – fixed-price meal with two or more courses; see also *formule*
musée (m) – museum
musette (f) – accordion music

navette (f) – shuttle bus, train or boat

orangerie (f) – conservatory for growing citrus fruit

pain (m) – bread
palais de justice (m) – law courts
parc (m) – park
parvis (m) – square in front of a church or public building
passage (couvert) (m) – covered shopping arcade (also called *galerie*)
pastis (m) – an aniseed-flavoured aperitif mixed with water
pétanque (f) – a game similar to *boules*
place (f) – square or plaza
plan (m) – city map
plat du jour (m) – daily special in a restaurant

pont (m) – bridge
porte (f) – door; gate in a city wall

quartier (m) – quarter, district, neighbourhood

RATP – Régie Autonome des Transports Parisiens; Paris' public transport system
RER – Réseau Express Regional; Paris' suburban train network
rillettes (f pl) – shredded potted meat or fish
rue (f) – street or road

salle (f) – hall; room
salon de thé (m) – tearoom
SNCF – Société Nationale de Chemins de Fer; France's national railway organisation
spectacle (m) – performance, play or theatrical show

tabac (m) – tobacconist (also sells bus tickets, phonecards etc)
tartine (f) – a slice of bread with any topping or garnish
télécarte (f) – phonecard
TGV – train à grande vitesse; high-speed train
tour (f) – tower

Vélib' (m) – communal bicycle rental scheme in Paris
vélo (m) – bicycle

↘ BEHIND THE SCENES

THE AUTHORS
CAROLINE SIEG
Coordinating author

Caroline's relationship with Paris began at age 16, when a teenage obsession with Jim Morrison placed a Père Lachaise pilgrimage at the top of her must-see list. A few years later, she returned to spend six months learning French at a language school and living around the corner from the Eiffel Tower. Subsequent trips to the city yielded countless picnics on the Champs du Mars, firecracker-filled Bastille Day celebrations, the best New Year's Eve – *ever*, and more hours spent toiling away the hours in cafés and wine bars in Montmartre and the Bastille area than she can count. She also believes one of the best ways to embrace Paris is to indulge in as much cheese and bread as possible. (She's had the luxury of testing out this theory numerous times.) These days, Caroline hangs her hat in Berlin, Germany, but she visits Paris as often as she can.

Author thanks

Merci to my parents for instilling in me a lifelong zest for travel. Thanks also to Sally Schafer and Jo Potts, as well as to Sasha Baskett for managing this project and to Angela Tinson for her careful edit.

STEVE FALLON

Steve, who has worked on every edition of *Paris* and *France* except the first, was surrounded by things French from a very young age when his best friend's mother thought it would be a 'bunny day' (or was that a *bonne idée*?) to rock them in the same cradle. Convinced that Parisians were seriously devoid of a sense of humour after he and said best friend dropped water-filled balloons on the heads of passers-by from a 5e arrondissement hotel balcony at age 16, he nevertheless went back to the 'City of Light' five years later to complete a degree in French at the Sorbonne. Based in East London,

Steve will be just one Underground stop away from Paris when Eurostar trains *finally* begin departing from Stratford.

CATHERINE LE NEVEZ

Catherine first lived in Paris aged four and has been returning at every opportunity since, completing her Doctorate of Creative Arts in Writing, her Masters in Professional Writing, and postgraduate qualifications in editing and publishing along the way. Catherine's writing on Paris includes *Paris Encounter*, and newspaper and radio reportage covering the city's literary scene. Beyond Paris, she's written numerous Lonely Planet guidebooks and web reviews, including Lonely Planet's *France* and *Provence & the Côte d'Azur* guidebooks. Wanderlust aside, Paris remains her favourite city on earth.

CHRIS PITTS

Christopher Pitts has lived in Paris since 2001. He first started writing about the city as a means to buy baguettes – and to impress a certain Parisian (it worked; they're now married with two kids). Over the past decade he has written for various publications, in addition to working as a translator and editor. Visit his website at www.christopher-pitts.net.

NICOLA WILLIAMS

Lonely Planet author, independent travel writer and editorial consultant Nicola Williams has lived in France and written about it for more than a decade. From her hillside house on the southern shore of Lake Geneva, it's a quick and easy hop to Paris, where she has spent endless years eating her way around and revelling in its extraordinary art and architecture – solo and *en famille*. Nicola has worked on numerous other titles for Lonely Planet, including *France, Discover France, Provence & the Côte d'Azur* and *The Loire*. She blogs at tripalong.wordpress.com and tweets @Tripalong.

THIS BOOK

This 1st edition of *Discover Paris* was coordinated by Caroline Sieg, and researched and written by her, Steve Fallon, Catherine Le Nevez, Chris Pitts and Nicola Williams. This guidebook was commissioned in Lonely Planet's London office, and produced by the following:

Commissioning Editor Joanna Potts
Coordinating Editor Angela Tinson
Coordinating Cartographer Peter Shields
Coordinating Layout Designer Nicholas Colicchia
Managing Editor Sasha Baskett
Managing Cartographers David Connolly, Herman So
Managing Layout Designer Celia Wood
Assisting Editor Carly Hall
Assisting Cartographer Corey Hutchison
Cover Research Rebecca Skinner
Internal Image Research Jane Hart
Language Content Annelies Mertens

BEHIND THE SCENES

ACKNOWLEDGMENTS

Thanks to Glenn Beanland, Lauren Egan, Ryan Evans, Joshua Geoghegan, Michelle Glynn, Brice Gosnell, Indra Kilfoyle, Alison Lyall, Wayne Murphy, Darren O'Connell, Trent Paton, Alison Ridgway, Sally Schafer, Amanda Sierp, Juan Winata

Internal photographs
p4 Statue on the Trocadéro and the Eiffel Tower, Craig Pershouse; p10 Parc du Champ de Mars with Eiffel Tower in the background, Bruce Bi; p12 Jardin du Luxembourg, John Elk III; p31 Taking photos of the Eiffel Tower, Jan Stromme; p39 Inside the Musée du Louvre, Greg Elms; p3, p50 Jardin des Tuileries and Musée du Louvre, FRA/Image Broker; p3, p81 Interior of Cathédrale de Notre Dame de Paris, Izzet Keribar; p3, p97 Place des Vosges, Jonathan Smith; p3, p125 Basilique du Sacré Cœur, Dallas & John Heaton/Photolibrary; p3, p143 City and Arc de Triomphe as seen from the Eiffel Tower, Christopher Groenhout; p3, p163 Pigeons and the Eiffel Tower, Lee Foster; p3, p187 Jardin du Luxembourg, Neil Setchfield; p3, p213 Panthéon, Jean-Bernard Carillet; p235 Daffodils in Monet's garden, Giverny, David Tomlinson; p244 Chapelle Expiatoire, Bruce Bi; p269 Diners in the Latin Quarter, Glenn Beanland

All images are copyright of the photographer unless otherwise indicated. Many of the images in this guide are available for licensing from Lonely Planet Images: www.lonelyplanetimages.com.

ACKNOWLEDGMENTS

Many thanks to the following for the use of their content:
Paris Metro map © 2010 RATP

↘ INDEX

See also separate subindexes for Drinking (p289), Eating (p289), Entertainment & Activities (p291), Shopping (p291), Sights (p292) and Sleeping (p295).

INDEX

D-L

INDEX

L-S

INDEX

DRINKING

000 Map pages
000 Photograph pages

INDEX

EATING

INDEX

ENTERTAINMENT & ACTIVITIES

INDEX

SLEEPING

MAP LEGEND

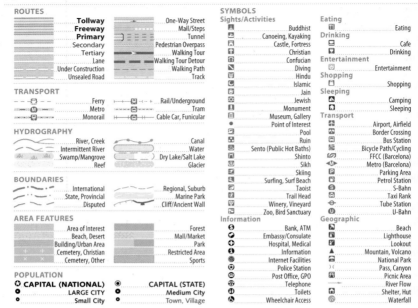

ROUTES

Tollway
Freeway
Primary
Secondary
Tertiary
Lane
Under Construction
Unsealed Road

One-Way Street
Mall/Steps
Tunnel
Pedestrian Overpass
Walking Tour
Walking Tour Detour
Walking Path
Track

TRANSPORT

Ferry
Metro
Monorail

Rail/Underground
Tram
Cable Car, Funicular

HYDROGRAPHY

River, Creek
Intermittent River
Swamp/Mangrove
Reef

Canal
Water
Dry Lake/Salt Lake
Glacier

BOUNDARIES

International
State, Provincial
Disputed

Regional, Suburb
Marine Park
Cliff/Ancient Wall

AREA FEATURES

Area of Interest
Beach, Desert
Building/Urban Area
Cemetery, Christian
Cemetery, Other

Forest
Mall/Market
Park
Restricted Area
Sports

POPULATION

◎ CAPITAL (NATIONAL)
● LARGE CITY
● Small City

◉ CAPITAL (STATE)
◉ Medium City
◦ Town, Village

SYMBOLS

Sights/Activities
Buddhist
Canoeing, Kayaking
Castle, Fortress
Christian
Confucian
Diving
Hindu
Islamic
Jain
Jewish
Monument
Museum, Gallery
Point of Interest
Pool
Ruin
Sento (Public Hot Baths)
Shinto
Sikh
Skiing
Surfing, Surf Beach
Taoist
Trail Head
Winery, Vineyard
Zoo, Bird Sanctuary

Information
Bank, ATM
Embassy/Consulate
Hospital, Medical
Information
Internet Facilities
Police Station
Post Office, GPO
Telephone
Toilets
Wheelchair Access

Eating
Eating
Drinking
Cafe
Drinking
Entertainment
Entertainment
Shopping
Shopping
Sleeping
Camping
Sleeping
Transport
Airport, Airfield
Border Crossing
Bus Station
Bicycle Path/Cycling
FFCC (Barcelona)
Metro (Barcelona)
Parking Area
Petrol Station
S-Bahn
Taxi Rank
Tube Station
U-Bahn

Geographic
Beach
Lighthouse
Lookout
Mountain, Volcano
National Park
Pass, Canyon
Picnic Area
River Flow
Shelter, Hut
Waterfall

LONELY PLANET OFFICES

Australia
Head Office
Locked Bag 1, Footscray, Victoria 3011
☎ 03 8379 8000, fax 03 8379 8111

USA
150 Linden St, Oakland, CA 94607
☎ 510 250 6400, toll free 800 275 8555,
fax 510 893 8572

UK
2nd fl, 186 City Rd,
London EC1V 2NT
☎ 020 7106 2100, fax 020 7106 2101

Contact
talk2us@lonelyplanet.com
lonelyplanet.com/contact

Published by Lonely Planet Publications Pty Ltd
ABN 36 005 607 983

10 9 8 7 6 5 4 3 2

Printed in China

MIX
Paper from
responsible sources
FSC™ C021741
www.fsc.org